Social Figures

Theory and History of Literature
Edited by Wlad Godzich and Jochen Schulte-Sasse

For other books in the series, see p. 242.

Social Figures

George Eliot, Social History, and Literary Representation

Daniel Cottom

Foreword by Terry Eagleton

Theory and History of Literature, Volume 44

University of Minnesota Press, Minneapolis

A revised version of "The Romance of George Eliot's Realism,"
Genre 15 (Winter 1982): 357-77 appears in chapter 6, "Realism and
Romance."

Published by the University of Minnesota Press
2037 University Avenue Southeast, Minneapolis, MN 55414.
Published simultaneously in Canada
by Fitzhenry & Whiteside Limited, Markham.
Printed in the United States of America.

Library of Congress Cataloging-in-Publication Data
Cottom, Daniel.
  Social figures.   14,95

  (Theory and history of literature; v. 44)
  Includes index.
    1. Eliot, George, 1819-1880—Political and social views. 2. Social
history in literature. 3. Social problems in literature. 4. Literature and
society—England. I. Title. II. Series.
PR4692.S58C68 1987   823'.8   86-19249
ISBN 0-8166-1547-0
ISBN 0-8166-1548-9 (pbk.)

48069

For Deborah

Contents

Foreword
Terry Eagleton

If "military intelligence" is one of the more striking oxymorons of modern society, the "crisis of the humanities" is perhaps one of its most notable tautologies. To see the humanities as a firmly grounded formation that at a particular point in its historical development enters into difficulty and self-doubt is to miss the truth that "crisis" and the "humanities" were born at a stroke. Crisis is permanent and structural to the humanities, not a regrettable confusion or failure of nerve that afflicts them from time to time. If the humanities are taken to be a body of discourses enshrining the richest, most imperishable values of humanity, how could they not be pitched into continual crisis in a social order where violence, repression, and cultural deprivation are the order of the day? In such conditions, it is part of the chronic bemusement of the humanities never to know whether they are central or peripheral, grudgingly tolerated parasites or indispensable ideological apparatuses. Radical critiques of their activitities can be launched from either of these two quite opposed viewpoints: in a celebrated pincer movement, the impotence of the humanities in the face of a philistine capitalism may be lamented at just the moment when their pernicious dissemination of bourgeois values is being denounced.

If the humanities seem merely supplementary to a society with quite different priorities of value, that supplementarity would nevertheless appear to fulfill a structural and hence, paradoxically, "central" function. It is part of the vital role of humane discourses within capitalism to occupy a modestly marginal position, always conveniently at hand to offer support when required to the currently hegemonic models of "humanity," but not, it is hoped, required too often. When historians, political theorists, and literary critics are summoned from their libraries to debate the fundamental "human" values by which modern societies live, it is a sure sign that all is not well with the ruling order, which is on principle uneasy about such searching self-reflection and rightly discerns in it the symptoms of ideological disarray. The humanities are in this sense most efficacious when least visible, the taken-for-granted conventional wisdom or spiritual stock-in-trade of a society that can then busy itself with more properly pragmatic affairs. It may do so secure in the knowledge that someone else, in the great division-of-labor scheme, will always be mobilized to furnish an impressive-sounding rationale for these more pragmatic pursuits, should it prove necessary. For their part, the role of the humanities is to refine and elaborate the spiritual stock-in-trade of society to a point specialist enough to justify their own autonomous existence as professional disciplines, but closely allied enough to that empirical wisdom to allow them to appear ideologically acceptable and even useful. This is not always a tension easy to maintain, as the traditional quarrel between "literary scholarship" and "literary criticism" demonstrates.

The structurally essential marginality of the humanities is one of the many features bequeathed to them by their historical predecessor, religion. As the man said, it is when religion starts to interfere with your everyday life that it is time to give it up. One of the traditional roles of religion was to provide the kind of spontaneous, intuitively accessible, taken-for-granted context to one's quotidian activities that, like the Almighty, was so unspeakably fundamental and omnipresent as to be effectively irrelevant. That these mysterious matters should be thrust rudely into self-reflectiveness would be of benefit neither to religion nor to practical life, as anyone who has taken a stroll around Belfast may attest. It is perhaps in part because the United States of America spends its time being tediously pitched from one imperialist crisis to another that its religious and other ideological discourses have about them a solemnity and explicitness odd and embarrassing to European ears. An American politician will invoke God, freedom, or patriotism in a way that a European public (and not just the professionally cynical intelligentsia) would find tasteless or overblown; there is a Victorian earnestness about American ideological language, a high, hollow seriousness, which rings strangely in the ears of those European societies that have long lived past their founding revolutionary moments and have had more time to diffuse and naturalize ideological doctrine as "culture," "manners," or "civilization" rather than histrionic appeals to nature or heaven. This is also the case with American debates in the humanities, which are characteristically more urgent, vigorous, and portentous than the shyly murmured obliquities of the jaded British.

Like religion, the humanities represent the heart of a heartless world, a phrase which Marx by no means intended wholly dismissively. The heart is so utterly the central source of life that we can get along most of the time without giving it a thought. If the humanities are conceived as the secret spiritual essence of society, this lends them a supreme centrality at exactly the moment it renders them elusive and invisible. If the humanities are in permanent crisis—if the affliction, so to speak, is genetic rather than environmental—this is because the soul they signify is in Cartesian fashion at once the very essential identity of the crassly material body of society and yet inexplicably mysterious in its effective relations with it, exterior and a priori to its mechanical operations. In the more affirmative versions of the humanities, the body of society is meaningful and valuable because a spirit informs it throughout, and humanistic hermeneutics devote themselves to deciphering this spirit's motions through its fleshly casement. In the more tragic or Gnostic version, the soul has sucked all meaning from the body, which is then reduced to a lifeless hulk. The soul retains the form of a center, but it is also a noncenter since it can no longer adequately engage or inform the body. God continues to be the mysterious source of all creation, but he has withdrawn his presence from the world, making all the difference while not mattering a damn. The humanities represent an idealized discourse of humanity, whose idealism is at once their capacity to pronounce with universal authority and their incapacity to speak to the point. As the metanarrative of human historical practices, the humanities can take as a historical object or problem everything but themselves; their efficacy drains into the very gap they open between themselves and their object-practices as an enabling reflective space. Such idealism is a necessity of bourgeois society, which requires a space within which it can project, preserve, and insulate the "humane" values it expunges from its own social practice. Entranced by this space as its own ideal identity while estranged from it as radically Other, bourgeois society lives in an aporetic relation of difference from and identity with "culture," establishing the separateness and marginality of this realm as structural and necessary.

If the humanities are self-divided, it is not because of the modern proliferation of specialist knowledges but because they are part of the problem to which they propose themselves as a solution. In the discourses of humanism, material historical practices are decomposed and reassembled in idealist form, which is to say that the act of extracting from them their true essences is inseparable from the process of knocking the stuffing out of them. The more society violates the values that the humanities supposedly incarnate, the more vitally relevant the role of the humanities will appear; but the very same conditions will unmask them as more abstract and impotent than ever. In a familiar dialectic, intensified repression in social reality generates ever more fantastic sublimations, the two phenomena at once sworn antagonists and comrades-in-crime.

What is sometimes seen as the "crisis of the humanities" in late bourgeois society could more accurately be seen as the death throes of a specific historical ideology of the intellectual. The contradiction we face is that a historical ideology that has in the past served the bourgeoisie marvelously well—that of liberal humanism—is still discharging a number of crucial functions and yet, in other ways, is progressively outmoded and discreditable within the very terms of developed capitalist society itself. Unable either to stay or to leave, haunting the locales of its old pursuits like a ghost suspended between life and death, this ideology represents a kind of superstructural "lag" within late capitalism, a residual heritage of a more buoyant, classical stage of capitalist development. It is precisely this earlier stage that Daniel Cottom takes as the subject of this absorbing study to throw light on the political exigencies of the present. What we witness in "George Eliot"—the name can be presented thus to signify one major instantiation of this liberal humanist formation—is the strenuous consolidation of an ideology of impressive power, depth, range, and intricacy whose historical hour has now come. The dramatic force of Cottom's book, then, is that it takes us phase by phase and figure by figure into the very process of constitution of a discursive formation that has governed the political life of the West for generations, whose supersession would have been in Eliot's own time utterly unimaginable, but which now, in a vertiginous historical moment, it is finally possible to begin to feel and think our way beyond. Readers of this book should therefore make no mistake that they are, so to speak, in on their own deaths, children as we all are in some sense of this immensely successful hegemonic project of the traditional middle class.

Systematic reflections on this or that human practice come and go; but the moment of the humanities' consolidation corresponds to the founding of a certain "humanity" in the sense of a total, universal order of human social life. "Humanity," in short, is constructed at a certain historical point by a class society urgently in need of naturalizing and universalizing its dominion. It is this historic moment to which we are witness in this study: the active production, on the part of a newly dominant English middle class, of a total order of human meaning transparent to the gaze of the disinterested liberal intellectual. With the advent of the middle class, as Marx reminds us, a truly universal history becomes for the first time possible; what is then necessary is that this universal order should achieve its rational representation, and one of the major forms of such representation for the Victorian bourgeoisie is the realist novel. Other discourses—philosophy, sociology, psychology, the natural sciences, political theory—naturally play their key roles in the production of such totalized representations; but it is not as though the Victorian bourgeoisie is out to fashion a complete political and institutional image of itself. It is neither fully capable of such a totalization, given its endemic empiricism, nor in the least enamored of it, given the fact that any such politically concrete configuration must mark the *limits* of a social formation and so veer ineluctably toward critique. The great histories, sociologies, political and economic theories of Victorian England will always be found to disarticulate any such political totality into some other, apparently more fundamental principle, whether this is called natural law or psychological necessity, the unfolding of spirit or the lawlike combinations of matter. The appropriate totality, then, is one that refuses the mere social, political, and institutional "appearances" of the social order for some secret, silent, subjacent unity—a unity that, as Cottom brilliantly demonstrates in the case of George Eliot, finally escapes definitive representation. The unity of the social formation is thus expelled beyond its frontiers in the very act of being located at its heart. Removed as it therefore is from routine inspection, it becomes accessible only to an intellectual elite, one whose "cognition" of the laboring masses consists in uncovering, beneath their unpalatable empirical and political lives, that knowledge which they themselves have projected there.

That "outside" point to which the unity of the social order is expelled may also be thought of as a certain "inside." Displaced from the terrain of practical, institutional existence, homogeneity claims its ghostly home in human hearts and minds, in that obscure, unfolding, stubbornly persistent subtext of suffering and desire that binds all men and women, regardless of social rank, to a common subliminal nature, and that will finally give the slip to the formalizing perceptions of science. One can see well enough, then, why it is the novel rather than political or economic theory that emerges as the supreme mode of cognition of the Victorian ruling class—why it is *Middlemarch*, not John Stuart Mill's works, which necessarily becomes a privileged paradigm of social knowledge. For it is exactly this terrain of unified inwardness that the realist novel seeks patiently to chart, this ultimately unformalizable depth which evades all but the most artistically nuanced, affectively alert representation. "Sympathy," not just science, is the keystone of the liberal intellectual's enterprise, which is simply another way of saying that England is now in precarious transition from the institutions of religious and political coercion to the apparatuses of moral-psychological consent.

The familiar term for the latter project is hegemony, which Antonio Gramsci derived from the internal strategic debates of the Second International and generalized in a bold gesture to the struggle between the social classes. Coercion and consent are not of course to be thought of as simply antithetical: indeed Gramsci occasionally uses the word hegemony to suggest a complex amalgam of both, as the typical conditions of class power. It is clear that the days of any ruling class that governs through coercion alone are likely to be not only unpleasantly turbulent but also strictly numbered. All ruling classes thus strive for hegemony—except for the most brutally imperious; but even though the phenomenon is not restricted to the history of the bourgeoisie, there is a curious sense in which bourgeois rule is the very paradigm of hegemony and delineates in more palpable, emphatic form a structure of dominance that is not its sole possession. With the advent of the bourgeoisie, the ratio of coercion and consent within state power is sharply modified in the direction of the latter, and this for a host of reasons, only a few of which may be broached here. For one thing, the very material conditions of capitalist society, with its massive mobility of labor and dissolution of regional communities, its diffuse, atomized collectivities, necessarily result in a weakening of immediate political authority and so throw a considerably greater onus on the individual internalization of social discipline. For another thing, the bourgeoisie wishes typically to pursue a pacific policy at home, whatever its colonial depredations abroad, as a crucial condition of economic development. It can thus proudly contrast its own techniques of gentle persuasion—"culture" and "education," as Cottom names them—with the barbaric militarism and aristocratic hauteur of superseded social formations. The rampant individualism of bourgeois society tends ideologically to discredit purely external constraints, relocating them in the self-motivation of the subject, just as materially speaking such traditional forms of politico-religious coercion give way to what Marx referred to as the "dull compulsion of the economic." Bourgeois society, moreover, is the only class-formation in history in which the subordinated classes are ideologically expected to believe that they are the ruling segment, through the apparatus of liberal democracy. Although this is ideological delusion, the subjected classes must nevertheless be, if not "fit to rule," at least fit to *believe* that they rule—to accept and internalize, as part of what makes them formally equipped to govern, the forms of subjectivity which in fact render them more pliable as wage-slaves. It is in this sense, then, that we can speak of the bourgeois epoch as the time of the "birth of the subject"—not, absurdly, that subjects, techniques of consent and collusion, institutions of persuasion, and forms of moral inwardness had no existence before then, but that the very material exigencies of the capitalist mode of production foreground them in peculiarly graphic style.

It is the gradual consolidation of these new practices of hegemony that Daniel Cottom maps in this study, and for which the name George Eliot is metonymic. As part of this project, a division is installed at the very core of social life between those proficient in a certain discourse of universal reason and those who, currently lacking access to this idiom, may be expelled to the minatory realm of the merely violent, egoistic, and insensate. "*Currently* lacking access," however, is a vital emphasis, and one that distinguishes this ideology from its precursor in the age of Enlightenment. Victorian society relativizes and historicizes a dichotomy which in the eighteenth century was much more absolute, since, given the common moral subtext that weaves all individuals into affective unity, there is no reason in principle why those now banished from the language of reason may not come in time to speak it and every possible ideological reason why they should. What is overcome in this myth of uneven historical progress is a contradiction that dogged the "public sphere" of polite universal Reason in the Enlightenment period. For although that sphere represented itself as open to all who could deploy the formulas of civilized discourse, it was plain enough that no one without a certain amount of property—an "interest" in society, as was said—need bother applying for membership. A successful transition from power, wealth, and rank to the criteria of "moral worth"—one mapped here by Cottom in the vicissitudes of that most socially eloquent of all English terms, the gentleman—will circumvent this contradiction, defining as one's admission ticket to the public sphere nothing more than one's internalization of the principles of moral reason. In the eighteenth century, only those with an "interest" could be truly disinterested; beyond that charmed circle lay those who, lacking a material "interest," were brutishly "interested" in all the wrong ways. In the nineteenth century, every individual is en route, however falteringly, to the appropriation of that best self which, through suffering, experience, and education, will die to selfish, sectoral interests and rise again to disinterested solidarity with others. It is tempting, indeed, to say that this, in a nutshell, is exactly what George Eliot's fiction is about.

To believe this, of course, required considerable courage and self-confidence on the part of the bourgeoisie, since there was no doubt that empirically speaking its own discourse of reason was under siege from a contervailing discourse of the Other. Whereas for the eighteenth century this Other—the laboring masses, the rude, raucous, and illiterate—had no proper civic or political existence at all, could simply not be figured or articulated within the language of the public sphere, the Victorian period, confronted by a now organized Other, is forced to be more liberal about the matter, dissolving power entirely into reason. The lower orders have always been unknowable, but now they risk becoming dangerously so; they are like the heart itself, a low murmuring discourse with the odd shocking spasm, and like the heart must be attended to patiently so as to decipher in their raw desires symptoms of that rational telos toward which they are obscurely travailing. The appropriate form of liberal-democratic hermeneutics—call it the realist novel—will read within the clamorous voices of insensate lower-class greed, the empty-headed egoism of women, and the incessant clucking of benighted petty-bourgeois tongues those subliminal impulses that prod you up the evolutionary scale. Since these low destinies are already cast by the bourgeois novelist in the image of her own consciousness, this hermeneutic, like most, turns out to be somewhat circular. In the most euphoric inflection of this Whig ideology, the poor individual is one who is destined to be rich but has not quite arrived. What guarantees this continuity is an all-encompassing nature, at once always elsewhere, a goal to be asymptotically approached and a reality installed in the interior depth of every individual subject.

If the petty-bourgeois intellectual is the representative voice of this nature, it is because the two figures are secretly coupled in their common transcendence of all sectional interests. Nature, like the realist novel itself, miraculously constitutes such partial commitments in the very form of their ultimate harmonization; and the proper embodiment of this harmony can then be none other than the newly professionalized intellectual, absolved as he or she apparently is from all social interests but the very life of the mind. The paradox we have already noted in the humanities thus comes into being: the truth of all particular discourses can be distilled from them only in an idealizing, rational metadiscourse which, necessarily removed from them, ends up delivering nothing more than an interminable dialogue with itself. It is, however, precisely this sealed, self-generative space of the public sphere, this endless exchange and circulation of opinion in the stealthily accumulating consensus of truth, that can plausibly offer itself as a model of the very social totality from which it is so desperately estranged. For that totality, as we have seen, is dissolved and reconstituted beyond all phenomenal appearances as the unfurling conversation of heart with heart. The idealism of intellectual discourse thus comes to project its own grounding referent in an idealized social order, bypassing en route both the sordidly political and an empirical readership whom the vagaries of the market have struck alarmingly anonymous.

There is, however, a dilemma at the very heart of the bourgeois public sphere, which can be summarized by claiming that whereas this free, unconstrained circulation of rational language mimes the exchanges of the capitalist marketplace, it is also continually threatened with being undermined by them. There are too many voices, opinions, claims to veracity in this spawning proliferation of texts, with no necessary guarantee, at least in one's less sanguine moments, that they will all somehow spontaneously coalesce into just the kind of truth needed to keep the working class at bay. Just as a growing degree of state intervention is needed in the economic marketplace, so a desire for regulating principles amid this cacophony of idioms arises within those, like Eliot and Mill, most anxious to preserve free discussion. It is this anxiety that will force Matthew Arnold into a direct betrayal of his own liberal tenets. Reason is a metalanguage against which competing claims may be checked, but then again, Reason would seem nothing but the open-ended exchanges of a certain style of discourse. How are such enunciations to be supervised by a higher Reason, and thus insulated from political error, without merely lapsing into the illiberal absolutism of pre-Enlightenment England? This epistemological crisis is triggered by a political one: the fact that the lower orders, with their own quite different styles of rationality, are even now knocking loudly on the door. For the bourgeoisie to reply to them *una voce* would seem to demand just the kind of unified Reason that its own marketplace models of linguistic circulation threaten to disrupt.

Perhaps this is another reason for the dominance of the realist novel, which permits a tolerant degree of dialogue with voices other than the author's own, but finally always inflects and idealizes them in that singular authorial discourse. Such a form allows maximum play to the concrete, particular, and individual, while drawing them covertly into a supremely well regulated whole. The synoptic vision of a *Middlemarch* is at once the sign of free-ranging plural sympathies and bleak testimony to just how much of social life now needs to be supervised and disciplined within a typifying scheme. That typology, always surreptitiously slid beneath the apparently irreducible particular, represents a regime of knowledge and control, as the concrete is distilled and abstracted into universal types only to be instantly reinvested with all the lived force of the immediate. The devices that construct this unity of the universal and the individual continually efface themselves so that the disciplines producing the novel are no more visible than those producing the bourgeois subject. The effect of this naturalization of conventions is in both cases what is known as "freedom": on the one hand, a writing constrained by nothing but its own wide-eyed, stubborn fidelity to the real; on the other hand, a human subject that works "all by itself" (Louis Althusser) precisely because the ideological determinations that produced it have now been sublimed and displaced to the moral. That configuration of sympathies which is the realist novel is itself the effect of a whole cluster of disciplinary techniques and pedagogical devices, constructing in its readers the very appropriate forms of subjective inwardness it disinterestedly purports to examine in its characters. In this way doctrine is dissolved into experience, politics into moral psychology, the universal into the individual, constraint into freedom, history into nature, and pedagogy into art. Eliot's novels, therefore, mark that historic point in English class-society at which ideology becomes literature; and later bourgeois critics have not been slow to demonstrate their gratitude.

Daniel Cottom's critical, powerfully distancing study of this phenomenon is almost, one might venture, too successful. For it leaves us uneluctably with a single question, which is nothing less than: Why, after this, read Eliot at all? Two comments may perhaps be made in conclusion.

First, in any examination of the hegemonic project of bourgeois society, its *progressive* elements should never be lost sight of. I mean by that not only those features of such hegemony that in whatever way eased the barbaric violence to which the poor were subjected within previous regimes, but also those aspects of it which became historically available to the working-class movement itself. The bourgeois public sphere of Victorian England is ridden with contradictions between its more "universal" and more class-specific dimensions, so that its impulse to incorporate the proletariat unavoidably bequeathes to them certain political and cultural goods, which they can turn against their oppressors. Culture, education, free speech, and liberal democracy must always be *dialectically* assessed by revolutionaries as being both instruments of class-power and potential levers in its subversion. Behind this book stands the work of Michel Foucault, whose accounts of the institutions of consent are as illuminating as they are one-sided, and who occasionally evinces even a certain nostalgia for the less insidious epochs of visible coercion.

Second, it should be remembered that there is indeed that in Eliot's fiction which surpasses a simple project of class-hegemony, which is nothing less than the whole question—self-declaredly passed over in this study—of sex and gender. If there is the Eliot of Adam Bede and Tertius Lydgate, there is also the Eliot of that disturbed, fraught, apocalyptic conclusion to *The Mill on the Floss*, the Eliot suffering passionately with Maggie Tulliver and Dorothea Brooke as well as superiorly ironizing them, the Eliot whose hunger, pain, and frustration could not be contained by any project of hegemony without the most lacerating self-discipline and self-violence. No hegemonic project can succeed unless it engages the unconscious desires of those it aims to subjugate; but it is always hampered in this aim by the fact that it has an unconscious too, which will always return to plague it at the very peak of apparently confident control. Eliot's articulation of the masculine imperatives of nature, Reason, and humanity entailed a painful *de*naturing of her own sexual identity; and the shadow of that injury is cast across her texts. Even after this forcefully subversive study, then, it remains true that there is more than one George Eliot, and that they do not always speak in a single voice.

T.E.

Preface

Generally speaking, the liberal intellectual tradition has bequeathed to us two approaches to literature, both of which can be found in George Eliot's writing. One has been to interpret rhetoric: to peer through the literary figure to truth, experience, the world, and so on. In this approach the "rhetoricity" of rhetoric is dissolved in favor of a reality identical with itself, capable of representing itself without distortion or dissimulation. Following this approach, Eliot would elevate her own fiction, with its supposed fidelity to everyday life, above works of romance. She described romances as idealized distortions of the plain-faced reality with which one ought to be content. This popular brand of literature appeared to her to be composed of a language dreamily floating above the reality of society, a language "merely" rhetorical. She would characterize her own work in terms of its dedication to the actual surface of experience, no matter how unpoetic or ungenteel that surface might appear to readers whose conception of art was formed by works of romance.

In the second approach, one accepts rhetoric as an essential part of the body of language, not just its disposable costume or ornamentation. Like the first, this approach assumes there exists a radical difference between rhetoric and reality. However, it assumes this difference can never be entirely overcome through language. The typical solution of the liberal intellectual to this situation is to posit a kind of faith—in the progress of reason, in humanity, in a community of sympathy, or whatever—that serves to bridge the distance between flawed representations and the world. Thus, in her writing, Eliot would sometimes emphasize the irreducibility of its metaphorical nature, as when she commented ironically on Aristotle's praise of metaphor in *The Mill on the Floss*. And yet, through the consciousness of this problem she displayed as a narrator, Eliot would make it appear that she had transcended rhetoric and reached a certain truth that her readers could share with her.

Jacques Derrida and Paul de Man, among others, have analyzed the impasses reached by any kind of idealist approach to language. In brief, the problem is that such approaches must both deny and affirm an identity between language and reality. To try to go beyond this problem in analyzing the discourse of the liberal intellectual and, in particular, the work of George Eliot, I have taken what may be called a materialist view of language and literature. In place of idealism of the sort with which Eliot identified, in which reality must always be other than the language that tells of it, I analyze uses of language in relation to those structurings of social life for which these uses constitute reality. Within this approach, one assumes language has no existence independent of the relations in which discourse is produced, circulated, and changed. For this reason, in analyzing the works of Eliot and other nineteenth-century English writers, I describe the conditions of their production, found in the historical relations in which these works appeared. These relations are not the context to the literary text but the very possibility of the literary text. They are the possibility of even the very notion of literature that we may tend today to assume is natural. Therefore, they are taken within my work to be the object of literary criticism.

My argument assumes that acts of discourse not only take place in a society but are constructions of a society. They are bound to authorize certain conceptions of truth, legitimacy, and power that represent specific groups or classes in society. "Discourse" in this view refers to signifying practices of all kinds, including those found in the operations of institutions such as publishing and charity work, in legal theory and practice, in fields of organized knowledge such as psychology and sociology, and even in the way day-to-day relations among people within a given society are played out. Discourse within this definition is heterogeneous, as I have indicated by the qualifications I place upon the term throughout this book. Nevertheless, discourses in widely different fields of social activity may fall into common political constructions at important points, despite the political conflicts they may also generate.

Within my definition, discourse does not simply comment on the forms social authority takes; it constitutes these forms of authority. To take a materialist view of language is to see every instance of discourse as a political as well as a social act. Rather than trying to formulate in a rational and systematic form the relation between language and reality, one analyzes the rhetoric of reality.

Within this approach, varieties of discourse are evaluated in terms of the social relations, identities, histories, absences, utopias, crimes—in short, the figures—that they call into being. In this work I have used the term figure in the traditional sense—as in my discussion of synechdoche in chapter 6—but also in a wider sense, consonant with the view that the elements of language are not properly separable into the literal and the figurative. Certain elements, such as "the truth of feeling," will indeed be seen to function within a given discourse as the ground to other elements, which appear in contrast to be figurative or symbolic. However, this ground to language is not any less rhetorical by virtue of this discursive situation. Whether they be certain *topoi*, grammatical patterns, narrative strategies, literary genres, or whatever, the elements composing this ground are figures that—as Nietzsche put it—no longer appear as such. Thus, the "author," the "individual," the "ordinary human life," or the typical Victorian association between violence, drunkenness, and the working classes may be referred to as "social figures." They are examples of the elements of a discourse that have been taken to be natural or to represent reality without displacement. Therefore, if analyzed, they may be seen to represent the politics of that discourse. In viewing the production of discourse as a political as well as a social act, one must analyze the rhetoric constituting a discourse and evaluate its implications in terms of the historical relations that allowed this discourse to appear and have the power of meaning.

It may be banal to say that criticism, like literature, is always political—although the dominant intellectual tradition in the humanities still rejects this idea. In any case, it is not banal to note that it is only in identifying these historical relations as its object that criticism can become conscious of its own enterprise. Only by this means can it work against its submission to the authorities of academy, culture, society, and history. For these contemporary authorities—especially in the field of literature—remain to a great extent bound by the middle-class construction of reality that I analyze in Eliot's writing as well as in the works of other nineteenth-century writers. This is one reason Eliot's writing continues to be of great significance to the student of politics, society, and literary history.

It should be understood from the outset that my approach in this study does not pretend to be a comprehensive one. Indeed, as I argue in my concluding chapter, the idea of a comprehensive view in literary criticism is theoretically incoherent, even though it is extremely important to the discourse of the liberal intellectual. Still, in describing my concentration on the discourse of the liberal intellectual in the nineteenth century, I want to emphasize that I am not doing justice to other perspectives that can be just as valuable in considering the literature of that time. For instance, in treating Eliot as a liberal intellectual, I am treating her as a figure of patriarchy. There is a nominal justification for this treatment in the pseudonym she adopted as a novelist, as well as a more important justification in the way intellectual power was generally denominated a male quality in the social practices of nineteenth-century England. Despite the fact that she was often critical of the contemporary condition of women in her novels, letters, and other writings, Eliot was by no means exempt from adopting the stereotypes involved in these social practices; and insofar as she identified herself with a form of thought she considered to be neutral, she identified with a form of thought that systematically demeaned women as well as other groups of people, such as the poor and working classes. This is not to say that a feminist analysis of Eliot's writings in terms of her identity as a woman in this time and place, rather than in terms of her identity as a liberal intellectual, is not valuable. It is simply to say that this approach differs from the present approach. In any case, I have tried to indicate at points throughout the present study—as in the part of chapter 4 that considers why Eliot views woman as being especially subject to and hurt by egoism—ways my emphasis might intersect with a feminist analysis.

Still other approaches are not canvassed here. For instance, my concern has not been particularly psychoanalytic, although I touch at times upon issues that have relevance to psychoanalytic concerns; and I have not been particularly concerned about tracing changes in Eliot's writing throughout the course of her career, although I have noted some in passing. What I have concentrated on— the discourse of the liberal intellectual in relation to the social history of the nineteenth century, especially as it involves the middle classes of the time—I have judged significant enough to warrant this emphasis.

In my introductory chapter, "'George Eliot' and the Fables of the Liberal Intellectual," I review the historical situation that made possible the appearance of the modern intellectual. More specifically, I describe the liberal intellectual: the social figure who takes the ideal of intellectual discourse to be the reality of society. By focusing on the role Eliot assumed in her writings, I explain what kind of a figure she conceived the author to be and relate this figure to the social, political, and institutional position of the English middle classes in the nineteenth century. Moreover, I sketch some of the consequences of this conception of the author by analyzing a number of fables, or rhetorical schemes, that accompanied the conception of this figure within the world of middle-class discourse. These consequences are described more extensively in the succeeding chapters.

Chapter 2, "Education and the Transfigurations of Realism," is devoted to the analysis of education as the new mode of social reproduction developed by the English middle classes over the course of the nineteenth century. Through an analysis of the rhetoric of truth, ignorance, and violence within the discourse on education in this age, I assert that Eliot's world of realism in her fiction is policed by the same educational conception that was thought to be at once the genesis, the continuing order, and the promise of the middle classes. In particular, I deal with the "gentleman," "society as a whole," and "ordinary human life." I argue that the appearance of these figures within the discourse in which Eliot participated may be taken to exemplify a new, rationalized scheme of meaning within this new scheme of social order.

Chapter 3, "Literary Consciousness and the Vacancy of the Individual," begins with a consideration of the way genteel and ordinary human beings, as they appear within liberal intellectual discourse, approach a social unity by meeting on the ground of individuality. I am concerned, then, with the metaphysics of the individual that Eliot brought to her fiction from this discourse. In finding a way to describe the individual as a novelistic character, Eliot had to come face to face with the problem of her own social identity. By concentrating on the way she "fills" this figure of the individual with her own literary consciousness, I analyze the rhetoric of experience in Eliot's fiction and the politics of this rhetoric.

In chapter 4, "Genteel Image and Democratic Example," I show how Eliot's art was meant to give birth to a new power of communication appropriate to a society moving toward democracy. According to this argument, a traditional order of representation based upon the fashionable image, which is fixed and absolute in nature, is contrasted in Eliot's work to an order of representation based upon the moral example, which is inflected by change and contingency. However, these orders in Eliot's fiction do not merely represent a difference between the historical past and present; they also represent aspects of the history of consciousness within individuals undergoing the process of enlightenment. Therefore, the ahistorical rationality of Eliot's discourse dominates her art even as this art exhibits the hopes and the anxieties with which the middle classes of Eliot's time responded to the prospect of a democratic social life.

In chapter 5, "Imperfection and Compensation," I question why the announcement of ordinary human life as the basis of art is the occasion in Eliot's writing for the conception of an art even more exclusive than that which she pictures as being typical of the world of traditional gentility. The answer is that Eliot describes true art as having this character because her aesthetics is formed by a demand for control over the significance allowed ordinary human life. In other words, her aesthetics is based on the power of interpretation constituting the identity of the liberal intellectual. This chapter, then, is devoted to explicating the relation between Eliot's conception of aesthetics—in which the novel represents a model consciousness mediating all the differences of society as well as all the imperfections in representation—and her conception of the liberal intellectual as a cultural figure dedicated, through the power of reason, to a tragic transcendence of social life.

Chapter 6, "Realism and Romance," is concerned with the relation between Eliot's conception of realism and the genre of romance opposed to this conception throughout her fiction. As the image of romance against which Eliot directs her own writing can be seen to be necessary to the articulation of this realism, so, too, can the conception of error throughout Eliot's writing be seen to be implicated in its conception of truth. Therefore, an analysis of romance or of error in general can be used to define the politics of Eliot's "truth." More specifically, I analyze the figure of synechdoche in nineteenth-century discourse. My argument is that this figure, as it is used to describe the relation of the individual to society, forms a social discipline of the individual. This discipline is as evident in Eliot's writing as it is in the organizational practices of the increasingly urbanized and competitive capitalist order in which she wrote. My conclusion is that the discipline embodied in the form of Eliot's novels and in related examples of nineteenth-century discourse is significantly related to the disciplines being formed for the government of factories, businesses, communities, and the nation of England.

In chapter 7, "The Supervision of Art and the Culture of the Sickroom," I show how Eliot's rhetoric is always utopian in nature, although tragic in tone and dramatic effect, by tracing the way the scene of suffering in her writing exemplifies her art. I analyze this scene in relation to the fields of charity, education, governmental organization, psychology, and labor (as these fields appeared in the discourse of Eliot's day) to point out the significance of the supervisory role she assumes in her art. My conclusion is that her artistic practice can serve to reveal how the liberal humanitarianism of her age was a rigorous social law, the promotion of sympathetic feeling an ideological construction, and the observation of individuals the rhetoric of this ideology.

In chapter 8, "Private Fragments and Public Monuments," I take a personal letter Eliot wrote to Johnny Cross in 1879 as a basis for interrogating the division in her writing between "the private" and "the public." This study then becomes a means for bringing into question other pairs of controlling categories in her writing, such as desire and duty, past and present, consciousness and unconsciousness, and fragmentariness and monumentality. Through this analysis I describe more precisely how Eliot's characters are composed of her historical consciousness and how this consciousness is composed of a rhetoric drawn from the discourse of the middle classes of her time.

In chapter 9, "Domesticity and Teratology," I focus on the language of sympathy in Eliot's writing to show how it appears as a summary name for her conception of the structuring of intelligence, communication, power, and identity in society. By analyzing this "sympathy"—which Eliot took to be the manifestation of truth in immediate social experience and, as such, the ultimate end of artistic representation—I try to give a conclusive view of the picture this book develops of the politics of Eliot's writing. I show why Eliot's politics cannot always find a coherent expression even within Eliot's rhetorical scheme of things. In other words, I explain why the domesticity that figures in Eliot's narratives as the ideal terminus of the inquiring mind must at times appear as a domain given over to monstrosity.

In my concluding chapter, "Reproduction/Quotation/Criticism," I use some of Walter Benjamin's writings as a basis for considering the advantages and the problems of a criticism that concentrates on the politics of rhetoric. I focus especially on the difficulties of writing about art as a historical creation, but I also discuss the vital importance of historical analysis as a means to political understanding. My argument is for a critical practice that resists the unconscious reproduction of culture by devoting itself to social change.

All quotations from George Eliot's works are taken from *The Personal Edition of George Eliot's Works*, 12 vols. (New York: Doubleday, 1901); *Essays of George Eliot*, ed. Thomas Pinney (London: Routledge and Kegan Paul, 1965); and *The George Eliot Letters*, ed. Gordon S. Haight, 8 vols. (New Haven: Yale University Press, 1978). Citations are given within the text according to the following abbreviations: "Amos Barton," "AB," "Mr. Gilfil's Love-Story," "MGL," and "Janet's Repentance," "JR" (from *Scenes of Clerical Life*); *Adam Bede, AB; The Mill on the Floss, MF; Silas Marner, SM; Romola, R; Felix Holt, FH; Middlemarch, M; Daniel Deronda, DD; The Essays of Theophrastus Such, TS; Poems, P; Essays, E;* and *Letters, L.*

Acknowledgments

I would like to thank my colleagues Nancy Armstrong, Charlie Baxter, Michael Bell, John Franzosa, Jerry Herron, and Ross Pudaloff, all of whom influenced this work through their criticism and conversation. Nancy Armstrong and Ross Pudaloff in particular have helped me to think through many ideas and reject many others—I hope this book is worthy of the time they have given to it.

I would also like to thank Homer Brown, who was especially encouraging while I was preparing this work for publication; Ed Dryden, for many favors; and Todd Bender, ditto. Donna Przybylowicz and Jochen Schulte-Sasse read the manuscript carefully and made valuable suggestions, and Terry Cochran has been a most helpful editor: I thank them.

Len Tennenhouse merits special appreciation for his generosity with time, advice, and criticism during the period when I was writing this book.

A Summer Research Award from Wayne State University made possible my work on chapter 6, "Realism and Romance."

Social Figures

Chapter 1
"George Eliot" and the Fables
of the Liberal Intellectual

*I wonder whether you at all imagine the terrible pressure of
disbelief in my own duty/right to speak to the public, which is
apt with me to make all beginnings of work like a rowing against
tide.*

Letter from Eliot to Frederic Harrison, 1877

When Mary Ann Evans wrote "The Sad Fortunes of the Reverend Amos
Barton" in 1856, she was already an accomplished translator, editor, reviewer,
and essayist. Then, as throughout the rest of her life, she was conversant with
contemporary developments in theology, philosophy, sociology, historiography, the natural sciences, the arts, and public affairs of all sorts. Her expertise in these matters had helped her make her way in the world, and she
identified herself as one whose role in society was devoted to the interpretation
and dissemination of knowledge. Having thought herself out of a provincial
and sectarian girlhood and into a position in which she could conceive herself
to be at one with all of humanity, she wrote only nominally as an individual,
and pseudonymously at that. The "George Eliot" who wrote "Amos Barton,"
and the works after it, won her narrative authority from an understanding
transcending individuals. In her conception, as the epigraph to this chapter indicates, she had to run counter to the current of her own mind if she was to
deserve her name as an author, that public identity that she took to imply the
attainment of a shore beyond the egoistic individual.

In effect, Eliot argued that realism was the true author of her writing.
Whether one addressed this authority as Art or Truth or some other personification of universality, it served to legitimate a discourse that prescribed
the superiority of the community over the individual and of humanity at large

over the individual community. Since a discourse of this nature requires that its author identify with the power of its most general term, a logic develops in which the writer as an individual is responsible only for such flaws as may appear in the work. For Eliot, it was at such points that she had failed in her effort to superimpose her writing upon the pattern of transcendent understanding. She had slipped back into the stream of egoism, or run aground upon transient shoals of circumstance, so as to leave as a place of legend the realm of universality that alone could guarantee successful communication. On the other hand, such power as her writing could claim would be attributed to the system of authority that gave it its nature.[1] She was not so much the creator of her art as she was the trustee of an artistic gift, the fruit of that journey beyond herself. "After our subtlest analysis of the mental process," she wrote in *Adam Bede*, "we must still say . . . that our highest thoughts and our best deeds are all given to us" (*AB*, 117). Following this logic, Eliot would insist to correspondents that her personal life be separated from her public persona and that her writing be seen to originate in the impersonal pressure of duty or right, not in individual will.

To be sure, any piece of writing may be analyzed for the logic to which it lays claim, and Eliot's arrangement of terms is hardly extraordinary in and of itself. This logic gripped the pens of a broad range of cultural figures in the nineteenth century and is far from being markedly unconventional. More remarkable is the self-consciousness with which this logic is articulated as an aesthetic theory in Eliot's writing, the detailed elaboration given to it, and the fact that the fiction thus produced shows us an artist who was also an intellectual, in a peculiarly modern sense of the word that is important to the understanding of her art. Eliot's stories, novels, and poetry were not written merely by an individual author, by a female author, or even by a female English author in the nineteenth century. Eliot was above all else one whose intellectual identity was of a type inconceivable before her age and incomprehensible apart from the changes that had been brought to England over the last hundred years. This status as an intellectual accounts for Eliot's conception of herself as an artist and may even be considered the most compelling influence in the art she produced. To understand her work, one should understand the provenance of this identity.[2]

The first point to be made in this regard concerns the professionalism of the modern intellectual. The term intellectual came into common usage in England in the 1820s,[3] the phrase "an author by profession" having been popularized by the mid-eighteenth century;[4] and the social changes exfoliating in these linguistic developments are vitally related. The first characteristic of modern intellectuals of any type is that they are bound neither to a system of patronage nor to a rigidly defined class within society, and yet they confront society with a distinctly articulated identity. Eliot became an intellectual at a time when the extension of literacy, changes in the publishing industry, and the growing need for expertise in all areas of social life could bestow an unprecedented professional status on individuals concerned with matters of knowledge. The nature of the intellectual was redefined within these historical changes, which would continue to be a great influence on the nature of this role in our own day.[5] Only in a modern society do intellectuals survey the world from a social position that may seem to insulate their claim of philosophical independence from all "accidents" of birth, class, and history. And this sense of independence is likely to be especially strengthened in an author like Eliot, who had "unusual freedom in the writing of her novels."[6]

Still, this independence would not have been so important in Eliot's case if it had not conformed to the fable that became a common nineteenth-century explanation of the stages of social evolution. For instance, chapter 5 of Carlyle's *Past and Present* is entitled "Aristocracy of Talent," and in it he looked forward to the day when a leadership based on free intellectual merit might take power and respond to his outcry about the wretchedness apparent in the midst of English prosperity: "How come these things? Wherefore are they, wherefore should they be?"[7] Hippolyte Taine saw an "insensible change" already in progress when he wrote his *Notes on England*, "the end of which," he predicted, "will be that the leading place will belong to intellect" rather than to "the aristocracy of birth or fortune."[8] Other contemporary writers such as de Tocqueville, Comte, and John Stuart Mill accepted this genealogical fable that represented the will of the future to be the bequest of leadership from the hands of aristocrats and priests into those of intellectuals not unlike themselves;[9] and the popularity of this historical forecast is not surprising. The scepter of power never could have been passed as simply and progressively as these writers imagined it ought to be, even supposing power to be a kind of possession that can belong to a limited group of people in society; but the relay was predicted in this form because of the changes that followed the creation of a modern industrialized nation, especially the spread of education to the middle classes, which accompanied their increasing economic and political power.

The most important institution in this regard was the publishing industry, which produced increasing quantities of books, magazines, newspapers, and pamphlets directed to the middle classes. As *Blackwood's* and the *Edinburgh, Quarterly*, and *Westminster* reviews especially assumed a position as cultural arbiters, they catered to distinct political and religious interests but, more importantly, to the growing assumption among the middle and upper classes that matters of public interest were matters of intellectual argument before all else. Ultimately, these matters were to be decided on grounds superior to sectarian interests of any kind. That this should be the case was of course forever an ideal, but an ideal toward which the educated public was prodded by the very form in which issues came to be presented in such publications. For instance, one can see the encouragement of this ideal in the language given to the audience for ideas at this time. This may be exemplified by the statement of William

Chambers's *Edinburgh Journal*, established in 1832, that its "grand leading principle" was "to take advantage of the universal appetite for instruction which at present exists."[10] The nutritional metaphor indicates how ideas might be turned away from the terms of parties and politics. It represents a neutrality that could seem to be progressing through the new forms of publication and the new audiences for literature.

Symbolically enough, the *Edinburgh Review* established the principle, later adopted by its competitors, that all contributors were obliged to accept payment for their work. So it seemed that henceforth neither amateurs nor superior priests would appear in the world of intellectual discourse. All writers would be equally denominated professionals when they met in these pages, and their words would be equally subject to critical judgment. According to this ideal, their words would determine their status, not vice versa, once the process of professionalization was accomplished.

In effect, authors would be nothing more or less than their words. These would become the real actors of the world of discourse. They would represent in a clarified form the engagements, conflicts, and resolutions of social history. Just as an aerial view of the earth, suppressing details and grasping relationships invisible to the mundane eye, may clarify the spatial terms of human existence, so too would this world of discourse offer a transcendent advantage to the understanding.

Thus arises the distinctiveness of the authority to which the modern intellectual pledges allegiance. On the one hand, this authority results from historical changes that largely did away with systems of aristocratic and political patronage, among many other features of social life. On the other hand, it may be taken to exist apart from these changes and the new institutions attendant upon them. Modern intellectuals need not believe themselves bound to any social world of the past, present, or future. On the contrary, they may imagine they are bound only to the form of their thought: to the world of intellectual discourse. Consequently, professionalized intellectuals may take the practice of their role as the nature of the world, their commitment to their words as a pledge to social unity and purpose, and the developing form of their own social existence as the flowering hope for a rational society.

One can see this professionalization at work in the prospectus prepared by George Eliot and John Chapman for the revived *Westminster Review*, which Chapman was in the process of buying in 1851. It reads, in part,

> In contradistinction to the practical infidelity and essentially destructive policy which would ignore the existence of wide-spread doubts in relation to established creeds and systems, and would stifle all inquiry dangerous to prescriptive claims, the Review will exhibit that untemporizing expression of opinion, and that fearlessness of investigation and criticism which are the results of a consistent faith in the ultimate prevalence of truth. Convinced that the same fundamental truths are

apprehended under a variety of forms, and that, therefore, opposing systems may in the end prove complements of each other, the Editors will endeavour to institute such a radical and comprehensive treatment of those controverted questions which are practically momentous, as may aid in the conciliation of divergent views.[11]

Somewhat less polemically, as editor of the *Fortnightly Review* in the last quarter of the century, John Morley dedicated it to the spirit of "patient and disinterested controversy";[12] but the principle is the same. One difference between sentiments like these and antecedents to their expression, such as Milton's *Areopagitica*, is that it was actually possible in Eliot's time to furnish them with institutional support and, in fact, to feel they were demanded by the institutions springing up everywhere.

Of course, there was no notion of a democracy of ideas, despite the belief that agreement might play hide-and-seek in diverse shadowy forms. Truth remained qualitatively exclusive and more accessible to some than to others, as is indicated by the terms in which Eliot urged Chapman to write to Mill about their intention to make the *Westminster* "the organ of the ablest and most liberal thinkers of the time."[13] But the social changes that had occurred in England made it possible and even imperative to conceive of ideas being adjudicated in a democratic marketplace. Truth might have an ideal and exclusive form, but one could no longer measure it with instruments suited to an aristocratic society. Quality in a society becoming middle class, mobile, and economically progressive could no longer be stipulated according to a fixed outline of the class structure. It had to be conceived in the form of a process at least theoretically open to wider participation and more extensive revision. The result was the distinctively nineteenth-century conception of "the harmonizing hand of liberal culture," to use Mark Pattison's phrase.[14]

It was the spirit of this process that brought Chapman and Eliot to plan the inclusion of an Independent Section in the review, "in which writers who differed widely from the editors might freely express their opinions. Vital political questions and diverse social theories were to be considered, not for their bearing on party or class, but for their relation to the public good."[15] This plan failed, as did the review itself, partly because of its supporters' anger at the inclusion of differing views. Nevertheless, the form in which the review was planned remains the conception of intellectuals confronting not only the idea of social democracy but also the material pressure for it. The plan was meant to lead the age forward and to accommodate leadership to a new age. Now that legitimacy no longer seemed the domain of an exclusive class, one had to translate authority into "a variety of forms" of expression. To speak to society, the intellectual now had to command a universal tongue.[16]

This change in the nature of intellectuals is even more evident when they are considered in relation to the wider world of book publication. The material change from a system primarily based on patronage to one primarily based on the commercial marketplace was also a great symbolic change. No longer subservient to the church or parasitic upon an individual or party to whose tastes they must submit themselves, intellectuals might seem to produce their thought as completely free and autonomous individuals. In this new publishing situation, one's audience might seem virtually invisible. It could become so faceless that writers might conceive it to be nothing more or less than a personification of the world of discourse. Within a curious inversion by which the physical audience and the metaphysical mind switch identities, all the features of this audience—its actual composition, its distinctive qualities, its personality or class—might be discounted as influences on one's work.

When the audience's relation to writers became sufficiently mediated, thus allowing it to appear as a completely abstract entity, it was easier for writers to believe that the audience had no reality in the production of their writing. They could imagine they addressed themselves only to the cause of unfolding truth. They could think themselves free of compulsion and constraint except for what was intrinsic to their imperfect nature as individuals. Being granted such imperfection as the fate of humanity, writers could imagine that the principled nature of their work—its devotion to universal truth—might qualify them for entrance into that paradise in the world of discourse reserved for those whose work shows its temporality only in its inevitable, marginal flaws.

From this situation the paradox of modern intellectuals arises: that their claim to complete freedom as individuals is the source of their claim to have transcended individuality and reached those shores where universals disport themselves in their unfettered ideality. It is from this paradox that they gain the duty/right to speak to others: the authority that is at once the freedom of the individual allowed its expression and a command from above to which the individual must acquiesce.[17] In this situation, just as the audience may appear as an abstract figure to authors, so may they appear as abstract figures to themselves. They may appear as a trope—"the author"—that exists in an ideal state in the world of discourse, from which it is assigned by discourse to individuals. Rather than thinking of themselves as individuals addressing others or as members of some group or class addressing a specific body of persons, authors may take themselves to be something like the voice of society itself, or of abstract Duty or Right, or even of all Humanity.

It is virtually impossible to overestimate the importance of this difference in the consciousness of intellectuals when writing became so much more public in its scope and yet, for writers, more private and seemingly detached from the influence of an audience. More than anything else, this publishing situation fostered the impression that intellectuals owed no allegiance to a particular class, although, of course, the mobility of middle-class society also nurtured this belief and commonly provided its ideological explanation. Certainly writers of all kinds might still aim to please, but in the very structure of these new conditions, there was encouragement for the belief that such an aim was at best a compromise of principles and at worst a pandering of the mind. It is this belief that Eliot's Sir Hugo Mallinger recognizes, in his rather thick way, when he says to Daniel Deronda, "'I don't go against our university system: we want a little disinterested culture to make head against cotton and capital, especially in the House'" (*DD*, 1: 183). Eliot took this idea very seriously, as when she wrote in reference to the financial imbroglio Sir Walter Scott brought upon himself late in his life: "An author who would keep a pure and noble conscience, and with that a developing instead of a degenerating intellect and taste, must cast out of his aims the aim to be rich" (*E*, 440-41).

In this way the publishing conditions that first made it possible for writers to envision economic independence also made it imperative that these conditions be mystified when one was concerned with art. For instance, John Wilson Ross, writing in the *London Journal* in 1845, referred to popular literature as "ECONOMIC LITERATURE."[18] In so characterizing it, he was relying on the prevailing assumption among intellectuals that literature sloughs off its economic skin when it becomes art. It must be so, for otherwise art in a middle-class age would be just another middle-class commodity. Instead it must be a different kind of object entirely, just as intellectuals must claim they do not belong to the field of commodity relations. The fact that their image of independence arose in relation to the economic situation of writers had to be repressed in favor of the metaphorical independence of the spirit.

This process of constructing metaphor through the repression of social reference was the fable of culture in the Victorian age and generally provided the plots of its novels. The magical transformation of money into culture was the fable outlined for the middle-class aspiration toward a redefined gentility, and also the fable of culture itself in a society becoming middle class in its values. One had to find "'the true golden gold,'"[19] in Mr. Boffin's elegant statement about this cultural transformation. The double redundancy of this image in *Our Mutual Friend* bespeaks the achievement of the metaphorical conversion necessary to turn dust into gold, a money-grubbing girl into a domestic saint, and the economic world of the middle classes into the world of cultural riches.[20] This same achievement is signaled in *Silas Marner* by the redundancy in the rediscovery of Silas's gold after it has been replaced by a golden-haired girl, who was taken by Marner in the first place to be a spiritual transfiguration of "his little sister whom he had carried about in his arms for a year before she died, when he was a small boy without shoes or stockings" (*SM*, 329). In both cases, the marked semiotic excess is the sign of cultural transcendence.

In fact, the catalepsy that overcomes Silas in his doorway so that Eppie may toddle magically inside—"'The money's gone I don't know where, and this is come from I don't know where'" (*SM*, 340)—might be interpreted as a name for the exemplary trope of culture in this age. Figuring the symbolic seizure of the body by art, it would represent the transference of the subject from the realm of natural parentage Eppie leaves behind to the realm of social identity

Silas comes to represent. For what grasps Silas in his doorway is not simply a melodramatic or fantastic plot device but the Victorian conception of culture as it seizes upon Eliot's text.

As Eliot's comment on Scott indicates, one who wrote for a largely middle-class public needed to locate a new origin for authority. Modern authors could not depend on the glamour of the aristocracy to furnish their work with the imprimatur of taste. It seemed one could argue that writing was art only by discovering within the artist the standards theory used to say were apparent to all in the hierarchical structure of society. It makes sense that Eliot should employ eighteenth-century diction when castigating the economic motivations of the writer who did more than any other to make the novel respectable and whom she otherwise greatly admired. This language indicates an attempt to negotiate the difference between the traditional regulating functions of taste and the more modern functions of morality and truth.

It is understandable, too, that artists' biographies were so closely tied to appreciation of their work, for Eliot and many others, from the time when the romantics apotheosized the heroic artist until late in the nineteenth century. The character of the author became vitally important to readers at precisely that point in English history when the character of literature was thrown into question by social changes that raised the new genre of the novel into prominence while simultaneously weakening the authority that formerly had dispensed aesthetic judgment. As Eliot decided, "A nasty mind makes nasty art, whether for art or any other sake. And a meagre mind will bring forth what is meagre. And some effect in determining other minds there must be according to the degree of nobleness or meanness in the selection made by the artist's soul" (*L*, 5: 391). Committing herself to this idea of the artist, she wrote to her publisher, "I will never write anything to which my whole heart, mind, and conscience don't consent" (*L*, 3: 417). Or, as she had written to Blackwood about *Scenes of Clerical Life* in 1857, "The moral effect of the stories of course depends on my power of seeing truly and feeling justly; and as I am not conscious of looking at things through the medium of cynicism or irreverence, I can't help hoping that there is no tendency in what I write to produce those miserable mental states" (*L*, 2: 362).

This emphasis on the personal character of the artist might seem to contradict the logic that separates the abstract author from the private individual, but the case is exactly the opposite. For what is this assumption of a necessary connection between the nature of the work of art and the character of the artist except the abstraction of the artist from the realm of mundane individuality, in which nastiness and meagerness may be dissimulated, to a utopian realm of truth in which they cannot hide? One fails to understand the conception of biography in the nineteenth century if one does not see that its famous lack of candor is not so much the result of prudishness or protective censorship as it is the result of this abstraction in the relation between artist and audience. Information that might mar the idealized picture of the artist is not as likely to be repressed from self-serving or hypocritical motives as it is from the simple assumption that such material is excluded categorically from the nature of the artist. For this abstracted character, hagiography is the normative, not the unrealistic, form of biography.

One should also note that Eliot, following the custom of her age, made a moral idiom out of the concept of "nobility." In the eighteenth century the meaning of this concept had been fixed by the governing order of society, however much it might have been extended metaphorically. Now, though, the fable of culture was at work, repressing social reference in favor of transcendent metaphor. The hierarchy of society would be entirely within the mind of authors—and within the mind of readers responding to their work. In this way the discourse of Eliot's age reconciled the theoretical openness of culture with the actual distribution of cultural privilege in society. The danger of the fable of social mobility was countered by the assumption that a variance existed within the nature of individuals that would assign them discrete levels in relation to each other. The corollary assumption was that this variance was roughly measurable by the relative success of individuals in society, even though plenty of elbow room might be left for progressive reforms. It was thus that the demand for a hierarchy of birth within aristocratic ideology was supplanted by a description of social hierarchies as an effect of human nature, in accordance with the typical middle-class strategy of representing its ideology as natural science.

It is no accident that the same age that invented mass literacy and mass communication also invented an attitude of intellectual distrust toward certain works simply because they were too popular. The potential for this attitude was implicit in the same changes that gave intellectuals their new role in society. Associated with the exhilarating freedom of ideas, which this role seemed to promise, was the necessity for the independence of intellectuals to be measured by a certain limitation of their audience. The range of education in the public was expected to set boundaries where the obligations due to a patron and the restriction of literacy to a privileged few no longer enforced them. Hence the significance of Eliot's reference to her readers in *Daniel Deronda*: "I like to mark the time, and connect the course of individual lives with the historic stream, for all classes of thinkers" (*DD*, 1: 90). As soon as "the public" became the audience of literature, it became common in one way or another to distinguish classes within it, such as the "educated" or the "enlightened" public. Similarly, artists like Eliot would distinguish themselves and their works from authors and works of a more popular tendency.[21] In this way categories that appear to be determined by the neutral consideration of intellectual development dislodged those discredited for originating in the "accidental distinctions" of class.

Even more fundamentally important to this time is the novelty of the fact that literacy was becoming the basic prerequisite for knowledge and education the definitive process of its refinement. Literacy was becoming the horizon of human existence in this century, which witnessed the popularization of the slogan Knowledge is Power among the middle and working classes. The consequence of the commercial, industrial, and administrative developments taking place in England, as reinforced by the emphasis on literacy among Dissenters and Evangelicals, was a society that redefined nature according to the prescriptions of literacy and education.

Henceforth, a new process of exclusion would be instituted in the governing discourse of the time, whereby the lack of literacy or of further educational "growth" explained social distress, marginality, discontent, or deviance. Ignorance could no longer be casual, natural, or innocent, although this is not to say it was considered a bad quality. It simply was no longer a quality or aspect of character at all. It was a vacancy: a deficiency of human nature precisely equal in its dimensions to the disturbances raised against middle-class ideologies. So Lord Chancellor Brougham in 1831 could say, "If there is the mob, there is the people also. I speak now of the middle classes . . . the genuine repositories of sober, rational, intelligent and honest English feeling."[22] In the perfection of this discourse, its contravention would not be taken as a denial of assent but as a failure of ascent. Thus one could condescend to rebellion, as the novels of the 1840s and Eliot's *Felix Holt* make clear. In this situation any person, circumstance, or event that was not of the cultured middle classes would bear the stamp of negativity, of an incomplete evolution, as Friedrich Engels indicated when he described 1858 England by saying that "this most bourgeois of all nations is apparently aiming ultimately at the possession of a bourgeois aristocracy and a bourgeois proletariat as well as a bourgeoisie."[23]

No sooner did literacy and education become assumptions of social life than they were used to dismiss from the realm of discourse the language of any person or group that did not display their standards. These were not merely "politeness" and "intelligibility" (although momentous enough in themselves); they were also the fully elaborated values of the intellectual world to which figures like Eliot belonged. Eliot's description of three laborers struggling to learn to write and cipher "almost as if three rough animals were making humble efforts to learn how they might become human" (*AB*, 243) was not a casual phrase. While she drew the characters in her novels toward "a sort of difficult blessedness, such as one may imagine in beings who are conscious of painfully growing into the possession of higher powers" (*FH*, 237), it was her sense of her own intellectual condition she was holding out for their pursuit and eventual delectation.

Just as this intellectual condition is characterized in Eliot's writing by its grasp of universality—the catalepsy in which the individual is seized by society—so is ignorance characterized by a deficiency of the power of abstraction. Hence her description of the society of "Mr. Gilfil's Love-Story": "At present, to find fault with the sermon was regarded as almost equivalent to finding fault with religion itself" ("MGL," 93). The society Eliot took for granted in this description as throughout her works is that described by Henry Brougham, the early Victorian reformer and one of the founders of the Society for the Diffusion of Useful Knowledge, when he said, in a famous phrase, "The schoolmaster is abroad."[24] This schoolmaster's emergence signifies the birth of a new standard of humanity based on the middle-class redefinition of knowledge to match the source of this class's growing power. The fact that the power of a specific class thus came to be identified as a universal force definitive of man and definitively based on educated discourse is a development essential to the historical understanding of a literature like Eliot's.

Of course, this development was neither instantaneous nor perfect. Arguments over the extent and nature of the education that ought to be practiced were rife throughout this period; and curricular reform in the public schools, for instance, did not begin until quite late in the century. However, in this case as in the question of the literary marketplace, the very debate over what changes ought to occur testified to the fact that a radical difference in the form of discourse had already been instituted. When literacy and education became formal prerequisites for humanity—and it is no exaggeration to say this was the change that took form in the discourse of the nineteenth century, despite the continuing piety in the dispensation of Christian souls to even the most ignorant members of society—words, including the words of novels, took on a different nature than they had had before.

The fable of this social change was that the development represented by education was an evolution of man and his spirit, not the articulation of the power of a class in society. Ultimately, the extent of human growth came to be measured by cultured middle-class standards of behavior, dress, speech, and belief, as a result of this fable's power. Thus it was that J. A. Roebuck, in a parliamentary debate over government support for education in 1833, might look forward to the day when "a proper education for the people" would result in "a thorough understanding on their part of the circumstances on which their happiness depended, and of the powers by which those circumstances were controlled." They would learn, he continued, "what a government could, and . . . could not do to relieve their distresses."[25] In other words, they would learn middle-class law, as such educational reformers always expected. Robert Lowe, a key figure in the development of education in the second half of the century, made this promise even more forthrightly:

> The lower classes ought to be educated to discharge the duties cast
> upon them. They should also be educated that they may appreciate
> and defer to a higher cultivation when they meet it, and the higher
> classes ought to be educated in a very different manner, in order that
> they may exhibit . . . to the lower classes that higher education to
> which, if it were shown to them, they would bow down and defer.[26]

So, although a number of social changes established the ground for this new emphasis on literacy and education, they took on meaning only through this change in the nature of humanity invented within the governing discourse of the age. No matter that a writer like Dickens could so violently disparage the values and practice of contemporary education: his insistence on a definition of human nature as something apart from the wrong sort of education shows him bound to the terms of the same discourse as Eliot. The opposition he expressed is significant, but in the analysis of this social change, it illustrates only how thoroughly the issue of humanity had become the issue of education—even if one chose to argue with this eventuality. The special relevance to intellectuals of this fable, in which the social power instituted in education was redefined as a quasi-biological and quasi-spiritual aspect of human growth, is that they depended on this metaphorical construction to sanction their roles and extend their influence in modern society.

Related to this consideration is the development E. L. Woodward has termed "the rise of the expert."[27] The growth of industrialization, the expanding complexity, centralization, and bureaucratization of state power developing with it, and the correspondent burgeoning of cities and population established conditions in which new types of professionals in business and government were needed.[28] One result was that great storms of rhetoric were raised in the nineteenth-century debate over the comparative merits of liberal and technical studies. However, this division is not the most salient one for the understanding of education in the nineteenth century, as one can see from the fact that the rise in the importance of the expert is closely associated with the rise of even that intellectual most passionately devoted to liberal values. Not only were these roles at times occupied by the same person—John Stuart Mill was a civil servant and Arnold an inspector of schools—but the values of the expert were allied in many ways with those of the intellectual.[29]

In addition to their shared concerns with education and a gentility based on culture rather than class, there was a parallel concern that a meritocracy should supplant traditional or aristocratic inheritors of power. It was the second half of the nineteenth century that first saw standards established for professions in medicine, teaching, the civil service, and other occupations. Although these could not be established easily, as Eliot's Lydgate had come to realize earlier in this age when he found how "dangerous" it was "to insist on knowledge as a qualification for any salaried office" (M, 1: 164), the conditions of the time led to the ideal of a systematically developed rationality in such occupations as in the general development of ideas, just as Lydgate would have hoped. It was in the latter half of this century, too, that competitive exams for the civil service and other posts became important. Although the civil service exam established after 1870 was largely based on knowledge of classical literature,[30] the very fact of its creation indicates how far the pressure for meritocratic standards had come: that is, for standards deemed objective because they were based on education. In this fact that education should become the matrix of objectivity, one sees how it became the theoretical standard for nature even as it practically defined nature through the behavioral norms that were being dispensed through educational disciplines such as medicine, psychology, and sociology.

As a result of the nature of their work, experts, like intellectuals, could seem to be independent of class, party, and patronage. Whether they were scientists, engineers, school inspectors, or members of government commissions on factory workers' conditions, they might seem to owe an obligation only to the facts with which they were concerned. One remembers that Dickens did not quarrel with Thomas Gradgrind's objectivity, only with his definition of humanity, just as Eliot never questioned the disinterested nature of Lydgate's medical work, only the nature of his decisions in circumstances associated with this work. "Alas! the scientific conscience had got into the debasing company of money obligation and selfish respects" (*M*, 2: 327).[31] Similarly, Eliot shows how Mr. Tulliver's tragedy in *The Mill on the Floss* lies only incidentally in his rash passions, which would not have had such profound consequences if he had not applied them to his business and legal relations, thereby losing all professional objectivity. In this case, too, Eliot does not question the professionalism Wakem brings to the practice of law or Tulliver to business but only the way they make decisions in their "private" lives.

It hardly needs to be said that the professional's independence was a fable and was so recognized by many at that time. The more important point in the present context is that the conscious recognition of a need for experts and the way they became institutionalized during this period could encourage the ideal of disinterest reflected in one of the meanings now given to the word "professional."

Scientism is the bottom line of this nineteenth-century devotion to education, despite the disputes between the advocates of scientific and liberal values. What needs to be understood of scientism is precisely this: it is no more allied to "technical" studies than to "humane" letters, although it underlies both of these subjects for most contemporary intellectuals. This scientism is a variety of middle-class ideology. It ensures that rationality is definitively human and destined to prevail in the direction of human affairs if society can only be made conscious of its power. Thus, Knowledge is Power. This fable is a development of the liberal values of the Enlightenment and owes its persuasiveness to the sense of progress with which the middle classes typically looked to the future as a result of the successes in their own recent history. Belief in this fable was forwarded even more during the course of the nineteenth century by its institutionalization in the theory and government of society, especially in the increasingly systematic practice of science. For instance, in Eliot's case, modern critics of her work are aware that it is shaped by scientific or naturalistic underpinnings, a fact that did not go unnoticed by her contemporaries.[32]

One does not have to argue the precise degree of Eliot's adherence to Comte's Positivism to see that a faith in science as a rational enterprise and in reason as the positive essence of man informs her works as it does those of writers such as

Matthew Arnold and Thomas Huxley. During this time when science went so far in supplementing or even supplanting divinity that stars were seen to "stink as they twinkle," in Ruskin's phrase,[33] even writers who might seem to have ignored or fought the change may nonetheless be seen to have absorbed its implications.

Eliot's was not the conservatism of Burke, or even that of Scott with which Ruskin so strongly identified. It was the conservatism inherent in a discourse rooted in the rationalist ideology of science and scientific logic. This kind of discourse does not confront the opponent with tradition but with truth—or realism. And part of the significance of Eliot's commitment to this progressive form of discourse is that it could contribute further to the meritocratic illusion: the belief that one can isolate merit within a society by means of a neutral rationality and thus promote a society that stratifies itself according to the laws of nature.

This is the fable of competency—or, in a more popular version, the fable of the self-made man—by which the middle classes justified their assumption and use of power. According to this fable, power in modern society is not grasped in any particular hands, as it would be under an aristocratic reign, which is likely to have as one of its consequences the production of a peasantry whose "rude mind with difficulty associates the ideas of power and benignity" (*SM*, 217). Instead, power is a formal effect of the structure of reason. Theoretically, society is seen as accommodating itself to that structure so as to allow individual merit to find its level. Thus it is that nature, within the new devotion of society to literacy and education, appears as the laws of reason, which, happily, fit the destiny of the middle classes.

The essential point is that the progressive potential of meritocratic institutions is invariably exaggerated to grotesque proportions. This is the case because intellectuals committed to a belief in rationality take the form of institutions for their practical and substantial reality. In much the same way as gentlemen in Eliot's age would involve themselves in "post-obiting" when they borrowed money against the promise of a future legacy (the vice Fred Vincy's Uncle Featherstone accuses him of practicing), liberal intellectuals typically trade upon the future they believe to be implicit in ideas.

There were many critics of this practice as an aspect of middle-class ideology in Eliot's age. However, such criticism did not touch the core of the fable, which is the assumption that power governs society only when that society is tyrannical, while reason is progressive because it redefines power as a function of universal forms and so understands all individuals equally. And if this argument for meritocratic standards also sounds like Eliot's interpretation of history, in which individuals, societies, and countries are seen as gradually moving toward the comprehension of universal symbols in their relation to ordinary human life, it is justly so. To understand her nature as an intellectual in this time is to see that her aesthetics and other intellectual beliefs are not simply the result of the writers and intellectuals whom she read, translated, reviewed, or chatted with, but much more fundamentally the product of the kind of discourse in which she engaged herself in undertaking these activities.

A final point to be made about the conditions for the appearance of the modern intellectual involves both the rise of the expert and the changes in the publishing industry in the nineteenth century. These developments were facilitated by the fact that transport and communication grew to be more rapid as well as more extensive owing to the building of canals, improvements in road financing and building, the creation of the railroads, and related developments. Consequently, the change to an industrial economy did more than lead to a greater concentration of population in cities and eventually to a greater centralization of powers in the nation. It also led to a greater consciousness of life on a national rather than a local scale—a development to which Eliot adverts in several novels set in the time before it was accomplished. In fact, the pattern of her own life may be said to epitomize this development, as it physically took her from the Midlands to London and intellectually from a narrow sort of Protestantism to an all-embracing religion of humanity. Moreover, it might be argued that the form of each of her novels recapitulates this passage from a provincial and parochial past to a future projected as a national and universal whole. Very often this is even the form of her sentences, as observations of particular individuals or circumstances are expanded on a universal moral scale.

G. M. Trevelyan has noted that the penny post of 1840 enabled the poor, "for the first time in the history of man, to communicate with the loved ones from whom they were separated";[34] and this example may serve to indicate the even greater broadening of intellectual horizons made possible for the middle and upper classes by a cheaper press and more rapid communications and travel. It became possible—and, indeed, necessary—for culture to be conceived of on a much greater social scale than had been looked to heretofore. Unlike the situation in "the early ages of the world" when "it was believed that each territory was inhabited and ruled by its own divinities" (*SM*, 228), modern education would, in John Morley's words, be "an instrument by which [one] may know how the world fares outside his narrow penfold."[35] The idea of culture had to change to include the changing system of its distribution. Now that this was no longer a largely static and hierarchical business confined to a small class attached to the tastes of London society and to the values of great estates, the idea of culture had to become more flexible in its nature, progressive in its intent, and extensive in the area to which it looked for its application. Like intellectuals, culture, too, could then seem independent of classes and responsible to all society.

This idea of culture as a broad circulation and independent arbitration of ideas was made possible only because communication in general seemed to be attaining this character. A writer like Eliot might satirize this change by referring to "the all-wise" and adding, "I mean the newspapers" (*FH*, 492), but this change in the social structure of communication did entail a change in the popular conception of wisdom. The transmission of knowledge through the metaphor of circulation replaced its transmission through the metaphors of blood, breeding, or inheritance when it actually became possible for intellectual discourse to function as a popular national currency, or—to choose a symbolic example—when Mudie's helped to open the gentleman's private library to the middle classes. So Edward Lytton Bulwer, writing in 1833, encouraged the modern "circulation of intelligence," while John Morley in 1866 commended Eliot's authorial reflections and comments because he saw them to be promoting "the active circulation of ideas."[36] The conception of independence among modern intellectuals could include independence from provincialism, too, because the world of intellectual discourse could seem as materially separated from provincial limitations as from class interests and unreasoning tradition.

A further aspect of this new and more rapid circulation was the explosion of information that accompanied it in a society characterized by progressive modernization in science and business as well as in industry. Thus Carlyle wrote in "Characteristics" (1831): "We stand here too conscious of many things: with Knowledge, the symptom of Derangement, we must even do our best to restore a little Order."[37] At this time there was simply a great growth of facts, social as well as technical, created by the new communications and threatening in their divulgation to overwhelm the average individual who might have no capacity for discriminating among them. So J. Phillips Kay commented, in his *Recent Measures for the Promotion of Education in England* (1839), that "the physical development of the population has been more rapid than the growth of our intellectual, moral, and religious institutions."[38]

Or such at least was the fear of the governing classes, who believed themselves able to digest this new information but feared it might lead only to a metastasis of dangerous opinions among those not fit to absorb it. Thus, although there is no direct connection between Eliot's horror of trashy literature and the government's attempt to suppress cheap publications in the Six Acts of 1819—an effort to keep such writings from the lower classes—this feeling shared by so many certainly had a political dimension. As Sir Egerton Brydges wrote in the early 1830s in reference to the extension of the reading public, "All they learn is to deface what they once had been taught, and to have no opinions at all—except that every one may think after his own fashion, and that all old-received principles are narrow and unenlightened prejudices."[39] So Tennyson wrote of "the light ephemeris / That flutters in the popular breath,"[40] while Eliot was wont to inveigh against "that calamity of our age, superfluous literature" (*L*, 6: 409). Similarly, in one of her essays for the *Westminster Review*, she wrote unhappily about "Circulating Library fiction," following the popular practice of stigmatizing this new institution with the dangers it was felt to have stimulated (*E*, 133).[41]

A terrifying feature of modernity for such writers was that there was simply too much of it. This excessiveness of the world was deemed to be confusing and dangerous in general, but especially in relation to the less educated and lower ranking members of society, who would be identified with this excessiveness both literally and metaphorically from the time of Reverend Malthus until at least the time when Hardy wrote *Jude the Obscure* and had Little Father Time exterminate himself and his siblings because they were "*'too menny.'*"[42] Within this situation so alarming to the governing classes of the time, it might well appear (to adopt Ruskin's formulation) that information was becoming deformation.[43]

It is not coincidental in this regard that industrialism in England was accompanied by a huge increase in population and that the vast majority of the total population during the nineteenth century belonged to the working classes and to the poor. In opposition to the world of the past as the Victorians had enshrined it in their cultural memory—the world Hardy characterized as one of "old association—an almost exhaustive biographical or historical acquaintance with every object, animate or inanimate, within the observer's horizon"[44]—the modern world might seem one in which information had so far outstripped traditional modes of thought that it had put a completely new face on the world and thus made it an object extremely difficult to confront without fear. It is precisely the recognition of this situation that made the Victorians so self-consciously "modern," just as it led to the Saint Simonian designation of this age as a "critical" one. The world of the country and of the past became news in Sir Walter Scott's and Maria Edgeworth's fiction, and later in Eliot's and Hardy's works, because the novelty of the modern world of commerce, industry, and urbanization forced a reinterpretation of the old as much as it required its own interpretation. (Hence the pairings of these times in such works as Carlyle's *Past and Present*, Pugin's *Contrasts*, and Blake's *Songs of Innocence and Experience*.) In this regard, the fact that popular journalism proliferated throughout England during the same period that saw the novel burgeoning in popularity marks a telling affiliation between these two modes of discourse. They were not only nourishing a new appetite for print, as the contemporary metaphor would have it, but they were shaping the growth of that contemporary opinion whose power had just been invented by the extension of literacy and the developments in modern transport and communications. As Eliot said, a "man or woman who publishes writings inevitably assumes the office of teacher or influencer of the public mind" (*E*, 440).

It appeared to intellectuals like Eliot that interpretation of a radically new kind was required to subdue this modern world. Without this new kind of interpretation, the novel sheen of the world might leave one as bewildered as are those acquaintances of the Veneerings in *Our Mutual Friend*, who are puzzled about whether they are the couple's oldest or newest intimates. In Eliot's terms, the result might be a Tory "revelling in regret that dear, old, brown, crumbling, picturesque inefficiency is everywhere giving place to spick-and-span, new-painted, new-varnished efficiency, which will yield endless diagrams, plans, elevations, and sections, but alas! no picture" ("AB," 4). A huge outpouring of raw facts, new conditions, could make the surface of the world seem more impermeable to understanding and more fertile a ground for misunderstandings than it had ever been before. And, again, this situation was thought to be especially true in relation to the lower classes, who typically were imaged as being threatening in their numbers and as foreign to the observer as the benighted savages of darkest Africa.

The function of controlling all this news, of interpreting it, became the expert's and the intellectual's role. In this world the intellectual's power was conceived to be that of a rhetoric or shaping discourse. So Mill wrote in *The Spirit of the Age*, "A change has taken place in the human mind," and added,

> Those persons whom the circumstances of society, and their own position in it, permit to dedicate themselves to the investigation and study of physical, moral, and social truths, as their peculiar calling, can alone be expected to make the evidences of such truths a subject of profound meditation, and to make themselves thorough masters of the philosophical grounds of those opinions of which it is desirable that all should be firmly *persuaded*, but which they alone can entirely and philosophically *know*.[45]

Such is the background, in a broad and summary form, of what is distinctive in the emergence of the modern intellectual. However, the foregoing considerations take on meaning only when one places them in relation to a specific type of intellectual. These considerations are a necessary preliminary to the understanding of any type of modern intellectual, but they trace a range of opportunities for positions in society rather than circumscribing those opportunities.

The potential idealization of the intellectual role has been emphasized because one of the most important types that appeared to fill this role in modern society—a type exemplified by George Eliot—was the liberal intellectual. Intellectuals of this type take the nature of their own social existence as their ideal and in fact as the ideal for all humanity, as Karl Mannheim suggested when he dilated on the destinies he would look to for modern intellectuals: "Most important among these would be the discovery of a position from which a total perspective would be possible. Thus they might play the role of watchmen in what otherwise would be a pitch-black night."[46] Emerson wrote in much the same vein when he described "The American Scholar" as "the world's eye" and added, "He and only he knows the world."[47] Eliot herself described the nearest approach to this utopian perspective, which would later provide her with the narrative form of her fiction, in a *Westminster* essay of 1855:

There is not a more pernicious fallacy afloat in common parlance, than the wide distinction made between intellect and morality. . . . Now that highest moral habit, the constant preference of truth both theoretically and practically, preeminently demands the cooperation of the intellect with the impulses; as is indicated by the fact that it is only found in anything like completeness in the highest class of minds. (*E,* 166)

To describe liberal intellectuals more specifically, one must distinguish them from the Liberalism commonly identified as the middle class's politics in this age. The affinities between these two are clear enough. They are shown in the fact that political Liberals in the second half of the nineteenth century generally stood for individual rights and freedom and against aristocratic tradition and "excessive" governmental interference in the social and economic life of the nation. Whereas Liberalism did not by any means imply complete sympathy with democratic or individualistic aims, the middle class's democratic claims on society were generally represented by this ideology. However, even though the liberal intellectuals of this period shared a rhetoric of freedom, individualism, and progressivism with political Liberals, one finds that they felt it necessary at crucial points in their philosophy to distinguish between the intellectual and political significations of their discourse. Although these intellectuals were generally in sympathy with those interests of the middle classes represented by Liberalism, they would take liberal intellectual values to be more comprehensive than and thus a corrective to Liberal political goals. It was precisely from this appeal to values transcending politics that they defined their intellectual liberalism. It is as characteristic of liberal intellectuals to sublimate political within cultural interest as it is for them to assert an individual interest that overrides any group identity and yet ultimately consolidates that group identity.

What defines this type of intellectual is not a specific brand of political judgment but a means of approaching political and other affairs. The ideal of a liberal education formulated by Cardinal Newman comes close to defining this method of understanding, but Newman's concern with a specific institution made his object narrower than the concern that gives definition to liberal intellectuals.

What defines the liberal intellectual is a commitment to the ideal of liberal intellectual discourse. Such discourse may be applied to the goals of a university, but this discourse is taken to be applicable to society as a whole—in fact, to be the essential revelation of society. The liberal intellectual's special technique of power is the assumption that the practice of this discourse *is* society. According to this argument, it is within the procedures of this discourse that the whole of society in the past, in the present, and even in the future becomes available to human understanding, which otherwise will wear the blinders of partiality and mistake its own limitations for a darkness cast over the world.

The role of the intellectual is taken to incorporate the very possibility of social truth. In this way the liberal intellectual defines the modern age as one that offers the possibility of unprecedented enlightenment.

What distinguishes this ideal from traditional philosophical claims to transcendent understanding is the framework of opposition and alliance that provided the specific conditions of its appearance. In the first place, any discourse directly related to a particular class within society is opposed to the liberal ideal. It is not the limitation or partiality of views in general that gives rise to the liberal intellectual's contrasting claim, although an intellectual of this stripe would claim otherwise and typically would thematize the contrast in universal terms. As one can see in the discourse of Eliot's time, it is a specific form of limitation, that which comes from class, which is abhorred. This opposition indicates the significance of the claim to a view of society as a whole. The ideal of a classless discourse would not have arisen without conflicts among classes to give point to it.

It was the rise of the middle classes and the development of an industrial society that provided the impetus for this ideal. The concept of social class developed only in the late eighteenth and early nineteenth centuries,[48] and the idea of liberal intellectuality is inseparably, although antagonistically, related to it. Characteristic of this relationship are the speaker's words in Harriet Martineau's *Illustrations of Political Economy* (1832-34): " 'When we reason upon subjects of this kind it is not our business to take the part of one class against another, but to discover what is for the general good; which is, in the long run, the same as the good of individuals.' "[49] The ideal of a classless discourse remained the refrain of the middle classes and of the intellectuals representing them throughout this period, as when R. G. Moulton in the latter half of the century commended the cause of University Extension by claiming, "We know nothing about classes in University Extension."[50] It is this ideal that spurs the plot of *Felix Holt*, in which one learns that "the picture-writing of Felix Holt's troubles was of an entirely puzzling kind: if he were a martyr, neither side wanted to claim him" (*FH*, 364). In Eliot's terms, this lack of class appeal is Felix's salvation and his claim to martyrdom.

The intellectuals' alliance is indeed with the middle classes but not with them as a class. For it was the virtue of the middle classes in this age to conceive their interests to be those of everyone in society, as the quotation from Martineau, her intellectual biography, and such novels as *North and South* and *Middlemarch* make clear. It is this belief that is adopted in the intellectual's claim to be above class interests and in the further claim that intellectual discourse represents the truth of society.

Whereas the traditional argument of the aristocracy had been that its superior prospect in society conferred upon it the ability to be disinterested in the adjudication of society's needs and problems, the characteristic middle-class argument was that the untrammeled pursuit of middle-class goals would, in fact, represent the interests of everyone in society. This attitude underlies the whole of middle-class discourse in the nineteenth century. It is the fable of middle-class enlightenment: the identification of the middle classes, or of the liberal intellectuals representing them, as the watchmen of society. The fable is that the middle classes are not the powerful or the rich element in society but rather the normative element, and thus the future incarnate of that society. The first great political implementation of this perspective was in the Anti-Corn Law agitation of the 1830s and 1840s, but it was also basic to middle-class discourse in relation to education and a host of other social issues.

When a social program was prepared by working-class leaders influenced by middle-class values, it would represent the same rejection of class that characterized the middle classes. Thus, Sir Francis Burdett in 1831 described the National Political Union, which was formed in reaction against the socialist National Union of the Working Classes:

> This is not a Union of the Working Classes, nor of the Middle
> Classes, nor of any other Class, but of all Reformers, of the masses
> and of the millions.
> The *National Political Union*, is essentially a Union of the People,
> and is the first instance on record of the nation breaking through the
> trammels of class, to associate for the Common interest in the
> Common cause.[51]

And when education was designed for the working classes, it was designed to impress them with the idea that the middle classes represented truth. Despite all the criticisms made of the middle classes by intellectuals like Eliot—criticisms directed precisely against those aspects of middle-class thought and manners that did not display an adherence to the classless goal—they were still indebted to the middle classes for their ideological positions in society.[52] It is for this reason that in her "Address to Working Men, by Felix Holt," which she wrote when the 1867 Reform Bill was passed, Eliot could argue for the "turning of Class Interests into Class Functions or duties" (*E*, 421). She could do so because she took middle-class interest to be truth and as such the moral basis for a doctrine of working-class duties.

It was on the basis of this assumption that the liberal intellectual sought a common, classless identity established among individuals by means of the free circulation of ideas. Mannheim described the intellectual as striving "to create a forum outside the party schools in which the perspective of and the interest of the whole is safeguarded,"[53] and this in fact was Eliot's aim. As she wrote to a friend, "One wants a temple besides the outdoor temple—a place where human beings do not ramble apart, but *meet* with a common impulse" (*L*, 3: 452).[54] So Arnold wrote that culture "enables us to look at the ins and outs of things . . . without hatred and without partiality, and with a disposition to see the good in everybody all round."[55] Similarly, Tennyson prayed, "And in its season bring the law; / That from Discussion's lip may fall / With Life, that, working strongly, binds— / Set in all lights by many minds, / To close the interests of all."[56] This is where the liberal intellectual finds the independence, equality, and common humanity of all individuals: in the forum of rational discourse.

In Mill's formulation, "the forbearance which flows from a conscientious sense of the importance to mankind of the equal freedom of all opinions, is the only tolerance which is commendable, or, to the highest moral order of minds, possible."[57] This tolerance was to order the mind as it was to be the order of society, in accordance with the typical assumption of the liberal intellectual that these ought to be treated as analogues of each other. So Mill wrote that in all areas except those of the exact sciences, no one's opinions deserve the name of knowledge "except so far as he has had forced upon him by others, or gone through himself, the same mental process which would have been required of him in carrying on an active controversy with opponents."[58] It is not that the mind is to society as microcosm is to macrocosm or as synechdoche is to the whole object, but rather that both are equally dependent on the metaphor of the free circulation of ideas. They are tropes of this trope, despite the fact that the discourse of the time would seem to lend them much more concreteness than the avowedly idealistic image of free discussion to which Mill dedicated *On Liberty*. To interpret their conception in this age is to analyze the procedures by which a certain order of figural language comes to be represented as an equivalent to science in Mill's philosophy or in Eliot's art, not to debate their accuracy or adequacy.

For instance, it can be noted that Mill's model for both the mind and society is the kind of discussion group that played such an important part in his early life. This kind of group may be said to be the model for liberal intellectuals in general. It incorporates the intellectual's claim to classlessness and independence, as these are the two key assumptions in the procedures of such a group, while the nature of its practices implies a society coterminous with rational discourse. In this model the source of society is not found in God or in hallowed traditions—the *"idola theatri"* Eliot dismissed in her first essay for the *Westminster Review*, "The Progress of the Intellect" (*E*, 29). One looks for this source (which is also the future) in discourse itself. This is conceived to have such prescriptive power as a process that any individuals able to participate in it will be so enlightened that they will recognize, sooner or later, the intellectual's ends as their own. In fact, Mill wrote, "Liberty, as a principle, has no application to any state of things anterior to the time when mankind have become capable of being improved by free and equal discussion."[59]

Although the development of liberal intellectual thought in England can be associated largely with middle-class Dissenters in the eighteenth century who had political and economic as well as religious reasons to adopt Enlightenment ideology and to promote freedom of discussion—and to begin an agitation against the establishment of a national system of education, which was successful throughout most of the nineteenth century, for fear that the established church would dominate its teachings—no limited interests are acknowledged in the ideal of this freedom. Similarly, no note is taken of the "taxes on knowledge" deliberately designed to inhibit the circulation of ideas among the working classes and the poor in an England swept by fears of Jacobin revolution, even though these were not entirely repealed until the second half of the nineteenth century. Other impediments to discussion were ignored just as easily. As Bertrand Russell dryly noted, "It is remarkable that Mill, in his book on liberty, never mentions the restrictions which law and public opinion in his day imposed upon even the most serious discussion of topics which the Victorians preferred to ignore."[60]

History is treated as an effect of discourse, and any impediments to free discussion that may exist are viewed as a lamentable but remediable reversal of this relationship. History is never implicated in the definition of free discussion, even though it may be admitted that it is only at a certain time and in a certain state of society that such discussion becomes possible. The essence of liberal intellectual discourse is this cancellation of history. It is on this basis that one feels capable of interpreting the past as it never could understand itself, of surveying modern society from a perspective superior to individual interests, and in projecting a future for society that is held to be the "truth" of society no matter what "errors" may seem to discompose it if one pays attention to limited circumstances, problems, conflicts, injustices, or disaffections. According to the viewpoint of the liberal intellectual, once it becomes possible to project a rational future through discourse, it is this prospective future that becomes the basis for morality and all other forms of social commitment, despite whatever the historical past and present may be. It is this viewpoint that composes the narratives of Victorian progressivism and optimism in all their variations, including Eliot's meliorist doctrine. Hence the characteristically expansive structures of Eliot's writing, as described by a reviewer for *The Spectator* in 1863: "You have to unroll a large surface of the picture before even the smallest *unit* of its effect is attained."[61] Her writing calls attention to its meaning more on the level of discourse than through particular narrative events or descriptions because of this overreaching grasp of time within her intellectual position.

Just as it is in the nature of the middle classes to identify their interests with those of everyone in society, so it is in the nature of liberal intellectuals to see their own ideal of rational discourse as in its very nature a comprehension, mediation, and transcendence of all interests. It is the business of liberal intellectuals to shun discontinuity in the realm of ideas, as in society, by categorically excluding from humanity and from discourse any phenomena that do not bear the ticket of admission to the forum of rational discourse.

In a more precise sense, then, the peculiar technique of power exercised by the liberal intellectual is the dissimulation of prescriptive legislation as descriptive analysis, whether this be exercised through the work of science or through the values of the culture promoted by a novelist like Eliot. Discourse in any age may assume a naturalized form, but the discourse of the liberal intellectual made this appeal to universality a sophisticated program of analysis that was continually able to reconfirm the identities of intellectuals, of the middle classes, and of middle-class truths. The universal procedures of rational discourse are a technique of power under which intellectuals representing the middle classes consolidated the practice of their role in society and through which they exercised their historical will, and only in a society characterized by the changes previously described could this technique have developed in this way. It required a modern society to give the figural language of nature and universality—the language of Duty and Right—the form of science along with the institutional apparatus in society to make this form appear as empirical and cultural fact, confront the members of society as neutral procedures, and thus make itself appear inviolable to any contravention except that which would appear to be destructive and antisocial violence.

Of course the participation of all individuals in rational discourse was only an ideal, even to the intellectual. The very development of a popular audience that helped to give modern intellectuals their role was indeed a problem for them. No wonder Eliot's comments on the "trash" that threatened to suffocate literature like hers in the popular marketplace are so frequent and forceful in her letters and more elaborately developed in her essay on authorship:

> Among those callings which have not yet acquired anything near a
> full-grown conscience in the public mind is Authorship. Yet the
> changes brought about by the spread of instruction and the consequent
> struggles of an uneasy ambition, are, or at least might well be, forcing
> on many minds the need of some regulating principle with regard to
> the publication of intellectual products, which would override the rule
> of the market: a principle, that is, which should be derived from a fix-
> ing of the author's vocation according to those characteristics in which
> it differs from other bread-winning professions. (*E*, 438)

As previously noted, this concern is characteristic of romantic literature and the literature that followed it. (In "Civilization" [1836], Mill suggested the Society for the Diffusion of Useful Knowledge as a rough pattern for "some organized cooperation among the leading intellects of the age, whereby works of first-rate merit, of whatever class, and of whatever tendency in point of opinion, might come forth with the stamp on them, from the first, of the ap-proval of those whose names would carry authority.")[62] In effect, the principle sought by Eliot as a means to institutionalize the character of the artist was the increasingly formidable barrier between "high" and "popular" culture that she constructed in her letters and that developed much further in Victorian culture as the age wore on. This barrier had been taken for granted in the past, when "popular culture"—manifested in such material as folk songs and tales, chap-books, and even novels—was simply assumed to be of a different species from the literature of the dominant classes in society. It became necessary to remark upon this distinction and to call for its proper theoretical formulation only when this other culture, along with the social forces it was supposed to represent, became a significant threat to the cultured elite's peace of mind. Aesthetic judgment here, too, was guided by political perceptions. Hence the coincidence in the development of virulent outcries about the overwhelming production of trashy literature alongside the development of the study of "folklore" as a formally constituted discipline. In the first case, the technique is one of exclusion, in the second, one of subordination and appropriation; but both serve the same purpose in regard to the official culture of the day.

Mill explicitly argued what liberal intellectuals in general maintained, implicitly or explicitly: that ideas are such only if they are educated. According to this argument, the freedom of discourse and the status of individuality are available only to those who have been initiated into the mysteries stipulated in this discourse. This enlightenment of course is taken to be a purely formal development of thought that does not limit the productions of discourse, just as reason is not taken to be a limit to but rather the threshold of meaning; and of course it is much more than this. It is the technique of power characteristic of the middle classes and of the liberal intellectual. It is the power to make nature appear as purely formal laws, whether of thought, economy, culture, or society, so that through these laws class interest can appear as universal truth.

Thus the ideal proceeds. In place of a hierarchy of classes—so the liberal intellectual believes—education makes degrees of enlightenment available. Individuals do not receive their place in society as a birthright or as the fruit of patronage; instead they rank themselves according to their ability to receive enlightenment. Under the sway of this idea, individuals become responsible for themselves in a radically new way. Their very "selves" are fashioned differently. Along with many other works of various sorts in this period, it was the business of Eliot's novels to plot this historical change as moral discovery and as psychological insight. In a larger perspective, what this development means is that the forum of discourse is treated as were public institutions, in which the middle classes strove throughout the nineteenth century to abolish patronage and in its place to establish competitive exams as the basis for appointments. The presumption in this effort, as in the orthodox political economy of the age, was that competition would result in a society of discrete levels with differing factors of power assigned to them, but that this distribution of power would not be an act or institutionalization of power. It would be the system of nature itself, into which everyone could enter and in which each person could find his or her level through education.

Thus, in 1836, long before *The Origin of Species*, the *Westminster* described competition as "a principle existing throughout organized nature, whenever production is too rapid," to explain why trade unions were foolish in thinking they could bargain to raise the level of wages.[63] Similarly, Henry George still argued in 1891, "we see no evil in competition, but deem unrestricted competition to be as necessary to the health of the industrial and social organism as the free circulation of the blood is to the health of the bodily organism—to be the agency whereby the fullest cooperation is to be secured."[64] In this manner the divisions within competition, like class divisions and the historical circumstances of events, could be taken as epiphenomena subsumed within the greater harmony of nature. So Eliot would write, "But convenience, that admirable branch system from the main line of self-interest, makes us all fellow-helpers in spite of adverse resolutions" ("JR," 296).

As it is true in society at large, so is it true in the cause of ideas that competition is not conflict but the unfolding articulation of nature—so goes the argument. Ideas, like people, should be left free to prove themselves. It was for this reason that Spencer refused honorary degrees: because he thought they might introduce unfair distinctions into intellectual competition.[65] If competition in any realm should appear to take the form of irreconcilable conflict, the expression of this conflict is regarded as senseless noise or violence. As the form of even those Victorian novels that take exception to competitive practices makes clear, the fable of competition is that individuals upon approaching maturity "enter the world," which hitherto has been a foreign realm to them, and then proceed to learn the difference between legitimate and unreasonable ambition when they learn they must find their place in society by looking within themselves.

In short, the fable of competition is the fable of "character," as that term comprised the essential interiority and human nature of the Victorian subject. In following this fable, the special role of the liberal intellectuals is to answer every appearance of discord with a demand for this regulating rule of discourse. They must believe that free and enlightened discourse is the solvent of all conflict and the way to make social reality apparent to all humanity. In this way they may place themselves in society in a position to mediate every social question. One can understand, then, why social forms or institutions do not play the mediating role in the plots of Eliot's novels that they play in the novels of Jane Austen. Instead, it is the discourse from which she wrote that provides this mediation. Her resolutions happen only figuratively, or in the minds and emotions of those characters who are brought to an approximation of the figural consciousness of her narrators.

The assumption of classlessness governing this discourse means liberal intellectuals will always look to society as a whole, or so they will argue. They will consider any category short of this whole as, at best, only partial truth, at worst, a positive evil, whereas people who reject this idea of the whole will be said not to know their own best interests. Those who will not accept the intellectual's mediation must accept the intellectual's paternalism. In accordance with this logic, a crucial role played by the novel as Eliot understood it—a role that later was overtaken by the mass media and earlier was unnecessary or fulfilled by religious, legal, military, and other customary institutions—was one of showing a nation to itself. Then as now, this was not so much a matter of mimetic representation as of establishing a tradition of structures for discourse, or of fables for her time, including though not limited to those analyzed above, which "explain" the origins of power and of culture, the nature of knowledge, rationality, competition, and social inequality, and the destiny of society. More generally, always to look to the whole means truth will not adhere to the surface of things but rather will be found in their spirit or in the progress to be looked for in their future. It is not for nothing that these latter are key terms in liberal sociology and historiography. The assumption of the liberal intellectual is that ideas are refined over the course of time, as are people and societies. The freedom of discourse implies a teleology: a polishing of ideas in their agitation against one another that results in the issue of a finer idea, a better society, a more enlightened individual.

The liberal intellectual considers this teleology to be visible in the range of ideas, from the most complex to the most simplistic or vulgar, among the different members of society. One need not see inequality in the different degrees of enlightenment visible in society at any particular time. Instead, one sees the structure of time itself. It is not incidental in this regard that education of the sort Eliot made for herself would be likely to be experienced in terms of a perception of having continually gained more and more knowledge and thus of having repeatedly shed less developed versions of one's self. For Eliot, as for those other intellectuals who were introduced to nineteenth-century ideas in a more conventional way, it could seem only natural to regard education as a progressive process and as a model for historical and social understanding. As peasant superstitions could be taken to resemble those of the ancients, throughout all the levels of society these intellectuals could see imaged the course of time and even the spirit of the future, as one reached "the highest class of minds."

Liberal intellectuals do not see difference in looking at all those in society who do not have their perspective. They see an identity with themselves that is imperfectly realized but that is promised fulfillment by the richness of time in the world of discourse. They can see the present as an allegorical image of the future and the past as such an image of the present, as in Eliot's interpretation of religious history, which is also her interpretation of such art as deserves the name: "Surely the acme of poetry hitherto is the conception of the suffering Messiah—and the final triumph 'He shall reign for ever.' The Prometheus is a very imperfect foreshadowing of that symbol wrought out in the long history of the Jewish and Christian ages" (*L*, 4: 71).[66]

It is for this reason that in her fiction and in her comments on it, Eliot always tried to push beyond "opinions," as she often put it, or "machinery," in another term she shared with Carlyle and Arnold, to a sense of mystery beyond or within the surface of human life. She disdained individual opinion (even though she was not shy in studding her novels with her own) in favor of procedures for formulating and adjudicating opinion. Her assumption was that these procedures could be neutral and so did not represent a coercive form of power. It is in this sense that her function was "that of the *aesthetic*, not the doctrinal teacher" (*L*, 7: 44). As she said, "I only wish I could write something that would contribute to heighten men's reverence before the secrets of each other's souls, that there might be less assumption of entire knowingness, as a datum from which inferences are to be drawn" (*L*, 3: 164). Or, as she put it in *Felix Holt*, "none of our theories are quite large enough for all the disclosures of time" (*FH*, 92). Or, again, she made this point in *Daniel Deronda*, in a passage that illustrates in a particularly striking way the rhetorical function art and feeling play in her writing as terms for the process of a rational discourse based on scientism:

> No formulas for thinking will save us mortals from mistake in our imperfect apprehension of the matter to be thought about. And since the unemotional intellect may carry us into a mathematical dreamland where nothing is but what is not, perhaps an emotional intellect may have absorbed into its passionate vision of possibilities some truth of what will be—the more comprehensive massive life feeding theory with new material, as the sensibility of the artist seizes combinations which science explains and justifies. At any rate, presumptions to the contrary are not to be trusted. We must be patient with the inevitable makeshift of our human thinking, whether in its sum total or in the separate minds that have made the sum. (*DD*, 2: 120-21)

The point of such an emphasis throughout her writing is not to deny her intellectual and artistic claim to a comprehensive vision (although she was always happy to note the inevitable flaws of even her own perspective, the lumber in her own eye). The point is to create a plane of discourse that is this vision. This is the plane on which argument is always deferred to time or to the illimitable correction of other viewpoints, while the assumption is concurrently made, through the reverent characterization of this deferral as a mystery, that there is an agreement or common identity implicit in this field. This is precisely the theory of competition in liberal economics and politics and ideas: that blatant conflict should be regarded as mysterious consensus, the diversity of individuals as the common abstraction of society, and diverse societies as one humanity. This is the fable of universal truth, and by it the spirit of the liberal intellectual is made essentially independent of time and place. It is made a social figure in the broadest sense of that term: a figure of the very possibility of sociality.

So it is no wonder that the languages of social vocation and of individual freedom should be conflated when Eliot joined "duty" and "right" to express her uncertainty about her authorial role, quoted in the epigraph to this chapter. In fact, the logic of this passage may be seen most clearly if it is read as a fable whose conclusion is implicit in the formulation of its beginning. Eliot's uncertainty may be attributed to a confusion—virtually inevitable for one in her social position—as to whether her role was one demanded of her or owed to her. Her writing was meant to fuse these divergent terms just as they characteristically were fused in the discourse of the middle classes and the liberal intellectual, in which the delineation of morality is always described to be a result of the free discourse of individuals. However, in this instance, and throughout her writing, Eliot showed a keen awareness of the novelty of this discourse in the domain of art and so inevitably expressed anxiety about her role.

Of course other personal factors may have entered in, too. For instance, one notes that throughout her career Eliot was extremely sensitive about reviews of her work and often would not read them herself, leaving to Lewes the task of telling her such bits and pieces of them as he judged fit to present. But just as it is characteristic of liberal intellectuals to insist on a distinction between the public and the private self, so is it characteristic of them to submit the latter to the former, as one can see in the practice of Victorian biography. Thus Eliot would note, "there has been no change in the point of view from which I regard our life since I wrote my first fiction in the 'Scenes of Clerical Life.' Any apparent change of spirit must be due to something of which I am unconscious. The principles which are at the root of my effort to paint Dinah Morris are equally at the root of my effort to paint Mordecai" (L, 6: 318).

The plane of enlightened discourse, this spirit, always appears identical. This is the right and the duty by which one speaks to the public, however tremblingly: the conscious commitment to a writing style in which the right to discourse and the idea of discourse as a duty are finally taken to be identical. Eliot desired a way to banish from authorship those who did not recognize this identity; who did not drive differences into unconsciousness or depict them as violence or patronize them as ignorance; who instead represented their individual "vanity and ambition" as they asserted their "troublesome disposition to authorship" (E, 441). Meanwhile, she could prove her aptness for her authorial role by the personal anxiety with which she approached the public, and by the mastery over the public that she entertained within this style of art.

Chapter 2
Education and
the Transfigurations of Realism

L'education peut tout.
                                    Helvétius

As if in fulfillment of Enlightenment ideology, a new mode of social reproduction was conceived by the English middle classes over the course of the nineteenth century. Surveying their history in relation to other classes, they took their mission to be the creation of education as the matrix of social continuity.[1] They would make human nature the offspring of enlightenment and thus confirm their role in society. Rather than have a social system designed to guarantee the maintenance of order by reproducing itself along class lines, the middle classes found they could turn a blind eye to class differences as long as their absolute was education, which had come to represent to them the rationale of their own historical progress. As John Wade expressed this situation in his *History of the Middle and Working Classes* (1833), education might be considered "the best form of social police, inasmuch as it destroys the chief seeds of crime, want and ignorance."[2] So, too, could Thomas Chalmers, writing in 1821, conceive an education in political economy to be "a sedative to all sorts of turbulence and disorder."[3] Not all were so confident in their views as this Scottish Presbyterian minister was, but it is true in general that education came to be worshiped as the divine origin of middle-class authority. It was for this reason that a supporter of an 1850 bill to fund public libraries called its provisions "the cheapest police that could possibly be established," while reformers in general referred to "a police of good understanding,"[4] and Eliot wrote of "the spiritual police of sentiments or ideal feelings" (*TS*, 339).

Even texts like Mary Shelley's *Frankenstein* or Browning's *Paracelsus*, which might appear to recommend a domestic or ignorant contentment in contrast to an enlightenment destructive to humanity, would do so with considerable reservations. Not the least of these involves the consideration that the narrator of such a work necessarily would compose it from a position incorporating the experience of education. Modern sentimentality is a highly cultured form of representation, like the classical pastoral, and is shaped by the biases of its cultural matrix. Even within such a critical perspective, the liberal intellectual's idea of independence can be seen to be related to education, which also promised to serve the cause of ideas pure and simple. No longer would education be a matter of "luck," or of "ill luck," as in "those distant days" of *The Mill on the Floss* (*MF*, 180). It would be rationalized. Instead of being bound by institutions, traditions, political authorities, divinities, or other *idola theatri* associated with the order whose decline was being predicted, the middle classes would put themselves in the service of this idea of their essence. By their own bootstraps, they would pull themselves up above the entire realm of history, which would become "the past" opposed to the continuously renovated "modern world."

Of course, in providing for the middle-class scheme of order, education also made ample provision for the portrayal of any challenge to this order as a form of violence. It was this portrayal that embroidered the discourse of this age with paranoid phantasms lurking about its borders and threatening to invade its pacific domain. This creation of education was equally a creation of ignorance and violence. As Eliot wrote in an epigraph in *Daniel Deronda* that perfectly captures the interrelation of these terms:

Of a truth, Knowledge is power, but it is a power reined by scruple,
having a conscience of what must be and what may be; whereas Ignorance is a blind giant who, let him but wax unbound, would make it a
sport to seize the pillars that hold up the long-wrought fabric of
human good, and turn all the places of joy dark as a buried Babylon.
(*DD*, 1: 233)

Because the features with which education was limned all formed a demand for middle-class reassurance, those social phenomena that would not or could not countenance this demand would not represent legitimate differences from the middle-class standpoint. They would be seen as threatening deviations from the normative truths of philosophy, psychology, anthropology, political science, or other varieties of middle-class justice. It is not going too far to say knowledge in this middle-class mode was only incidentally a mastery of information or skills. Far more essentially it was a complex structuring of regulations in society and in the character of the individual. As this knowledge was born of the need for a middle-class identity strong enough to face down the threats represented by the retreating authorities of the past and by the hungry masses advancing "as a lion creeping nigher" (Tennyson),[5] its history articulates the middle-class position in society; and, as it was worked out in the terms of education, George Eliot made this position the stuff of aesthetics in her conception of realism.

For this reason it is not sufficient merely to note the didactic form of her realism or even to analyze this feature and its resemblance to the forms of instruction offered in schools, churches, and other institutions at the time. A more specific understanding of the institutionalization of education and of the phenomenon of this process in middle-class discourse is called for in understanding Eliot's conception of art because the new power Eliot conceived realism to be was a version of the social destiny designed through the terms of education.

This destiny was not conceived easily, and it was not the product of one or even of several individuals experiencing a brainstorm. After all, it was one thing to say power should be transferred from the traditional aristocracy to a modern intellectual elite and even to judge that this event was occurring; it was quite another to lend this change a rhetorical sanction. As a simple event—if it were possible to view it as such—this change might be considered an evolutionary improvement in the nature of social life but just as easily might seem an appalling degradation of humanity. In fact, one can discover this change as an event only by observing the raveling of discourse along these lines, especially at the end of the eighteenth and the beginning of the nineteenth centuries, when these arguments were interwoven on such frames as the French Revolution, the growth of "excess" population among the poor, the Corn Laws, the New Poor Law, urbanization, and industrialization.

In this situation empirical or positive analysis could not be sufficient to the aims of the middle classes, however much the perfection of this technique might be the dream of Jeremy Bentham, James Mill, Harriet Martineau, and other reformers of their ilk. The middle classes needed the texture of a metaphor to lend the power of cultural truth to the transference of power assumed in their discourse. They needed a popular form of representation for disseminating their idea of enlightenment. They found this in the novel, as one can see in the way its principles were codified by Eliot, who was among the most self-conscious of writers in her approach to her craft and its bearings on society; but what they found in fiction like Eliot's, they also found elsewhere because all aspects of Victorian cultural life were irregularly, imperfectly, and yet massively reoriented to the magnetism of the middle-class conception of truth.

Most notable in this regard, especially in relation to Eliot's writing, is the fate of the gentleman in this age. Traditionally conceived to be the *summum bonum* of civilized life, gentility became one of the more important metaphors in which the transfer of power to middle-class enlightenment took place. According to the social history of the time, as interpreted by the middle classes, it was only logical that they should find legitimation, a fable of their identity, by appropriating the distinctive term of upper-class exclusivity for their own discourse of moral universality and democratic opportunity. This appropriation had already begun in the eighteenth century, as Defoe's *The Compleat English*

Gentleman and the writings of Addison and Steele testify. However, it did not find an institutional setting and thoroughgoing ideological acceptance until the Victorian era. More than any other change in this era, it was the transfiguration of this metaphor of gentility that enabled the middle classes to publicly identify their novel historical prominence as a destiny representing the progressive refinement of history and thus comprehending history, neutralizing it, and subordinating it to their interests.

What is exceptional about the case of education in Victorian society is the fact that it became a universal mandate. Whereas it had previously rested on the support of an exclusive class or order of men in society, it was now aligned with the spirit of humanity. This development was perhaps the most revolutionary result of those changes industrialization brought to England. Even though England lagged behind the Continent in its establishment of an educational system—it was not until the last two decades of the century that free compulsory education on an elementary level was made available to all—and despite the fact that prominent figures resisted the change at that time just as influential persons had been against it when the idea was first widely bruited near the end of the eighteenth century, the creation of this alignment was unequivocally the work of English society in the nineteenth century. The issue of education became a central focus in discussions on all sorts of social problems throughout the century, and it came to form the terms of those discussions, however much particular plans of education might be disparaged, defeated, or bound to failure.[6]

The idea of the gentleman became so difficult in this age, "a subject of dialectical inquiry and nerve-wracking embarrassment as readers of Charlotte Yonge and Trollope know,"[7] because the manners distinguishing this figure could be taken to embody the discourse of the middle classes as captivated by the issue of education. Just as the genre of the novel could be seen to have advanced its social standing at the expense of more exclusive arts and the ideologies they represented, so could the figure of the gentleman be taken to measure the success of the middle classes. It could be read both literally and symbolically, as a figure tracing the form and degree of this success while also imaging the pursuit of an even more satisfying destiny. The liberal intellectual of this period conceived of society as modeled after the discussion group, and the form in which this discussion was supposed to be carried on found expression in the figure of the gentleman, which was now redefined in terms of achieved rather than inherited social status. By the time Eliot wrote *Daniel Deronda* and had Sir Hugo Mallinger inform the young Deronda that he was sending him to Eton and later to Cambridge because he wanted him to have " 'the education of an English gentleman' " (*DD*, 1: 177), the emphasis was decidedly on the qualities education was expected to bring to the child, not on the innate qualities a gentleman might be expected to bring to that institutional setting.

In relation to education, gentility became middle-class morality. Social manners became moral graces and social status an issue of inward character: such is the historical change assumed in the topic of gentility in the discourse of this time. As far as the tendency of this discourse was concerned, gentility would become an acquirement wholly of moral culture. Hence the ironies of Dickens's *Great Expectations*: Pip is most a gentleman when least so, and the unlettered Joe is in fact the "gentlest" of all because this novel takes as its structure the transfer of power from an aristocratic conception of society to a more democratic middle-class conception. Even in so hapless a form as that of Mr. Pocket's school, presided over by the distracting but *distingué* Mrs. Pocket, aristocratic pedagogy had to be discredited in favor of a culture that was moralized and interiorized before all else. Thus, the greatest irony of this novel is that Joe in his simplicity depicts more than any other character the new worship of education in this age. The untutored nature he represents is precisely the nature that one was supposed to acquire through educational cultivation. It is not accidental that Joe marries a schoolmistress: the pathos of his struggle to acquire literacy symbolizes his essential character and his mediating social function. It is in this fashion that a writer who launched thunderous tirades at the "unnatural" emphasis on education may be seen nevertheless to have been as captivated by this emphasis as Pip was by Estella's "unnatural" character. In this respect Dickens was like Ruskin, who argued in *Fors Clavigera* that for the preceding fifty years modern education had "devoted itself simply to the teaching of impudence"—but made this argument in the course of outlining his own plan for education, which was devoted to the need to "manage our mobs."[8]

What needs to be especially emphasized, then, is the rhetorical nature of the figure of the gentleman. This figure was the composite of a narrative about the past, present, and future stages of human development. Not only was "gentility" a word undergoing a historical transfiguration, but in the contemporary representation of this process, it can be seen to have embodied the typical middle-class view of history as an essentially progressive and qualitatively discriminating process. As an 1862 article on gentlemen in the *Cornhill Magazine* put it, "there is a constantly increasing disposition to insist more upon the moral and less upon the social element of the word, and it is not impossible that in course of time its use may come to be altogether dissociated from any merely conventional distinction." Even such a conservative article as this one, which upheld the inevitable superiority of the higher over the lower classes, adhered to these assumptions about history.

Education was a process so uplifting in terms of all aspects of human character that it would promise improvement even in a Tory view of society that insisted on an eternally necessary hierarchical structure in society. The discourse of taste, which had dominated eighteenth-century aesthetics and in so doing had provided a vision of social stability for that period, was gradually supplemented or displaced over the course of the nineteenth century by this discourse of intellectual improvement. It was not for nothing that this century was popularly regarded as an Age of Intellect or Age of Intelligence and commonly imaged as being in the vanguard of the March of Intellect or, as Eliot's first essay for the *Westminster Review* had it, "The Progress of the Intellect."

A distinctive aspect of the gentleman within this scheme of improvement was that his social, intellectual, and even aesthetic significance could not be dissevered from his moral status, in contrast to the situation of this figure in the eighteenth and earlier centuries. Consequently, a logic was possible in which everyone might seem to have at least the potential for "true" as opposed to "merely superficial" gentility. One can see this logic in the plots of Sir Walter Scott's novels, which are largely devoted to discovering this distinctive truth, this middle-class subjectivity, although in a somewhat different fashion and with different emphases than one finds in Eliot's novels.

Within this scheme of things, it finally did not matter if a definition of the gentleman was of the most conservative or most liberal sort. Even the particulars given to the definition were beside the point, for by the second half of the nineteenth century, virtually all definitions would assume the same rhetorical form. Samuel Smiles, who wrote the famous *Self-Help*, would argue that the moral qualities of the gentleman were not confined to any particular class; and so would a writer as dissimilar as Tennyson define this figure by its moral character, when he wrote of Arthur Hallam, "And thus he bore without abuse / The grand old name of gentleman, / Defamed by every charlatan, / And soiled with all ignoble use."[9] Ruskin's definition was of a type with these when he made gentility an intellectual consciousness of the history and morality incarnate in language: "A well-educated gentleman . . . is learned in the *peerage* of words; knows the words of true descent and ancient blood at a glance, from words of modern canaille."[10] Although this latter formulation may seem reactionary and idiosyncratic, such a description would be misleading. It would ignore the way this definition takes for granted the transfiguration of the word that gave it its moralized middle-class identity.

By the very way they approached its definition, Scott, Ruskin, Tennyson, Smiles, Dickens, Eliot, Cardinal Newman, and the others who occupied themselves with this figure of the gentleman showed the change in its definition and the extensive implications of this change. Therefore, one could revise the words of the *Cornhill* article—"The division between those who are, and those who are not entitled to this appelation, is as real and important as it is indefinite"[11]—to say this division was real and important because it was indefinite and hence receptive to the middle-class drives toward democratic social opportunity and a highly charged personal interiority.

Social mutations commonly appear in the form of discourse long before they are clarified as the matter of that discourse, and such was the case in this instance. Even though "gentlemen," defined by the traditional standards, still largely monopolized positions of power in Victorian England, the middle classes were overtaking them, while exerting a pressure on their identity difficult to measure in the orthodox terms of historical understanding but readily apparent in the forms of the discourse from which these terms are so often derived. For example, consider the form of *Adam Bede*. Whereas many critics have found it notable that a common carpenter such as Adam should be made a hero with only the slightest of apologies for his social status—that he was not the average carpenter of the time—it seems to have appeared largely unnecessary to note that it is as a gentleman that Arthur Donnithorne is waylaid by the plot of this novel, and that the novel is so structured to transfer his gentility to Adam and thus to transform it. Arthur's moral failings are the failure of the traditional definition of the gentleman. To put it another way, they articulate the pressure being exerted for semantic revision in this term as in the terms of culture as a whole. Nevertheless, Eliot could mark his fault as being psychological and essentially universal in nature because in her art it almost went without saying that the traditional definition Arthur tries to assume is anachronistic.

Again, this is not to say gentlemen of the old school were not a social reality long after the time of Austen's novels. Nor is this to say these novels did not already show deviations in the definition, as in Elizabeth Bennet's surprise at the genteel comportment of her middle-class uncle when he gets along so famously with Darcy. The point is that this term was so increasingly squeezed by middle-class importunities that during the course of the nineteenth century its new, moral emphasis became indistinguishable from its traditional one. Carlyle's version of history in *Past and Present* and in his other works, the Young England movement, contemporary theories of paternalism, and the fable of decline that coexists with the fable of progress in Eliot's works—the notion that a formerly vital upper class has become spiritually bankrupt, as Daniel Deronda senses and Grandcourt shows in her last novel—all testify to this change.

It was through this transfiguration of the gentleman that the transcendence of classes, assumed to be the ideal of the liberal intellectual, was given a living rhetorical form. To be sure, Eliot was personally disqualified from this status on account of her gender, even apart from the question of how she conducted her private life. Nevertheless, the concerns composing this figure were her own. The concept of gentility was one dear to her art and, very strikingly, to her life. Hence her insistence after she began to live with Lewes that she be addressed as Mrs. Lewes and that her "marriage" to him should be seen as representing her devotion to this social institution, not her violation of it. Furthermore, the mystique of this figure in the culture at large may be compared to the mystery of humanity Eliot called upon as the basis of moral conduct. Her "humanity" is this figure of the gentleman writ large.

In Eliot's novels, as in all the discourse accompanying the revision of this figure, one no longer deferred to the overawing person of the aristocrat. Instead, one turned to this moral figure of the gentleman, which was so troubling, which could not be fixed securely, because truth under the new dispensation of discourse was made to exist in the virtual relations among men, not in the exclusive properties of a class or a calling that could be symbolized by neat distinctions of blood, heraldry, or landownership. (The fact that distinctions such as these had never been neat is beside the point: they appeared to have been so because they were regarded by representatives of a culture conceived as being essentially based on interiority or "character.") The ultimately insoluble debate over the precise definition of the gentleman in this period actually epitomizes the nature of the discourse of which he was the object. He was kept independent by the illimitable continuation of the debate, as this discourse in general always had to defer its resolution to a temporal or spiritual mystery; his identity was more an inner than an outer condition, as truth in enlightened discourse like Eliot's realism was never found entirely on the surface of experience; the breadth of view with which he was associated could not be defined precisely but only maintained through the sweep of that discourse with which he was involved; and there was no certain material or systematic measure to this identity, just as there was none for the judgment of truth in the writings of Carlyle, Matthew Arnold, and Eliot. This gentleman, this metaphor securing the advances of the middle classes, was the figure of a discourse in operation.

It was violence that the liberal intellectual would find opposed to the enlightened discourse represented by this figure. Whereas ignorance could be patronized and included within the history of enlightenment, violence could never be made part of a continuity between the traditional and the modern orders of society. Of course, violence appeared so categorically alien because it was so denominated within this discourse—"violence" is as much a rhetorical figure as is the "gentleman." But, even though the intellectuals of this age were occasionally self-conscious about the definition of gentility or of such related terms as enlightenment, reason, and taste, recognizing that they might appear to be involved in history even if they were finally recognized as having a definition that transcended historical change, there was no quarter given in the definition of violence. In this case the discourse of the time closed upon itself. It became as positive as it could be. It understood violence as a simple phenomenon for which the working classes and the poor had a special propensity, a phenomenon that could constitute only an unmediated rupture of the fabric of discourse that preserved society. In this character violence defined the boundary of middle-class discourse in relation to the lower classes, as one can see in the way the "rough" would be distinguished from the "respectable" worker according to one's perception of the violence or lack thereof in his being. So, too, would illegal combinations, criminal intimidation, and other crimes be distinguished from "the legitimate expression of a grievance," as the diction of the time would have it. Violence was the far side of middle-class identity. It was the darkness the middle classes had to overcome in their mastery of themselves and of their positions in society as played out in rhetorical movements like the transfiguration of the gentleman.

The crucial point is that "violence" was a figure not taken to be such, the metaphor taken as empirical fact, the phantasm of a class taken to be an unmediated perception of that class. So Arnold described the figure of the working class by saying, "now, when he does come, he comes in immense numbers, and is rather raw and rough."[12] So this figure was characteristically addressed from the beginning of the period until well after the "leap into the dark" of the 1867 Reform Bill, and always in opposition to this figure was the discourse into which one would be initiated by education.

Understanding this situation, one can see that the apparent exaggeration of union and mob violence in novels like Mrs. Gaskell's *Mary Barton* or Eliot's *Felix Holt* was not really an exaggeration at all. It was simply measured out in the terms of this discourse, which gauged the standards of realistic representation quite apart from what one might expect those standards to be if one attended only to the definitions of realism explicitly formulated by the writers of the time.[13] It is for this reason that the governing classes of England did not find their response to the agricultural disturbances of 1829-30 to be excessive, even though "the rioters had neither killed nor seriously injured anyone" and yet found they had moved justice to demand "nine lives of men or boys, the transportation of 457 more, and the imprisonment at home of about 400 others."[14] As E. J. Hobsbawm and George Rudé have noted, "Even so sympathetic an urban observer as T. L. Peacock presented the 1830 rioters in Crotchet Castle as the 'Jacquerie' and made them clamor for arms" despite the fact that "there can rarely have been a movement of the despairing poor so large and so widespread which used, or even threatened, so little violence."[15] The historical is not homologous to the literary event in a mode of causality or reflection but rather in terms of the formulation of events, judicial, literary, or otherwise, in the figurative procedures of the discourse of the time.

It is important to see that violence did not face educated or enlightened discourse in the form of a simple opposition. The assumption was that this discourse necessarily would reveal the truth of middle-class ideologies. Strictly speaking, it could not be opposed. Violence, then, was a term in a narrative: a term in the fable of education. Its relation to enlightenment cannot be understood apart from this conception of social reproduction. In a summary form, one can describe this conception of education by saying truth would be produced as ignorance was included within consciousness and violence excluded from it. It is a formula of great simplicity and yet it was of tremendous consequence. It is the narrative of hosts of Victorian novels, in which sentimentality unites the highest culture with the simplest forms of human experience and in so doing diverts the individual from violence into the safe haven of morality, because this is the narrative form governing the discourse of the time.

In this production of truth, this new form of social reproduction, one sees how the idea of intellectual discussion in this age was an assumption of intellectual consensus, and that consensus the image of the middle-class mind. This is the significance of enlightenment in the nineteenth century, especially in those cases in which it is represented as a normative question of art or psychology or philosophy or sociology, as in the argument Bulwer Lytton made in favor of popular education:

> We may observe (and this is a most important and startling truth) that nearly all social excesses arise, not from intelligence, but from *inequalities* of intelligence. . . . But where Intelligence is equalized— and flows harmonious and harmonizing throughout all society—then one man can possess no blinding or dangerous power over the mind of another—then demagogues are harmless and theories safe.[16]

It was simply inconceivable that the capacity to reason, correctly conceived, could lead anywhere except to the point of middle-class reassurance— even if the historical emergence of this "truth" might make it appear "startling." This is the sign of a middle-class age, that it takes its social order to be based on reason rather than "blinding or dangerous power." The special blindness of such an age lies in its style of irony, which in Victorian England primarily took a sentimental and patronizing form, as in the moralized transfiguration of the gentleman. The transference of power involved in this process was not acknowledged. The change was seen as a rationalization of power that liberated it from the possession of any limited class or group in society.

This assumption of rationality did not prevent various factions among the middle and upper classes from arguing among themselves, and often with extreme virulence. The only time it was really meant to come into play was when their arguments were directed against those by whom they felt threatened.[17]

In effect, the middle classes needed to feel threatened by the working classes and the poor so they could construct a logic of their power in society. They required an image of social order to replace the traditional image of fixed estates, or at least to give it a temporal and rationalized dimension that would open it to evolution. The middle classes needed to attribute violence to others so that their own exertions of power would appear to be reasonable rather than willful. The logic is the same as that which brought Eliot to conceive her psychology as an artist to be one in which she forever battled against herself to transcend herself. In both cases there is a need to produce the appearance of rationalized production.

At times this narrative of violence and its transcendence was noted blandly—for instance, in Lytton's reference to "social excesses"—but at least as frequently it was evoked more directly and even luridly, in novels like

Dickens's or documents like J. Phillips Kay's *The Moral and Physical Condition of the Working Classes Employed in the Cotton Manufacturing in Manchester* (1832). As this issue was put by Kay, who later assumed the name of Kay-Shuttleworth and became perhaps the single most important figure in the institutionalization of education in Victorian England, "A little knowledge is . . . inevitable, and it is proverbially a dangerous thing. Alarming disturbances of social order generally commence with *a people only partially instructed*. The preservation of *internal peace*, not less than the improvement of our national institutions, depends on the education of the working classes."[18] In this last sentence, one can see a perfect example of the syntax, positive and negative, given to the construction of truth in the terms of education. The enlightenment to which education was directed was always as much a policing function as was the literature John Morley called "a weapon and an arm, not merely a liberal art,"[19] and the "goodwill" of which Gladstone once spoke when responding to a critic of his policies: "Please to recollect that we have got to govern millions of hard hands; that it must be done by force, fraud, or goodwill; that the latter has been tried and is answering."[20] The contrasting terms—"force" and "fraud" on the one hand and "goodwill" on the other— are so close, syntactically and ideologically, that they are almost indistinguishable. Nevertheless, it was the business of education in this age to maintain the difference between them.

As previously noted, there were many who objected to the idea of education for the masses, especially in the late eighteenth and early nineteenth centuries; but the nature of their objections is often revealing. Many distinguished between the teaching of reading and the teaching of writing to the poor, as the one was conceived to be a passive and the other an active and productive skill. In Hannah More's belief that a knowledge of writing would lead the poor to sedition and in the objection of others that this knowledge would lead to an epidemic of forgeries, one can see wonderfully displayed the assumptions of power and legitimacy constitutive of the issue of education in this age. Moreover, there were characters like Thomas Arnold who would sidestep the issue with opinions like the one he expressed in a letter to the *Hertford Reformer* in 1839: "Most wisely has Mr. Laing said in his most instructive account of Norway, that 'a man may read and write and yet have a totally uneducated mind; but that he who possesses property, whether he can read or write or not, has an educated mind.' "[21]

Arnold's statement and the attitudes of those more directly opposed to education may indicate that disagreements over this issue, no matter how fiercely contested, are beside the point if one is concerned to analyze the forms of discourse in this age for the power they represented. For what went without question in these quarrels was the idea that the lower classes were a dangerously violent element in society, and the conclusion was that one needed a technique for controlling this element. Whether one argued that education would serve this purpose or that denying them education was the way to go about it, the aim was still the same, as was the inspiration for that aim. Just as those who argued for or against factory reforms in this century were united in their concern for disciplining the workers, so, too, were those on either side of the issue of education more profoundly in agreement than they were at odds with each other. They shared the same discourse in which morality, science, religion, nature, and all the other registers of knowledge prevailing at the time composed a single conception of social truth opposed to the tendencies attributed to the lower classes, despite the specific recommendations—conservative, liberal, or whatever—with which individuals might qualify this conception and so distinguish themselves from one another.

This situation can be compared to the way those who argued for and against the novel in Eliot's day were united in their concern for its moral purpose. In this case, too, education was at issue and formed a coherent scheme of power, even in the midst of a debate involving severe disagreements. As it happens, Eliot's work was often used as a test-case in this regard, and the reactions she gathered exemplified the wider debate—the terms of which she accepted and preached on her own behalf.[22] Moreover, the novel's indissoluble link to the issue of education in this age is attested to even in the most literal sense of its subject matter: the variety of governesses, tutors, schools, and autodidacts with which it swarms. In this respect, too, one sees how education, like the figure of the gentleman, provoked so many bitter differences because its fundamental conception was assumed to be so important.

In the rhetoric of this time in which education and then political rights began to be extended to the lower classes, political violence, protests, and class agitation were placed in a rhetorical series along with drunkenness and general mischief. In this way they were made categorically senseless, animalic, opposed to the language of education, civility, and reason.[23] When Eliot tells of the "obstreperous animalism" of a group of miners ("AB," 23), or when she describes the rector wishing he could stop "the political sermons of the Independent preacher, which, in their way, were as pernicious sources of intoxication as the beerhouses" (FH, 41), it is this series that comes into play. The second instance is marked by the narrator's irony, whereas the first is not, but even with this irony, the nature of the rhetorical series goes unquestioned. Decades after the era of Chartism, Eliot could still use this rhetoric to provide the form of *Felix Holt*, whose hero resists the mob with an emphasis on sobriety, civil obedience, and education, just as Dickens had used it for *Hard Times*, in which Stephen Blackpool is framed on the one hand by his besotted wife and on the other by the ignorant and violent union of his fellow workers. This rhetoric was used by all sorts of writers throughout the nineteenth century, and its point was always to proscribe any form of discourse and any arguments opposed to the interests of society as a whole, which was understood to be of the nature of the middle classes.

Violence especially—within the middle-class definition—was not allowed to be a language expressive of anything. Instead it was understood to be a sink of being in which humanity, raised from animalic ignorance by education, was turned to a demonic form. In this form, humanity was ignorant of and at odds with itself. Brontë's Shirley says, " 'At present I am no patrician, nor do I regard the poor round me as plebeians; but if once they violently wrong me or mine, and then presume to dictate to us, I shall quite forget pity for their wretchedness and respect for their poverty, in scorn of their ignorance and wrath at their insolence.' " [24] This creation of language in opposition to violence was as evident in the social reforms of the age as in its literature.

It was in the following terms that William Lovett, the famous Radical, characterized one of the aims of the London Working Men's Association: "To publish their views and sentiments in such a form and manner as shall best serve to create a moral, reflecting, yet energetic public opinion; so as eventually to lead to a gradual improvement in the condition of the working classes, without violence or commotion." [25] This opposition was always invoked between enlightened discourse and violence, and this opposition always served the argument that knowledge was middle-class law. Thus, as Brian Simon has written, it is no accident that a practical result of the 1869 Endowed Schools Act, which took over and "rationalized" existing endowments for schools, "was to cut away the traditional rights of the poor and other local inhabitants." Those few "who might succeed in making their way upwards would inevitably do so—and this was the intention—at the cost of alienation from their own class and local community." [26] On this point the educational practice of the age and its discourse on education, enlightenment, and knowledge were in agreement. There could be no language, no meaning, except that of the middle classes.

As a writer in the *Quarterly Journal of Education*, which was sponsored by the Society for the Diffusion of Useful Knowledge, conceived of the improvement of the poor in 1831, "The circumstances that give rise to those gradations of rank and fortune that actually exist" might be shown to be "as natural to society as differences of sex, of strength, or of colour." [27] Lord Abinger, speaking to the grand jury investigating the Plug Riots in 1842, relied on this sense of nature in expressing "compassion" for those classes "who, not having a competent judgment of their own as to the principles or the rights of property, or upon the questions on which their own property is involved, imagine that they can by force and violence dictate terms to their masters." [28] In all such cases, violence could not be allowed to produce language or to "dictate terms." This function was the prerogative of education. No wonder, then, that in her "Address to Working Men," Eliot had no compunctions about speaking to the working classes and as a member of those classes through the thoroughly genteel medium of *Blackwood's*. One assumes she regarded her assumption of this role "as natural to society as differences of sex, of strength, or of colour";

and her publisher appears to have felt the same way. It is by such means that the character of the middle classes was conceived to define the universal condition of humanity and, through education, was meant to colonize England with middle-class souls while England's forces were colonizing the world beyond its shores.

This emphasis on education had special importance in the late 1830s and 1840s, when the most significant division among Chartists was between the Physical Force and the Moral Force camps, with the crusaders for moral force being so by virtue of their absorption of middle-class influence, especially by way of education and the educational doctrines of the Philosophic Radicals. (It is also very significant that the partisans of moral force tended to be the better paid artisans or skilled workers among the working classes.) Despite this special importance, the formulation of this division in Chartist ranks was symptomatic only of the discourse of education, in which the opposition of the terms of morality and violence had already been well established by the time the events of Chartism had appeared on the scene to fulfill their form. One of the more violent of the Chartist agitators, Feargus O'Connor, recognized the implications of this conception when he described it in 1841:

> I object to Knowledge Chartism, because it implicitly acknowledges a standard of some sort of learning, education, or information, as a necessary qualification to entitle man to his political rights. In fact, the Whigs think opposition to Whiggery, and the Tories think opposition to Toryism, a perfectly good and valid ground, whereon to establish popular ignorance, and a consequent political disqualification.[29]

But O'Connor's consciousness of the scheme of power implied in this conception was not a common one. This age might find some figures like Victor Frankenstein's monster, destined to turn violent when apprized of the tormenting difference between the conception of education and the reality of social experience or, like Krook in Dickens's *Bleak House*, laboriously trying to teach themselves to write for fear that someone else might teach them untruths as deadly as those given birth in the atmosphere of Chancery. And there were some people like John Watkins, who was quoted in O'Connor's *Northern Star* in 1843 as saying, "We ask for the Charter, and they give us reading-made-easy. Out upon them."[30] However, as the fate of the monster and Krook's own exceptional end may indicate, critical attitudes such as these did not enjoy much success.

In any case, what is important to recognize is the way "education," "enlightenment," "knowledge," and the other words in this series were promoted as terms opposed to the senselessness of "violence" while in fact their meaning necessarily was constrained by the framework of ideological opposition and alliance comprised in the history of their development and use. Hence, Eliot's words: "I believe—and I want it to be well shown—that a more thorough education will tend to do away with the odious vulgarity of our notions about functions and employment, and to propogate the true gospel that the deepest disgrace is to insist on doing work for which we are unfit—to do work of any sort badly" (*L*, 4: 525). In this belief that enlightenment will generate a natural stratification of society in coincidental accordance with her interests, one can see the liberal intellectual ideal as well as the defense of her conception of herself as an author that Eliot derived from this ideal. Like liberal intellectuals in general, Eliot came to take education for granted as a social process and as a metaphor for humanizing growth. "Those who trust us educate us," she wrote in *Daniel Deronda* (*DD*, 2: 34). She assumed education was a morality and a social discipline and so concluded that any language that resisted this policing was disqualified from meaning.

This conclusion was the fate of "violence" and, on a higher social level, of "mere" material and technical interest. Like the uneducated laughter on which Eliot commented in one of her essays, such phenomena were taken to be irreconcilably alien: "The last thing in which the cultivated man can have community with the vulgar is their jocularity; and we can hardly exhibit more strikingly the wide gulf which separates him from them, than by comparing the object which shakes the diaphragm of a coal-heaver with the highly complex pleasure derived from a real witticism" (*E*, 217). Here is the new gentility, a social distinction supposedly founded in empirical observation of the world of nature but also taken to represent a moral interiority: the gothic "wide gulf" broached by the appalling agitation of a workman's diaphragm. It appears we have only to compare objects, and through the phenomenology of the cultivated consciousness, we can establish our superiority. It is significant that Eliot chose laughter as the basis for this distinction, since the rhetorical effect of this decision is to make the workman's voice inarticulate, senseless, violent noise and the cultivated man's response highly articulate even if it remains silent. (In this respect it recalls Daniel Deronda's sensibility: "There was a calm intensity of life and richness of tint in his face that on a sudden gaze from him was rather startling, and often made him seem to have spoken, so that servants and officials asked him automatically, 'What did you say, sir?' when he had been quite silent" [*DD*, 1: 166].) Just as the singular "cultivated man" is contrasted in his individuality to the massed "vulgar" ("them"), so is the gentleman's thought made to speak more loudly than the workman's voice. One also notes that the objects compared are material in the case of the workman ("the object which shakes the diaphragm") and psychological in the case of the cultivated man's "highly complex response." This dissimilarity of reference may be the result of an unintentional syntactic confusion, but it makes perfect sense in terms of the identification of moral interiority with the cultured individual. Indeed, it was in the form of this identification that Eliot established her intellectual independence at a crucial point in her life. When she had a terrific falling out with her father in 1841 over the issue of religion, she agreed to start attending services again as long as he did not command her inner assent. Such is the essence of freedom to liberal intellectuals and the kernel of all their moral prescriptions.

John Stuart Mill assumed this same intellectual consciousness in *Utilitarianism* and elsewhere when he argued that the cultivated members of society were more competent to judge the interests of the less educated than they themselves were. Ruskin followed this same line of reasoning, despite the great political differences between himself and Mill, when he argued that "both well-directed moral training and well-chosen reading lead to the possession of a power over the ill-guided and illiterate, which is, according to the measure of it, in the truest sense, *kingly.*"[31] Within this ideology of education, people who shake with rude simplicity, like unsophisticated readers and those who do not take their employers' will as their own, are not allowed to know what they are doing. They are not allowed to have expression or identity in such moments except when they may be interpreted in contrast to enlightenment, as negative examples of the production of truth. They are tasteless, senseless, alien, or—at the very least—as comical as Pip is during his first meal with Herbert Pocket and as pathetic as Joe is when he visits Pip in London. Thus far Dickens and Eliot are in agreement, whatever other differences there may be between their representations of the lower classes. Both show the discipline launched through education in its function as the "best form of social police."

The legal reforms instituted as victories of civilization against violence in the first half of the nineteenth century, such as the restriction of capital offenses and the abolition of the pillory and of sports involving animal baiting, belonged to the same discipline. The motivation of these reforms, their humanity, lay in the need of the governing classes in society to draw a more rigid distinction within their discourse between its forms of discipline and the kind of language, behavior, and experience reason would not sanction. Like the gentleman and violence and education itself, these reforms were cultural figurations before all else. They were arguments for the rhetoric of universality—the " 'sense of the universal' " so important to Herr Klesmer (*DD*, 1: 48)—and thus promoted the identity of the cultured middle classes, whose only "interest," to use the contemporary term, was the interest of society as a whole.

Of course, the social history within this conception of society is another matter. First of all, there is the consideration that the thought of society as a whole was a specifically urban or modern imperative, as Wordsworth indicated in *The Prelude* when he described the London of his youth by saying, "Above all, one thought / Baffled my understanding: how men lived / Even next-door neighbours, as we say, yet still / Strangers, nor knowing each the other's name."[32] A consciousness of society as a whole was demanded as a new source of authority because the historical changes that had led to the perception of the modern world as such were also taken to imply the debasing of old authorities. Within the logic that had led to the perception of the modern world as being frighteningly excessive—overwhelming in its production of supernumerary books, information, and novel phenomena of all sorts—was the assumption that it had taken on this quality because of the absence of a necessary power of authority. It is not only in the thematics of Victorian fiction—as in the representation of the past as a lost love still cherished in one's memory that suffuses Eliot's writing—but also in many other varieties of discourse in this time that change implies loss, and novelty, destruction. Studying this thematics is not a matter of deciding whether or not society actually was more fragmented and individuals and classes more at one another's throats than they had previously been, as the discourse of the time would have it. It is a matter of analyzing the social history productive of this rhetoric, tracing the forms it assumed, and thus coming to an understanding of the situation that gave meaning to Eliot's writing.

"Never since the beginning of Time," wrote Carlyle, "was there, that we hear or read of, so intensely self-conscious a Society"[33]—but of course there was no such thing. Intellectual figures, such as Carlyle, insisted that society be a "self-consciousness," a prescription for the self. In this role it was supposed to replace the influences of church and state that were thought to have lost ground and thus to have revealed a world bursting with novelty and begging for education. Carlyle was following the middle-class strategy of representing prescriptive as descriptive statements, ideology as nature, and historical change as unprecedented crisis. Eliot was no different, in the "Prelude" to *Middlemarch*, when she referred to the failure of epic striving where there was "no coherent social faith and order which could perform the function of knowledge for the ardently willing soul" (*M*, 1: 4). She was universalizing a middle-class anxiety as a structural defect in society and as a vacancy in knowledge. While representing the form of liberal intellectual discourse as a discovery of experience—of nature—she was also representing it as a sociological explanation for the epic's displacement by the novel as the characteristic genre of her time.

It is a distinguishing characteristic of realism to align aesthetic form and the form of experience in this fashion. However, what especially needs to be remarked about this aesthetics is its dependence on the structuring of discourse that invented modern consciousness for the liberal intellectual. The experience recorded within Eliot's novels is based on this invention and has no historical significance apart from it. Within these novels, "experience" represents the phenomena of this discourse, not of "the world" or of "humanity" in a historically or universally objective sense.

The idea of society as a whole was a demand that historical change be comprehended, organized, and controlled in the form of middle-class experience. As Carlyle put it, "Considered well, Society is the standing wonder of our existence; a true region of the Supernatural; as it were, a second all-embracing Life, wherein our first individual Life becomes doubly and trebly alive, and whatever of Infinitude was in us bodies itself forth, and becomes visible and active.''[34] Carlyle so defined society even though he also viewed it just as Teufelsdrökh did:

> Call ye that a Society . . . where there is no longer any Social Idea
> extent; not so much as the Idea of a common Home, but only of a
> common over-crowded Lodging-house? Where each, isolated,
> regardless of his neighbour, turned against his neighbour, clutches
> what he can get, and cries 'Mine!' and calls it Peace, because, in the
> cut-purse and cut-throat Scramble, no steel knives, but only a far cun-
> ninger sort, can be employed?[35]

As far as he was concerned, there was no contradiction in these two formula-tions because one referred to the truth of society—that is, to the prescriptions for experience allowed within culture—whereas the other referred to that sort of experience denied reality by intellectuals like himself. In this case unreconstructed middle-class materialism is castigated, but his target just as easily might have been—and was, elsewhere—the "violence" of the lower classes.

A second major consideration in this idea of the whole society is that it typically would have a religious form. This form commonly shaped experience for the middle classes, which included individuals like Eliot who had laid aside orthodox belief. Hence the horror manifest in the government Blue Books and similar documents of this period when children of the working classes were queried about Jesus and responded uncomprehendingly. This sort of condition at least as much as conditions of physical squalor and abuse led to reforms in the mines in the 1840s and in the gang labor on farms in the 1860s, as is evident not only from testimony at the time but also from the way the importance of education was stressed in this age.

The Anti-Corn Law agitation in the first half of the century provides a good example of the role religion would play even in the most "secular" issues, and even in the secret unions of the working classes, one finds religious appeals be-ing made as an injunction to unity. Arnold made implicit use of this religious context when he wrote that culture is "the *social idea*" and added that "the men of culture are the true apostles of equality,"[36] and he adopted it more ex-plicitly in *Literature and Dogma* and other writings. So, too, John Keble made social unity a religious form in *The Christian Year*, writing of "Four thousand sympathetic hearts / Together swelling high / Their chant of many parts,"[37] much as Eliot, one of his admirers, later composed "Oh May I Join the Choir Invisible" as a Positivist hymn. For Eliot as for most others in this age, the thought of society as a whole was as essentially religious as it was imperative.[38]

So much almost goes without saying. However, the connection between religion and the idea of the whole society in the discourse of this period goes beyond the way religion, like the figure of the gentleman, could provide an urgent narrative form and a fund of imagery for disseminating the idea of the transcendence of individual and class interests. It even goes beyond its provision for a Providential understanding of the history of the middle classes, the excesses of which were run to earth by Dickens in the notion of Podsnappery and by Eliot in the mores of the Dodsons but, in both cases, without prejudice to the virtues of a more cautious belief in the progress associated with middle-class virtues in the modern world.

More significant is the way this connection sacralized social experience. It charged the most trivial as well as the most important thoughts and actions of everyday life with an epic intensity. Thereby it contributed to the drive toward universality in middle-class ideology. The image of the Victorians' seriousness comes from this situation. By virtue of this connection, moral pressure could be applied anywhere in society, no matter how trivial or secular the spot. It could be applied to work, which was construed as a religion by writers like Carlyle, Eliot, and Ruskin as well as by the mill-owners and magistrates. Or it could be applied to amusements, including literature, for they also faced the demand to be productive in terms of moral, intellectual, and emotional improvement. It could even be applied to notions like space, time, leisure, and pleasure. Above all, it could be applied to feeling and, in fact, would come to define feeling in the sentimental mode, as in Eliot's description of Amos Barton: "Milly's memory hallowed her husband, as of old the place was hallowed on which an angel from God had alighted" ("AB," 78).

This is not to say this connection was made with the deliberate intention of creating a technique for exerting power, as if the Victorians collectively were kin to Virginia Woolf's Sir William Smith, whose goddess of conversion disguises a desire for power as "love, duty, self sacrifice."[39] Rather, the religious form assumed within middle-class experience, as this was "naturally" made intrinsic to the idea of society as a whole, helped to extend the demanding significance of this thought beyond the broader categories of social life and behavior to even the most eccentric pockets of existence. Deciding whether or not one should ride a horse or wear a necklace—even when there was no question of impropriety involved in these activities—could fall under the sway of this pressure, as Dorothea Brooke interpreted it, despite the fact that she was no Puritan according to the historical definition of the religion. Even more significant (since Eliot showed Brooke's interpretation to be supererogatory) is the force this pressure could lend Eliot as she made the consciousness of everyone in society the object of her aesthetic supervision. With the aid of this pressure, she could develop a general psychology of egoism much more demanding than any bans on horse-riding or adornment because it represented a religious enlightenment ruling over all, not a "mere" discipline or artificial code of manners. "Justice is like the Kingdom of God," she would write: "it is not without us as a fact, it is within us as a great yearning" (R, 2: 176). In dedicating her writing to the "faithful" representation of the nature of ordinary human life, Eliot was able to trade on the customary power of the form of religious thought even while she systematically replaced a theological with a rational form of transcendence.[40] Carlyle set a precedent in this case, too; for example, when he explained the need to educate the masses by defining intellect as "the discernment of order in disorder . . . the discovery of the will of Nature, of God's will; the beginning of the capability to walk according to that."[41] The narrative implied in this passage—a movement from a passive understanding to an active motivation—represents the identity between knowledge and discipline that could always be drawn when one was granted the sacralization of social life as an unquestioned assumption.

This connection made it all the easier for the liberal intellectual to see society and the reality of human experience as representing an undifferentiated whole. It is to a "web" of human lots (*M*, 1: 146) or to a "mirror" (*AB*, 181) that a novelist who is also an intellectual of this type might well look for an image of her art. She would look to an image of totality that appeared to be uniform throughout its surface. She would do so because such an image could be expressive of a social conception that was not given over to inalterable divisions or forms but rather dedicated to a transcendence of all that was arbitrary, violent, and merely traditional or material. As Eliot put it in the epigraph to chapter 57 of *Daniel Deronda*, "Deeds are the pulse of Time, his beating life, / And righteous or unrighteous, being done, / Must throb in after-throbs till Time itself / Be laid in stillness, and the universe / Quiver and breathe upon no mirror more" (*DD*, 2: 312). Thus formed, the basis of Eliot's art was conceived to be more a method of truth than an assertion of truth. Eliot formulated her novels in such a way as to suggest that the reader was being presented not only with a representation of society but also with the logic of this representation.

Her writing suggests this logic is a neutral and comprehensive scheme to which no one can object except those who are prey to narrow prejudices, class interests, or the like. In images like those of the web and the mirror, one sees a fictional matrix that defines the reality of society in the image of rational discourse. In this respect Eliot's fiction is one with the universalized conception of education developed as the new mode of social reproduction in her age. As she wrote of her aesthetic revelation of society, "Art is the nearest thing to life; it is a mode of amplifying experience and extending our contact with our fellow-man beyond the bounds of our personal lots" (*E*, 271). Similarly, "A statesman who shall be nameless," she told John Blackwood, "has said that I first opened to him a vision of Italian life, then of Spanish, and now I have kindled in him a quite new understanding of the Jewish people. This is what I wanted to do—to widen the English vision a little in that direction and let in a little conscience and refinement" (*L*, 6: 304). Her art was to be distinguished from the narrowly didactic or merely entertaining and even from the popular Victorian combination of "instruction and amusement." In her hands the novel was to be above all else "a real instrument of culture" (*L*, 3: 44). It was to be educational in the most sacred, humanizing, socially regulating sense of the word.

No wonder one may find in her novels descriptions like the following account of Seth Bede's feelings:

> He was but three-and-twenty, and had only just learned what it is to love—to love with that adoration which a young man gives to a woman whom he feels to be greater and better than himself. Love of this sort is hardly distinguishable from religious feeling. What deep and worthy love is so? whether of woman or child, or art or music. Our caresses, our tender words, our still rapture under the influence of autumn sunsets, or pillared vistas, or calm majestic statues, or Beethoven symphonies, all bring with them the consciousness that they are mere waves and ripples in an unfathomable ocean of love and beauty; our emotion in its keenest moment passes from experience into silence, our love at its highest flood rushes beyond its object, and loses itself in the sense of divine mystery. (*AB*, 36-37)

It does not matter that it is extremely unlikely that Seth ever heard the strains of a Beethoven symphony or saw a statue or a pillared vista. The texture of Eliot's intellectual culture is imposed upon his feelings, willy-nilly, on the assumption that the truth of society is an undifferentiated universality. Social truth is that seamless plane of discourse represented in the "unfathomable ocean," "silence," and "divine mystery" of this description. The escalating address of the passage reinforces this point when it shifts from Seth as a historical individual ("He was but three-and-twenty") to a particular type of "young man," and thence to all who love properly, until, finally, the author and her readers are emphatically embraced as a social community ("Our caresses, our tender words"). In this passage, as in Eliot's writing in general, the representation of ordinary life is both an exposition of philosophical principle and a formal demonstration of the logic justifying this principle. The form of this passage penetrates the particular to reach the universal, leading the reader through the transfiguration of the individual into society as a whole. The justification for this process is the characterization of representation of any sort as a symbolic entrance into the universal. This allows the rhetorical appeal of the passage to be based on an assumption of shared experience. Presumably, those whose love has not brought them the consciousness that their feelings are mere waves and ripples on an unfathomable ocean have not properly felt "a deep and worthy" love. The situation resembles that created by Eliot's references to the inevitable faults of her representation of human life, which serve to reinforce the legitimacy of that representation by formally including error within its principled presentation. Similarly, in this passage the characterization of representations as "mere" epiphenomena serves to make their impression all the more demanding. It is thus that Eliot, following the governing discourse of her age, made the culture of the middle classes a prescription for social experience while claiming she was describing only the truth of this experience.

It is interesting in this respect to consider the importance of memorization to the highly educated person of Eliot's time, as evidenced in the habit of quoting from memory common to Eliot and so many others of this period. While encouraging a sense of intellectual independence, this educational practice also encouraged a sense that the past might be incorporated into consciousness and that books, statues, concerts, and other cultural objects were the individual features of a comprehensive and integrating spirit that could be drawn from the individual's consciousness. Thomas Pinney has noted that Eliot's quoting of others is usually from memory and unreliable even when it is apparent that she is quoting directly from the text,[42] and this "fault" may be seen as a suggestive indication of the nature of the liberal mind. It is only a step from the gaining of this spiritual impression of consciousness encouraged by the habit of memorization to the making of a character like Seth, who experiences his feelings for Dinah in the same way Eliot would hear fine music. If the burden of the past was often felt as a crippling influence by the educated person of this time, one must also remember that the perception of this burden as such depends on an expectation that the situation ought to be otherwise and thus on a will to dominate and transcend the past.

To Eliot, knowledge took the form of her own intellectual consciousness, just as she took culture to be the basis of society as a whole despite her admission that this culture would be experienced directly only by a small group in society, "the world able to give away a sovereign without pinching itself" (*L*, 5: 335). This limitation of the experience of culture did not matter as long as Eliot could make culture appear to be the universal basis of experience so that the terms in which someone like Seth actually might have felt his love for someone like Dinah could appear to be derived from Eliot's more comprehensive conception of reality. It was thus that Eliot could succeed in asserting a sense of control over social history: by transfiguring the feelings of an ordinary man like Seth into the design of her own intellectual nature. In this procedure her style was very different from that used by Dickens to assert the gentility of Joe Gargery, but the ideological sense of the assertions of these two writers was very similar.

This example of Eliot's description of Seth is not a casually chosen one. Eliot argued that her conception of art necessarily demanded that attention be paid to common people and that this attention had a special importance. "All the more sacred is the task of the artist," she wrote, "when he undertakes to paint the life of the People" (*E*, 271). And she wrote elsewhere, "My only merit must lie in the truth with which I represent to you the humble experience of ordinary fellow-mortals. I wish to stir your sympathy with commonplace troubles; to win your tears for real sorrow" ("AB," 62-63).

The nature of this attention must particularly be noted, not simply the inclusion of common figures within the domain of art. For example, the religious diction with which Eliot defined the task of the artist is instructive, as it is this form of discourse her representation of Seth's feelings was designed to elicit. It is important to note how Eliot's painting of the people was meant to apply her fiction to society as a whole because of the ontological role they were assigned, not simply because of the fact of their inclusion within it. When Eliot insisted on "calling attention to the existence of low people by whose interference, however little we may like it, the course of the world is very much determined" (*M*, 1: 429), the self-consciousness with which she made this announcement may be seen as the aggressiveness of one who found herself in the relatively unexampled role of the intellectual novelist; but her emphasis on the determining importance of such people is also a tug on the web of her discourse meant to remind readers of its totality. In this case "the world" serves as the universality comprehended by her text, but it is clear here as throughout her fiction that social order is at stake, no matter what term this may fall under.

Consider the way this self-reflexive emphasis is developed in a passage from *Felix Holt*:

> For what we call illusions are often, in truth, a wider vision of past and present realities—a willing movement of a man's soul with the large sweep of the world's forces—a movement towards a more assured end than the chances of a single life. We see human heroism broken into units and say, this unit did little—might as well not have been. But in this way we might break the sunlight into fragments, and think that this and the other might be cheaply parted with. Let us rather raise a monument to the soldiers whose brave hearts only kept the ranks unbroken, and met death—a monument to the faithful who were not famous, and who are precious as the continuity of the sunbeams is precious, though some of them fall unseen and on barrenness. (*FH*, 191-92)

The images of the sunbeam, the monument, and the army are the reflex of an art in which society emerges from discourse undifferentiated and whole. Eliot wrote, "It is the habit of my imagination to strive after as full a vision of the medium in which a character moves as of the character itself" (*L*, 4: 97). What this statement meant in practice was that all her characters and all the phenomena of their world would be resolved in a common medium presented to the reader as more than the consciousness of the artist. They would be presented as the rational truth of society.

This is " 'that enlarged life which grows and grows by appropriating the lives of others' " of which Philip Wakem writes to Maggie Tulliver (*MF*, 537). It is this manner of representation that Eliot called realism. When she wrote to her publishers so devoutly, "And I cannot stir a step aside from what I *feel* to be *true* in character" (*L*, 2: 299), and when she told how she did not try to show anything "as it should be" but only "to exhibit some things as they have been or are" (*L*, 2: 362), it was such images of totality and the discourse they represented that she had in mind. It is significant in this respect that she underscored the words "feel" and "true." In this way she traced a continuity in the description of her creative psychology embracing a transcendent will ("I cannot stir a step aside"), a subjective order of feeling, and the interpretation of social truth ("character"), just as she used this continuity to represent experience in general. The sentence itself is a compressed narrative of the intellectual's transcendence of self in the service of the revelation of society.

If one has in mind only such rhetoric as Burke's characterization of the lower classes as a swinish multitude, Eliot's willingness to pay attention to individuals of the lower or lower-middle classes might indeed seem to represent "the enchantments of the wizard whose first article of belief is the truism which very few of us comprehend until it has been knocked into us by years of experience—that we are all alike—that the human heart is one," as E. S. Dallas said in his 1859 review of *Adam Bede* in the *Times*. He recommended Thackeray for the same virtue, in what appears to have been a common comparison at the time, along with the one frequently drawn between Eliot and Charlotte Brontë. Whereas Dallas saw this virtue as a radically new one in literature, a more cautious reviewer in *The Sun* congratulated Eliot for the "great tact and discrimination . . . displayed in the selection of the class of persons who figure before us in this eventful drama . . . taken from the ranks of the workers of the world, and yet the superior ones," a note that others also found important to make. In any case, it was commonplace then as now to notice that Eliot favored "average humanity," as a reviewer in the *Atlantic Monthly* put it in 1866.[43] This matter has been considered by one of her most prominent modern critics, Barbara Hardy, in the course of a commentary on *Middlemarch*:

> We cannot look at one character or one of the four main actions
> without seeing the "sameness of the human lot," in love, in marriage,
> in economic problems, in work, and in the moral process of growing
> away from self. "While I tell the truth about loobies," George Eliot
> says as she concludes her account of the reading of Featherstone's will,
> "my readers' imagination need not be entirely excluded from an oc-
> cupation with lords." This is more than an arch irony or an apology
> for humble material. It is a reading direction.[44]

But what are we to make of this reading direction and of the way so many readers from Eliot's day to our own, not excluding Hardy, have accepted it?

In "A Minor Prophet," Eliot wrote, "I cleave / To nature's blunders, evanescent types / Which sages banish from Utopia" (*P*, 386). In this way she contrasted her art to one of the misleadingly idealistic types that would be preoccupied only with "lords." However, as the reactions of readers like Hardy make clear, Eliot's effort was to make the evanescent, the imperfect, or the unrecognized identical to the cultural ideal of humanity. Eliot's emphasis on ordinary human life did not represent a broadening of the scope of aesthetics, as she argued, but rather a normalizing of this scope. For this reason one who looks back from Eliot's novels and other Victorian writings to romantic literature is liable to consider the impulses of this literature radically liberating, simply because the retrospect constituted by an aesthetics such as Eliot's can make any resistance to the ordinary appear to be so. In the very way she recognized ordinary human life, as well as in the sense she made of her observations of it, Eliot constituted this life as part of the utopia of culture. Even setting aside for the moment the consideration that she generally chose to write of the more presentable ordinary people, it still remains true that her ordinary characters are as much phantasms of the ordinary as the mob in *Felix Holt* is a phantasm of the lower-class character. They are figures designed to represent an ordinariness that is the existential equivalent of Eliot's supervising idea of rational discourse.

After all, how did ordinary life come to be so remarkable that one would have to give it one's "faithful" support in dedicating this new genre of realism to it? How did it become so estranged from "us" that "we" would need its appearance framed by the *apologia* in Eliot's commentary as well as by that in her sophisticated narrative techniques? This situation did not come about because some malevolent spirit suddenly had bereaved the prevailing literary forms of meaning. What is at issue here is rather the production of a new interpretation of these forms: an interpretation founded in the situation of historical change that made it possible for Eliot to be a liberal intellectual and that guided her in thinking that a fiction in which all people were taken to be essentially the same was a true representation of ordinary reality. In other words, Eliot's discovery of ordinary human life is an invention of that life just as her revelation of society as a whole is a demand that society be viewed this way. Like the figure of the gentleman to which it bears an ironic relation, the figure of ordinary life in Eliot's writing is a transfiguration of the plane of discourse she took as the basis of her writing, and this basis is itself a transfiguration of the intellectual identity made available to Eliot by the social changes that had come to England during the preceding century.

The lesson of Eliot's writing, as of her age, involves the transference of power from the supposed fixity of figures in the traditional society of the past to the rationalized circulation assumed within the transfigurations of the modern world. This is the power and the freedom made available by knowledge in its modern conception: the will to identify the representations of this new middle-class cultural order as the reality of society, its figures of speech as figures of life, its transfiguring art as the redemption of humanity.

Chapter 3
Literary Consciousness and the Vacancy of the Individual

> *I read, without design, the opinions, thoughts,*
> *Of those plain-living people now observed*
> *With clearer knowledge.*
>
> Wordsworth, *The Prelude*

Ordinary human life was remarkable to Eliot for the same reason that the gentleman became the subject of vexed debate in her time. This term represented a social change, not a creature that had been kept under wraps until it received its revelation at her hands. For Eliot, this term was the invention of an ignorance she could patronize. It was the sentimental complement to the transfigured gentleman. This is the relation one sees in the narratives of this time when an "ordinary" human being collides with the traditional figure of the gentleman and, through the impact, becomes a part of the gentleman's transfiguration. A corollary version is a meeting of this sort between an ordinary human being and an excessively respectable member of the middle classes.

The ordinary human being is as much a figure of discourse as the gentleman is, and it is inseparable from this other figure in the nineteenth century. Whether or not their relationship takes on a dramatic form—as it does between Adam Bede and Arthur Donnithorne, Felix Holt and Esther Lyon, and Mordecai and Daniel Deronda, to name some of the more prominent examples of this configuration in Eliot's novels—it is the relationship between them, as well as the wider clustering of figurative forms and devices attendant upon this relationship, that defines ordinary human life and gentility as such in the discourse of Eliot's day. When Eliot wrote, "And to judge wisely I suppose we must know how things appear to the unwise; that kind of appearance making the larger part of the world's history" (*DD*, 1: 343), she exemplified this relationship governing the modern conception of education and the transfiguration of the gentleman, just as Wordsworth did when he described how his perception of ordinary people had improved after he had spent a term at Cambridge.

Of course, the figure of ordinary human life involved in her fiction was not Eliot's individual invention, but rather an articulation of the terms of her culture. For instance, the process Eliot went through in the invention of this phantasm had been rehearsed by Carlyle. As he wrote in "Chartism" (1839):

> How inexpressibly useful were true insight into it; a genuine understanding by the upper classes of society [of] what it is that the under classes intrinsically mean, a clear interpretation of the thought which at heart torments these wild inarticulate souls, struggling there, with inarticulate uproar, like dumb creatures in pain, unable to speak what is in them!

In Carlyle's as in Eliot's invention of this figure of ordinary human life, the first step is an erasure of its consciousness and will and thus of its history and its historical relation to other elements of society. The meaning of this life becomes a problem, as the "under classes" become "dumb creatures in pain" without coherent voices, needs, or desires of their own, because the intellectual makes it a problem. In representing this life, Eliot found truth to be "so difficult" (*AB*, 183) because her system of representation created this appearance of difficulty, which served specific ideological ends.

This is not to say there is no significance in representations like Carlyle's and Eliot's but that the identity of the governing classes was at stake in this invention of the ordinary. Although the mention of ordinary or common life would seem to be the neutral designation of a universal level of experience shared by the higher classes even if transcended or refined by them, it was nothing of the sort. It was another application of the middle classes' idea of their own history to the nature of the world. Ordinary life emerged as a blank slate from a timeless traditional past (hence its muteness or its language of animalic incomprehensibility), then found its need for a rational basis (as in the "clear interpretation" sought by Carlyle and by the ordinary human beings who appeal to the understanding of Eliot's narrators), and then discovered its identity and the future reproduction of society through its submission to the process of education. As Carlyle went on to say,

> What are all the popular commotions and maddest bellowings, from Peterloo to the Place-de-Grève itself? Bellowings, *in*articulate cries as of a dumb creature in rage and pain; to the ear of wisdom they are inarticulate prayers: "Guide me, govern me! I am mad and miserable, and cannot guide myself!"[1]

For Carlyle as for Eliot, to pay attention to ordinary human life was to aggrandize the power of middle-class interpretation. It was to insert the fable of the middle classes' history into the being of the lower classes. They honored the existence of these classes by stripping it of any differences it might have with the experience allowed within the governing discourse of the time. This discovery of ordinary human life was thus an instance of the controlling rhetoric John Stuart Mill described as the special gift of the intellectual. (This is not to say this rhetoric was as conscious and deliberate a development as Mill would have had it be). Although it suggested growing intellectual enlightenment and broadening human sympathies, the insistence upon the problem of this class of life, on its need for interpretation, was a scheme of social order.

After all, how did the lower classes become such obscure objects? J. F. C. Harrison is among those who have suggested that one factor in this event was the development of modern towns in which "the labouring poor became segregated in exclusively working-class districts," whereas the medieval town and its descendants through the eighteenth century had found "rich and poor, merchants and labourers . . . more or less intermingled."[2] However, his observation cannot serve to explain this anxiety: this problem of comprehending ordinary human life. It does seem to be the case that social classes became more materially divided from one another during this period than they had been heretofore, but the notation of this fact does not serve to explain why this division was interpreted as such a pressing problem. Nor does it explain the solution given to this problem within the social criticism of Carlyle and the fiction of Eliot: a call for education reinforced by a claim to a new form of psychological and literary observation.

The motivation for this problem of ordinary human life is better expressed by the words of an 1861 commentary on *Silas Marner* in *The Saturday Review*:

> It is in the portraiture of the poor, and of what it is now fashionable to call "the lower middle class," that this writer is without a rival, and no phase of life could be harder to draw. George Eliot alone moves among this unknown, and to most people unknowable, section of society as if quite at home there, and can let imagination run loose and disport itself in a field that, we think, has been only partially opened even to the best writers.[3]

As this response indicates, the remarkable "discovery" of ordinary human life is not so much the result of a change in this life as it is the result of a new posture assumed by the middle classes in their relation to the lower. It is not caused by a material estrangement, although this was suggested at the time by Cobbett's nostalgic visions of an era when a farmer's workers would eat at the same table with him or by the conviction on the part of writers like Mrs. Gaskell that masters and men would understand each other if only they could meet fact to face and learn about each other's lives. Rather, the division between these two classes was a middle-class assertion of distance.

That this was the case is evident in the logic of this review of Eliot's work. The writer congratulates Eliot for revealing an unknown and largely unknowable class of life. However, in so doing he shows that the persuasiveness of Eliot's representations has nothing to do with social experience in any neutral or positive sense of the word (even assuming there could be such a sense). It cannot have this basis, for the reviewer, his audience, and even "the best writers" are excluded from any direct knowledge of the life that is Eliot's subject. And this is not even to mention the way the rhetoric of this passage excluded those below the middle class from understanding, for they composed by far the largest proportion of the population at the time and yet to "most people" were said to be unknowable.

Eliot's persuasiveness can have come only from the form of her consciousness of this life. This form was persuasive because it made the imagination "quite at home" in this field and yet securely distanced this life that generally would be liable to appear all too close and threatening. In Eliot's wonderful phrase, her imagination was "a licensed trespasser" (*AB*, 72). It could transgress boundaries and yet maintain a distinctive identity, which, as she carefully noted, might be said to have the force of law behind it. This form of imagination reassured people like the journalist contemplating the prospective "plebification of art" in 1866, who feared that "social boundary lines" were not as sharply drawn as they ought to be. "In other words," he wrote, "the old 'cordon sanitaires' have snapped under the pressure of multitudes, and we have not yet succeeded in twisting new ones."[4]

All the literature of the discovery of ordinary human life, which played so large a part in the reception of realism as a characteristically middle-class and nineteenth-century form, represents the middle-class imagination at play in a field created by the distance it rhetorically fashions between itself and the classes beneath it. During this time of consolidation in the middle classes' historical rise to power, as in the period of their development, their identity was nothing more or less than the imaginary center to the relationships they perceived to exist between themselves and other classes. Such is the nature of the consciousness of class in society. And because the key relationship from the first third of the nineteenth century on was that which the middle classes had with the lower classes, the largely "unknowable" nature of this latter part of society can be thought of as a creation of the need for middle-class differentiation. The contrary drive to know these classes can be seen to represent the middle-class imperative of education as the source of social reproduction. It is the stipulation of this distance between classes and the process of its manipulation that is the real subject of Carlyle's writing on the common people and of Eliot's dedication of her writing to them. The lower classes are caught both coming and going by this trap of their discovery within discourse. They are portrayed as empty of reality except when they fall away from or aspire to the status of the middle classes.

In Eliot's fiction, this life is always shown in a tragic and sentimental relation to its unfulfilled potential, which is simply a set of middle-class imperatives given an exemplary form in the moralized figure of the gentleman. In other words, ordinary human life is a vacancy for discourse in Eliot's writing as it is in Carlyle's. It is valuable precisely because its "intrinsic meaning" is mute or confused and thus may be taken to be a muddied version of middle-class aspirations, just as the figure of the gentleman was valuable because its definition was so difficult to pin down. Ordinary human life is not found at a distance but rather is an invention of this distance. In its universality, its normality, and its promise of internal coherence and future development, it is an idealized displacement of the institutional sites where discourse was actually produced. It makes knowledge appear to come from "life" rather than from governments, schools, experts, and similar sources. This figure is the vacancy of ignorance created within society by middle-class discourse so that it may be filled with ideologies and yet dramatically appear to learn these truths, to reach them after great difficulties, to pull them out of its own innards, and thus to prove, through the power of "self-making" that leads to "self-consciousness," the justice of the social system that instituted this discipline.

One can say of Eliot what Hazlitt said of her beloved Scott—that her works, taken together, "are almost like a new edition of human nature"[5]—as long as one notes that this new version of human nature is the design of a discourse gaining novel power, just as human nature is in Scott's writing. This is the case, too, with the writing of Wordsworth, another of Eliot's favorites. Wordsworth, we are told, observed ordinary human life "without design" and yet "with clearer knowledge" after a term at Cambridge; and he later found an understanding of the universality of man in "the best of those who live," just as Eliot and Arnold would.[6]

The use of this "ordinary life" did not end with Eliot—one can immediately think of later writers such as Hardy and Lawrence—and it did not begin with Carlyle. From the eighteenth century on, it was common for writers to invent the lower classes while claiming to discover them, just as it was common for any invention that dramatized itself as such to be dismissed as being overly sentimental. This situation is exemplified in the judgment Eliot and other critics passed on Dickens's portraiture of the poor. It is useless to look for one point at which this use of ordinary life was established, but it is characteristic of an age in which the middle classes achieved a position of strength in society sufficient to turn them to self-consciousness and thus to an interest in their relation to other classes and their consciousness. It is for this reason that Wordsworth's and Scott's mode of paying attention to this subject appears so different from that of a writer like Smollett, despite the great differences that exist between the works of the two romantics. By the time they were writing, a new quasi-spiritual seriousness and quasi-scientific attention had entered into the formula for the representation of this life.

Take the example of Wordsworth's poem "A Narrow Girdle of Rough Stones," which perfectly represents this articulation of middle-class consciousness in the form of a discovery of ordinary human life. It opens with the narrator and two friends sauntering along a causeway that extends into

Grasmere and casually observing the margin of nature, unproductive and disorganized, found there. "It was our occupation to observe / Such objects as the waves had tossed ashore— / Feather, or leaf, or weed, or withered bough / . . . And in our vacant mood / Not seldom did we stop to watch some tuft / Of dandelion seed or thistle's beard." While engaged in this desultory wandering through a nature that is itself desultory and wandering, the three friends hear "the busy mirth / Of reapers, men and women, boys and girls." They are "Delighted much to listen to these sounds," which they consume, taking this harvest labor as nourishment for their imagination— "And feeding thus our fancies." Then, what they espy "a Man / Attired in peasant's garb" fishing on the lake, the group breaks out in imprecations upon his improvidence in enjoying this leisure when he could be earning money and saving for the harder times of winter. They move closer, however, and see he is wasted by sickness, unable to work, and trying to use "his best skill to gain / A pittance from the dead unfeeling lake / That knew not of his wants." The friends are so chagrined that they name the place "POINT RASH-JUDGMENT" because it was there they learned "What need there is to be reserved in speech, / And temper all our thoughts with charity."[7]

This poem may be taken to represent the discovery of self-consciousness through a consciousness of others. One learns to distinguish accurate perceptions from distortions caused by a distant viewpoint, moral from spontaneous speech, feeling from deadened nature, and good from rash judgment through this experience in which leisure and labor are juxtaposed. At first these different categories of experience appear to be in harmony, at least from the viewpoint of the poet and his friends. Then this harmony is disturbed when the angling peasant is descried and cannot be made to fit the categories that divide the leisured from the laboring group and the casual from the organized nature. It is finally regained in a new, moralized version that appears to be all the stronger because it has endured this plot in which it must weather the complicating phenomenon of the angler. The poem thus composed is a formula for the process of perception, for the developing consciousness of gentility in the moralized nineteenth-century mode, for the poised composure of society as a whole, and, in addition, for the understanding of nature as the symbolic formula encompassing all these others.

This nature is not a simple thing. At first, the strand along which the poet and his friends walk—"A rude and narrow causeway," a "retired and difficult way"—seems a pleasant and peaceful shore despite its roughness, the detritus that washes upon it, and the mixture of "flower or water-weed" along its edge. Its heterogeneous and uncultivated nature may seem to parallel the disorganized wanderings of the group of friends with their "lovely images" of the morning. However, the discomposure of the spot may also seem to foretell the "serious musing and . . .self-reproach" that unexpectedly disrupt their pleasant consciousness. This reproach turns the heterogeneity of the leisured and the laborers into a conflict: a disturbing revelation to the leisured of a "dead unfeeling lake" in their pleasant consciousness. In the end, the place and persons are reconciled through the naming of the place with their experience. In this way nature may be seen to encompass the naive, the illusory, and the moralized perception and thus to embody the course of experience represented in the poem. The point in this scene is symbolically neutral until it is privately named by the poet and his friends and fully appropriated to their subjective response to their experience. Therefore, it appears nature is as neutral as language is when one is concerned with any sort of social judgment.

The complexity of this neutrality is raised through the issue of naming. This is the overriding issue of the poem, in both senses of the word. On the one hand, it is the outcome of the poem's drama: a point is named. On the other, it is the issue raised in the conflict preceding this outcome: a mislabeled phenomenon reveals disturbances within other categories of the protagonists' experience. The means of concluding the poem is thus implicated within the conflict that constitutes it. Therefore, the ultimate complementarity of language and nature that is developed in the poem can result only from their displacement of each other in a narrative that becomes an allegory of consciousness. The signifying potential of nature is revealed only when the perception of nature is discomposed by a misnaming. This error is necessary to the achievement of the higher moral consciousness symbolized by the identification of human consciousness and natural location at the end of the poem. Thus, an act of violence in which language is divided from nature so that both lose their ground must occur if the two are to be reintegrated in a moral and social mode of being, rather than in a mode that is basically unconscious. The most profound complication raised by the misnaming of the angler, then, appears to be the subsequent impression that any naming of nature, if it is to be accurate or true, must be subject to a potentially infinite deferral that can be limited only by a stipulated social consciousness. This poem serves to exemplify that consciousness in its form as a cultural object. In this respect, it is not a poem with a moral. It is the very basis of morality because it is a representation of culture.

Such are the exquisite complexities of a gentleman's analysis of consciousness. Even more notable, though, is the moral question not canvassed in this little drama. As the issue of the poem appears to involve the establishment of culture, the question of the legitimacy of these three friends making their initial judgment upon the peasant—aside from the problem of whether this judgment happens to have been "right" or "wrong"—goes without question. The issue not named, the issue buried in the "mistake" of this poem, is the appropriation of language by the poet and his friends. Just as the divisions between the laborers and the wanderers and between uncultivated and productive nature are not questioned in this poem, so is the question of language and moral judgment as a property exclusive to a certain class of people in society one that receives no attention. This is what is found equally in the "wrong" and the "right" of the poem: the assumption of a certain power of moral judgment allied to a proper conception of language.

For all its sophistication, the effect of this poem justifies the kind of sentimental judgment by which the genteel associate themselves with the lower classes and appear to take a lesson from them in the nature of true perception, morality, and meaning while actually remaining in control. And this is the control maintained in Eliot's writings, in which this sort of drama is played out in the relations between narrator and characters and narrator and readers, as well as in the relations among the characters in the text.

This becomes clear when one considers the figure that allows this kind of sentimentality to be produced because it comprehends both the gentleman and the common man without doing violence to either. This is the figure liberal intellectuals oppose to the "violence" of class distinctions: the individual. Here, again, one sees the intimate bond between the middle classes and intellectuals. A definitive characteristic of liberal intellectuals in this period was that they interpreted society as comprising individuals and regarded the individual as the first category for thinking about society as a whole. In this exaltation of individuality, they were providing a metaphysics for what was already the basic middle-class theory of economic and social practice.

True, no one was more fierce than the intellectuals of this period in pouncing upon and dismembering the actual products of this practice. E. L. Woodward alluded to this when he wrote, "From a sociological point of view it is an interesting paradox that the bourgeois writers of the age of high capitalism should have been almost unanimous in failing to discover beauty in the technique upon which middle-class life and the capitalist system were based."[8] Eliot, for example, was perfectly capable of describing a character such as Chubb, the publican in *Felix Holt*, with his "political 'idee', which was, that society existed for the sake of the individual, and that the name of that individual was Chubb" (*FH*, 136). But there is no real paradox here, at least if one is regarding liberal intellectuals. In this case, as with their rejection of class, it is within their definition, as it were, to be critical toward and even contemptuous of the material conditions that gave rise to their values and their position in society. These must be put at a safe distance just as "economic literature" must be quarantined to preserve the purity of "true" literature.

Even though it may be used as a tool to discipline the lower classes, as in Ruskin's writings or Smiles's tales of entrepeneurial successes, the idea of individuality cannot be recognized by liberal intellectuals as being in any way a product of society or of a particular social class. To so recognize it would be to implicate themselves within a historical process, whereas the effect of the conditions that engendered their role was that they should seem to assume a position in which, as individuals, they were above any material obligations to history and society. Consequently, because their idea of the individual is founded upon their own role, it is entirely abstract. It is the perfect abstraction of the Idea itself, as this now could be conceived to be liberated from tradition and given over to the neutral and impersonal operations of reason. Thus it is that society is conceived of on the model of the liberal intellectual's mind, with individuals as the elements to be thought into a social whole. As Carlyle put it, in a formula that also expresses the erasure of history in the middle-class conception of its character, "Social Life is the aggregate of all the individual men's Lives who constitute society; History is the essence of innumerable Biographies."[9]

The liberal intellectual conceives the essence of individuality to lie in selflessness because the individual is made to be subject to operations of reason that turn abstract individuality into ideal sociality. It is useless to look for philosophical logic in such a scheme: this "reason" is the plot of middle-class will and only need satisfy this to prove compelling. So Eliot's narrator could say, in "A Political Molecule," "Society is happily not dependent for the growth of fellowship on the small minority already endowed with comprehensive sympathy. Any molecule of the body politic, working towards his own interest in an orderly way, gets his understanding more or less penetrated with the fact that his interest is included in that of a large number" (*TS*, 316).

Even though they might disagree with aspects of Adam Smith's thought, liberal intellectuals pursue their thought just as Smith did when he characterized the individual as one who pursued his selfish ends and yet found his essential selflessness revealed when he was transfigured in the context of society as a whole. Liberal intellectuals exalt the individual but with no recognition that this is the archetype of middle-class identity, or at least—as in Arnold's, Ruskin's, and Eliot's cases—with no recognition that this archetype is significantly related to their own idea of individuality. As a pure abstraction and as a specific moral imperative, this idea of individuality is taken to be nature, as are the operations of reason in general, as they were understood in nineteenth-century discourse. It is thus that a society based on individuals in free competition and a rationality based on individual ideas that are supposed to be in the same state are paralleled in the discourse of the liberal intellectual. To refer to one is to make reference to the other, however imperfectly developed one or the other may be and however much one or the other may be less than perfectly aligned with the idea toward which it is intended to move, which in any case is taken to be its true meaning.

It is true that at times Eliot might have seemed to be arguing against just such a conception of human beings. When she wrote to her friend Charles Bray, in reference to his recently published *Philosophy of Necessity*, she mentioned her extreme dislike for a passage in which he appeared "to consider the disregard of individuals as a lofty condition of mind." She went on to say, "My own experience and development deepen every day my conviction that our moral progress may be measured by the degree in which we sympathize with individual suffering and individual joy" (*L*, 2: 403). Similarly, Eliot scattered a number of disparaging remarks upon "philosophers" throughout her fiction—despite the fact that she already was being remarked upon in her own day as the most philosophical of novelists, for example, in Henry James's reaction to her writing—and she always did so because in her eyes they disregarded the sanctity of the individual or regarded it only juridically rather than sentimentally and, in effect, novelistically.[10] Emotion, she wrote ironically, "is obstinately irrational: it insists on caring for individuals" ("JR," 356); and the philosopher is liable to appear in contrast to emotion in her fiction, as in Wordsworth's poems, in the role of "a fingering slave, / One that would peep and botanize / Upon his mother's grave."[11] In another letter she wrote, "I become more and more timid—with less daring to adopt any formula which does not get itself clothed for me in some human figure and individual experience, and perhaps that is a sign that if I help others to see at all it must be through that medium of art" (L, 6: 216-17). In this kind of statement the purposes of her art do indeed seem to diverge from the reasoning of the liberal intellectual—but only if one fails to consider exactly how Eliot treated the individual within the medium of her art.

In this regard, one might further look at the way Eliot announced the individual as if she were herald to the discovery of a new species of human subject. After all, it is a sign of her intellectual self-consciousness and one of the most distinguishing features of her art that she found it important to call attention to her recognition of the individual as the basis of any realistic representation of human life. Of course, in some cases this announcement may seem to be merely a reaction against a certain brand of popular romanticism—not unlike the practice of a writer like Jane Austen. However, even in such cases the significance of the contrast stems from Eliot's broader insistence that any knowledge will fall into delusion and victimization if it is not founded on a personal sympathy with individuals. Eliot did not simply oppose one genre to another, one type of character to another, or even the reality of individuals to the production of stereotypes. In heralding the individual, she announced that knowledge in general was contingent upon an understanding of this phenomenological category before all else.

Compare Austen's emphasis on the attention that ought to be directed toward social forms, however disagreeable and irrational these might be, to Eliot's description of the Reverend Irwine in Adam Bede. This description is preoccupied with the difficulty of isolating the individual so that his nature may be studied uncontaminated by the artificial forms of society. Eliot wrote, "See the difference between the impression a man makes on you when you walk by his side in familiar talk, or look at him in his home, and the figure he makes when seen from a lofty historical level, or even in the eyes of a critical neighbor who thinks of him as an embodied system or opinion rather than as a man" (AB, 69).

Eliot's hyperconsciousness of perspective throughout her works—as in the fault she found with telescopic and even microscopic views in Middlemarch, when she suggested "a stronger lens" might always clarify matters further (*M*, 1: 60)—shows the multiplication of viewpoints produced by this insistence on the individual in her fiction. This sort of representation is also found in her use of juxtaposed plots and scenes and characters, in her employment of an omniscient narrator, and in various other devices. In any case, the intensity of the attention she paid to the difficulty of isolating the individual, like her attention to the problem of establishing a description of ordinary human life, is a measure of her demand that the individual appear to be real and the real basis of all understanding. This difficulty cannot be said to stem from the multiplicity of perspectives available to her, for this multiplicity would not appear onerous if she were ensconced in its implications, taking society's measure of man as her own. These perspectives appear troublesome and alienating only because she was concerned about rejecting them. She wanted to reject the surface of society and to put a certain order of subjectivity in its place—this abstract individuality—to serve as the power of truth.

This is the distinctive aspect of her art: that she brought to fiction a concern with the representation of character that went beyond an interest in mocking, exploiting, criticizing, or correcting cultural stereotypes. Her representation of character was instead related to a certain conception of reason. Through this conception, it was further related to a general theory of society and its representation. Because her art was identified with reason, which the liberal intellectual thought to be the font of morality, Eliot could not represent characters without thinking that conclusions about the way society ought to be conceived and life ought to be lived would be implicated in the style of this representation.

Even the most casual or brief descriptions in her work might be viewed as theorems from which could be deduced a view of subjects such as morality, science, and political economy. No representation could be taken for granted because all her writing was cast in this demanding form intended to promote rational discourse. Therefore, Eliot continually had to insist upon the problem her writing was trying to solve, the individual it wanted to discover, the gentleman and the ordinary human being it was seeking to reconcile. As Eliot said in *Middlemarch*, she could afford none of the leisurely digressions over the extent of the universe that a historian like Fielding could enjoy because her subject—a few individual human lives—was so complex and engrossing.

For Eliot, the individual had become the text of the universe. And like the ordinary man and the gentleman whom the individual would serve to reconcile, the individual was a literary figure demanded by the position Eliot assumed in relation to society. It became the source productive of the complications of her narratives as a result of the form in which she, as a liberal intellectual, understood historical change to have occurred and her own identity to have been established. Narrative did not become a problem for Eliot as a result of her conception of the individual: this new conception was just as much the creation of the problem of narration. This need to make narration a problem is another version of Eliot's need to emphasize the possibility of variant perspectives throughout her writing. The style of her writing had to be deliberately inserted among a host of alternative representations so that its status as a representation could be marked, defined, and given the appearance of greater comprehensiveness and truth. Similarly, her characters had to be so arranged in relation to one another as to show that their selves were not stipulated by their birth or position in society but rather were discovered or evolved through the experience represented over the course of the novel.

Thus, the form of Eliot's novels was the form of middle-class psychology. According to this form, Eliot's writing could include the possibility of other descriptions, but they could not include hers. This is the epistemology characteristic of the liberal intellectual: the conviction that knowledge is refined to the extent that the discourse with which it is advanced is able to comprehend variant or competing ideas. Hence the imagery of narrowness, extremism, and abnormality typical of liberal intellectuals in dismissing competing ideologies.[12] Where an infinitely expandable breadth of concern is not evident—as in a purely material idea of progress or in an expression of irreconcilable class interests, to choose two of the favorite *bêtes noires* of liberal intellectuals in Eliot's time—writers can patronize the ideas in question by showing their comprehension within the scope of their own thought, and thus dismiss them. This in itself is enough to disqualify such ideas: that they do not convey the style of middle-class discourse, the style of the watchman's supervision, in which all arguments are required to express universality.

In this situation, the question of whether an argument might be true or false is practically beside the point. The point is to produce a discourse that does not seem to exclude from itself the competition of other perspectives but rather seems to see through or beyond the others. It is thus that the plurality of individuals is turned into a social unity within the formal structuring of this discourse. In Eliot's hands, this manner of representation is the novel rationalized, its own technique a systematic concern, its form as well as its drama an education in what was allowed to be reality within the discourse of education in her time.

Perhaps the most exquisite exhibition of this technique occurs in chapter 20 of *Middlemarch*. This chapter begins with Dorothea Brooke in tears, and so brings her into marked contrast with the last view the reader had of her in chapter 19, in which Will Ladislaw and Adolf Naumann saw Dorothea posed in the Vatican museum as if she herself were a work of art. One realizes at the end of chapter 20 that it has all been designed to lead the reader to a new vision of the significance of that human work of art seen by the two young men while simultaneously leading to the explanation, at the beginning of chapter 21, of the reason for Dorothea's weeping. Thus, in this chapter, Eliot created a narrative that cannot be said to be either temporal or spatial in its orientation. It is rather a transformation of such representational effects to the effect of a writing with the dimensions of pure reason. Individual character is discovered by the reader in the same way it is later discovered by Ladislaw in the story and, it is implied, by enlightened individuals in the actual course of life. In this design the reader's consciousness is not made to coincide with the narrator's or with any of her characters'. Instead, it is led to imitate the process of enlightenment undergone by the characters and, in so doing, to experience the narrator's theory of realistic representation.[13]

In this way this section of the novel serves as an allegory of Eliot's description of character. An individual initially taken to be an artistic type—changeless, self-contained, and distant—is disturbed from that status and made to epitomize the process as well as the subject of a different kind of art. The ideal reader not only learns but experiences the definition of realism. Just as those who promoted education in society at large assumed that an initiation into the process of enlightenment would necessarily result in a certain understanding of society and of the individual's place in it, so did Eliot assume in the design of this chapter as in all her work that an initiation into the principles of realism would necessarily result in a certain understanding, which she most often marked with the word "sympathy." And, of course, it is characteristic of a time when the audience of literature was changing that it should seem necessary thus to tease the consciousness of the reader into being.

It is in terms of this change that the self-consciousness in Eliot's approach to the novel can be seen to differ from that of earlier writers like Fielding or Sterne. In the works of these earlier novelists, self-consciousness is generally emphasized in terms of the writer's relation to his materials and to his creative activity. In Eliot's writing, self-consciousness is shown as the experience of reading is moralized, made subject to a certain kind of discourse. The self-reflexiveness of Eliot's art is seen only incidentally in the form of epistemological or representational quandaries raised by the activity of her writing. It is highlighted as the discipline of interpretation necessarily involved in both writing and reading. The demand is that the reader, like the author and the characters in her novels, be initiated into reason. This reason is constitutive of self-reflection, which—it is assumed—will produce moral experience and eventuate in the orderly and progressive reproduction of society.

Such is the reasoning of Eliot's art in one of its most subtle passages. It might well be argued that here "the individual" is depicted with a complexity and a fullness of relations rarely if ever to be found in the novel prior to this time. However, a question still remains. In considering how the individual was made the basis of Eliot's art and how the perception of the individual was made to require a new sort of consciousness, one still must consider why the individual in her writings became the subject of such an intense attention. Why did this figure become so extraordinarily difficult that Eliot had to design a way to its understanding, so obscure that Eliot had to announce its existence, at the very time when this figure's importance had long been self-evident to nineteenth-century intellectuals concerned with law, politics, and economics—and in fact when it had been an important legal and social type in England for centuries? Why was it such a difficult task for the novelist to scare this figure out of hiding as a way to reconcile the gentleman and the ordinary human being? After all, it seems to have been propagated on the very surface of the culture, right out in the open, completely accessible to understanding as the archetype of middle-class consciousness and the founding assumption of liberal intellectuality.

The answer is apparent in the similarities Eliot bore, despite her protestations, to those who treated individuality as an abstraction. For this in fact was the only form in which the individual could be given to her novelistic vision: as an abstraction. It could not be otherwise because this is all there was to the individual in the culture to which Eliot belonged. It was an abstract negation of class divisions, aristocratic traditions, and social history. This individual was a novel figure, but its novelty lay entirely in these negations.

To be sure, the middle classes were associated with aspects of society such as trade, industry, science, and Dissenting or Evangelical religion. Nevertheless, all these had nothing to do with the figure of the individual developed within middle-class discourse. However much these features may have been used in novels by Defoe, Richardson, and Smollett, Eliot could not use them to compose the individual she was concerned to announce. It was precisely such indexes to character that she would see as being contrary to culture because they specified the type of a social class rather than the essential element of society as a whole. In facing a similar problem when he tried to give significance to this figure, Rousseau had had recourse to an imaginary state of nature; but even such a ploy as this was unavailable to a novelist whose intellectual identity demanded the individual always be denominated within and subordinated to society as a whole.

This, then, is the dilemma in which Eliot was trapped as an intellectual and a novelist. As an intellectual she was dominated by the category of the individual, and as a novelist she would find this figure to be empty. Even though this individual posed no problem when it was invoked in intellectual discourse to refer to the basic unit of the Liberal politics aligned with laissez-faire economics, and even though it posed no problem to novelists like Dickens who were not so bound to an intellectual identity and therefore had no need to announce this figure with such self-consciousness, for Eliot the task was different. If she were systematically to articulate her brand of realism as an aesthetics as well as a philosophy, she had to give character to a figure that had not been conceived to have a character.

When it was found wanting, Eliot's later writing was often criticized for being too abstract or too philosophical; and Eliot admitted she would be condemned by her own principles if she had to think such criticism accurate. Therefore, she had to give face to an abstraction. In her terms, she had to show the ideal in the real or the abstract in the concrete. However, even when she tried to do so, she could not recognize the reason for the difficulties she faced. Such a recognition would have required that she separate herself from all the values that were hers as a liberal intellectual and look upon them as an ideological outcome of the changes that had been brought to society in recent times.

Eliot was no more able to transcend her social identity in this way than Wordsworth was able to transcend that privileged self he took to be his in his role as a poet. Therefore, in finding a way to describe the individual as a novelistic character, Eliot came face to face with the problem of her own role in society. Her obsession with the difficulty of representing this figure was that of confronting her own identity. Although she did not recognize this situation, the fact that it was herself that she confronted in dealing with this figure is evident in the way her narrative technique rushed in to fill this empty abstraction, in accordance with the logic that would obtain its fullest elaboration in the works of later writers such as Proust, James, Conrad, Woolf, Lawrence, and Joyce.

As one can see in the rhetorical design of Eliot's work, the individual was so obscure and difficult a figure for this intellectual novelist because the subject of her discourse was a figuration of that discourse. Any approach to the individual had to entail a self-reflexive discourse keyed in its every statement about human nature to this liberal intellectual's assumption of her own role in society. The complexities that result—such as the way perception is put through its paces in chapter 20 of *Middlemarch*—are the "truths" of "experience" that portray the discourse of the liberal intellectual as social reality. For this reason, novels by an author like Eliot require a historical criticism different from that appropriate to earlier and less relentlessly intellectual works. One must note not only how self-consciousness of this sort enters into the novel but also by what techniques it is made to appear as universal human nature. In other words, one must analyze the education built into the consciousness represented in Eliot's writing. In this education one sees the politics of Eliot's rhetoric and their relation to the institutionalization of education in the nineteenth century.

In this historical criticism, five approaches to filling the vacancy of the individual with a literary consciousness may be instanced as being among the most important in Eliot's work. She regards this figure as a social type, expands it to a general conception of humanity, makes it an occasion for philosophical generalization, transforms it into an allegorical drama, or—for those who might have missed this tendency in all her writing—makes it a text that is an image of her own.

As types, her characters' sensibilities are often defined in relation to their occupations. Thus, Adam Bede is described as possessing "the rough dignity which is peculiar to intelligent, honest, well-built workmen, who are never wondering what is their business in the world" (*AB*, 278). However, even when Eliot draws her denomination of types from categories other than that of occupation, the same end is accomplished. No matter what the typological register may be, individual characters gain significance from their representative qualities.[14] This pattern might seem odd in an art said to be dedicated to the individual, but this figure in Eliot's writing in no way suggests the unique or even the unusual. As she wrote in one of her letters to her publisher, "We are all apt to forget how little there is about us that is unique, and how very strongly we resemble many other insignificant people who have lived before us" (*L*, 2: 376). The degree of intensity with which characters are announced as individuals in Eliot's work will often correspond to the degree to which they are common or ordinary types, comparable to thousands of others and sometimes so compared even while the difficulty of their individuality is being heralded. After all, Eliot's realism is the demand that the subject of representation be representative according to middle-class norms.

The assumption of consensus in this type of description serves as rhetorical proof that individuality is the basis of society as a whole. In furthering this impression of consensus, the individuals of Eliot's novels fulfill basically the same cultural function as that performed by characters in allegories like *Pilgrim's Progress* or *The Faerie Queen* but with one notable difference. This difference arises in the way the social consensus marked by this style of representation coexists with the ideology of realism. The result is that Eliot's descriptions, no matter how broadly generic, have the effect of being observations of the world in its full particularity. It is by this characteristic that one can distinguish a middle-class from an aristocratic or sectarian style of art: it appears to have the power of all the world behind it.

In this demand for representativeness, one sees how the figure of the individual is just as abstract in Eliot's work as it is in a text like Mill's *On Liberty*. Nevertheless, this representative nature is fashioned so as to appear to have been discerned analytically within certain numbers of individuals within society, not unconsciously imposed on the author by the material structures or cultural traditions of that society. It is for this reason that Eliot would generally not identify one of her major characters as a middle-class type, a rural type, or a scientific type without insisting on the idea that in any identification of this kind she was making "nice distinctions" ("AB," 40) related to place, time, circumstance, and psychological peculiarity. She would suggest that such generic statements of character were induced from a complex examination of a field of details, not received in the manner of popular prejudices or social stereotypes. In fact, her novels' plots are designed to correct such false typologies by making experience prove to be an analytic crucible for them, as in the developments following the scene with Dorothea in the gallery, the changes in the perceptions Felix Holt and Esther Lyon initially have of each other, or the change in Daniel Deronda's view of Gwendolen Harleth from their first to their last encounter.

This is how individuality is defined and maintained in Eliot's writing: through the impression that common types occur naturally in society and may be identified without prejudice by the independent judgment of the intellect. This is the liberal intellectual's fable of character, which assumes that a rational organization of society would result in a natural stratification of individuals according to their innate deserts. In effect, the figure of the individual grows from this rule of realism, which assumes characters may be examined with intellectual neutrality and so be judged in terms of a universal human nature just as they are supposed to be judged in the perfectly meritocratic society. The particular typologies Eliot assigned to characters are merely the ideological working-out of this scheme of discourse. This discourse assumes the impersonal power of natural science in her fiction just as it did in the scientific, philosophical, and psychological descriptions of her day, which would specify the characters of people of different sexes, occupations, religions, classes, races, and nations. The figure of the individual in Eliot's writing is an abstraction that is distinctive because it may appear not to be an abstraction at all—not a rhetorical and narrative form—but to be a natural phenomenon.

This consideration becomes even clearer when one turns to those instances in which Eliot described her characters by generalizing their situations, attitudes, ideas, or feelings to make them expressive of all humanity. As she wrote, "Mr. Gilfil felt as if in the long hours of that night the bond that united his love forever and alone to Catherine had acquired fresh strength and sanctity. It is so with human relations that rest on the deep emotional sympathy of affection: every new day and new night of joy or sorrow is a new ground, a new consecration, for the love" ("MGL," 209). Or, as she commented on Dorothea's relation to Will Ladislaw: "There are natures in which, if they love us, we are conscious of having a sort of baptismal consecration: they bind us over to rectitude and purity" (*M*, 2: 360). Even though such generalizations tend to be repeated in a limited set of variations, as in these examples, thus representing a fixed stock of ideas about human nature in Eliot's writing, they appear as if they were inseparable from the individual situations of her characters. In fact, the only worry Eliot expressed about the selection made from her works in 1872, *Wise, Witty, and Tender Sayings in Prose and Verse*, was that the volume might encourage a view of her writings divided along these lines. "Unless I am condemned by my own principles," she wrote, "my books are not properly separable into 'direct' and 'indirect' teaching" (*L*, 5: 459). Eliot would not have wanted to be identified as another Martin Tupper *cum* novelist, even though she shared with the famous author of the *Proverbial Philosophy* this habit of thought that enabled her to identify middle-class opinions and experiences as universal truth.

Furthermore, as the narrative scene is sometimes presented prior to generalizations about human nature and sometimes after them in Eliot's writing, the consequent impression that the relation between the two is reversible can be seen to have been reflected in this worry she had over the extracts made from her writing. It is not that "direct" and "indirect" teachings (notice the term that goes without questioning quotation marks) are separable in her work but that her work so confuses an inductive with a deductive form that it makes manifest the ideology of its rationality, the social police at work in its aesthetic principles. Although Eliot would have it otherwise, it is evident that the concrete situations of her characters do not serve her narrators as texts on which they can ruminate. These situations and her generalizations are as one, having neither narrative nor logical priority over the other. Both are *writing*; and one can see this situation further represented in Eliot's habit of using epigraphs as chapter headings in her later novels. This repeats the doubled form of her descriptions within the chapters and so indicates the impossibility of a regression to an original subject. An epigraph to the first chapter of *Daniel Deronda* even takes care to point out this idea, as if in a reflection on its own existence: "No retrospect will take us to the true beginning" (*DD*, 1: 3). *Exemplum* and *interpretatio* are neither interchangeable nor radically distinguished from each other.

So in this aspect of her writing, too, one can see how Eliot's realism is not entirely a matter of subject, style, plot, or theme, in accordance with the narrower literary sense usually given the word. One sees that it is most importantly a technique for drawing an identity between the representation of human life and a certain kind of intellectual discourse. In the case of these generalizations, the argument is that the individual is the basis of society as a whole and the idea of all humanity so that these terms, in this order, form a thematic and temporal plot of progressive enlightenment and increasing universality. No matter what their moral and social denomination, all Eliot's characters are put into the service of this plot. Usually this tendency in her writing is taken on its own civilizing terms—as in Valentine Cunningham's description of Eliot's intent as one that "was serious, scientifically objective; no one, not even the Dissenter, was to be declared common or unclean"[15]—but the technique of power represented in this design is hardly so simple a matter.

For example, consider how the announcement of individuality is coupled with the description of a social type and also with the idea of all humanity in one of Eliot's meditations upon Gwendolen Harleth in *Daniel Deronda*:

> Could there be a slenderer, more insignificant thread in human history than this consciousness of a girl, busy with her small inferences of the way in which she could make her life pleasant?—in a time, too, when ideas were with fresh vigor making armies of themselves, and the universal kinship was declaring itself fiercely: when women on the other side of the world would not mourn for the husbands and sons who died bravely in a common cause, and men stinted of bread on our side of the world heard of that willing loss and were patient: a time when the soul of man was waking to pulses which had for centuries been beating in him unfelt, until their full sum made a new life of terror or of joy.
>
> What in the midst of that mighty drama are girls and their blind visions? They are the Yea or Nay of that good for which men are

enduring and fighting. In these delicate vessels is borne onward
through the ages the treasure of human affections. (*DD*, 1: 125)

One notes that whereas questions of social drama are contrasted to the individual, the individual is made to be the essence of these questions. This
figure—"this consciousness of a girl"—represents the very possibility for an
enduring society. The fact that the individual in question is a girl is of some
significance because it turns the development of this generalization toward the
specific characters of fighting men and culture-bearing women and thus
manifests the sort of opinions Eliot took to be universal statements. In the present context, though, it is the form of the passage that is more significant.
(After all, Eliot would employ this rhetoric of apparent contrasts and real continuity in relation to male characters, too, and in fact would make it serve to
reconcile men and women as well as all the other conflicting phenomena in
society.)

The form of argument in this passage is, in brief, the metaphysics of her
conception of the individual as the basis of society as a whole. In this case as
throughout her writing, society is not slighted in favor of the individual.
Rather, it is made over in the image of this abstract figure. This can be seen to
be the source of all figuration in Eliot's writing, so that according to her lights,
there could indeed be no radical division drawn between direct and indirect
teaching, narrative and commentary, or *exemplum* and *interpretatio*. Her
worry about the possibility of seeing such a division enables one to view this
possibility as the issue her writing was meant to articulate so that it might then
be denied. In this way, the style of her writing would prove itself a continuity
bespeaking the identity of the individual and society as a whole. Teaching and
experience would appear to grow naturally from the undifferentiated plane of
Eliot's discourse.[16]

Given this situation, it is only to be expected that the description of character
in Eliot's writing should call forth philosophy. As often as Eliot generalized
about human nature, she connected her characters to the nature of life in
general. As she wrote in *The Mill on the Floss*,

If we look far enough for the consequence of our actions, we can
always find some point in the combination of results by which those
actions can be justified: by adopting the point of view of a Providence
who arranges results, or of a philosopher who traces them, we shall
find it possible to obtain perfect complacency in choosing to do what
is most agreeable in the present moment. And it was in this way that
Philip justified his subtle efforts to overcome Maggie's true prompting
against a concealment that would introduce doubleness into her own
mind. (*MF*, 350)

Like her descriptions of social types and her generalizations about human
nature, reflections such as this one appear throughout Eliot's narratives in a
reversible relation to physical descriptions of her characters. Thus, they make

them the nodes of a discourse in which the physical, mental, and emotional qualities that individuate them (to name three of the basic registers of such description in her writing) are given no more importance than the philosophy of nature, society, and humanity with which they are filled.

These characters are maintained as individual figures only insofar as the reader accepts Eliot's formal presentation of them as such. Otherwise their identities would be seen to be composed of generic attributes and ideological expressions. A similar analysis might be made of the characters in any kind of fiction—in a sense, this is just a special instance of a formal tendency in any literary representation of character that goes beyond the bare announcement of a name. However, it is peculiarly important in Eliot's case because her aesthetics was articulated against the kind of representation that she would refer to as the stuff of Byronism or Silver Fork gentility; she conceived her representation of character to be different in kind from that found in other varieties of fiction. As previously noted, she conceived this difference to lie in the observation of the individual in her writing that would emancipate this figure from displacements such as romantic idealization, literary and social stereotyping, and genteel censorship. If they have accepted her characters in the terms of Eliot's realism, her readers and critics have paid attention only to their formal conception. They have not analyzed the language that actually composes these figures that people her fiction.

Eliot would never claim that she had achieved perfection in her fictional representations. As she said, "We must have some comradeship with imperfection" (*DD*, 2: 327). Still, this self-conscious acknowledgment of imperfection so typical of her writing (the egoism of the intellectual who requires this acknowledgment!) serves to distinguish her ideal of intellectual discourse. It shows the shadow of its fulfillment by the ironic light of reality. After all, the best way to comprehend all perspectives and thus to distinguish the true individual is by admitting imperfection in one's own perspective in such a way as to smuggle all potential differences into the shadows cast by one's irony. The formal individuality this admission of imperfection gives to Eliot's writing is analogous to the signature of tragic individuality that distinguishes her characters.

To Eliot, the meaning of individuality lies in the production of a discourse in which everyone might share if human nature were rendered independent of all cramping social conditions so as to become the pure idea of itself. However, the fact that Eliot's style is not always as dazzling as it is in chapter 20 of *Middlemarch*, so that the reflections composing her characters appear more plainly as a disorderly bazaar of nineteenth-century notions on topics such as race, phrenology, sex, nationality, and history, is significant. When one is not overwhelmed by her technique, one sees the typical fate of the liberal intellectual: to mistake wide-ranging opinion for comprehensive knowledge and universal sympathy.

Another way Eliot regards the individual is as an allegorical subject. It should go without saying that the characters in Eliot's fiction are allegorical in the broad sense of that term, as no writing can be understood except as it appeals to various semantic registers. However, the point still must be made because the supreme allegory to which Eliot's writing is bound, as one finds in all its imagery of perspective, observation, and science, is the allegory of experience. So Eliot remarks in one of her letters, "That every study has its bearing on every other is true; but pain and relief, love and sorrow, have their peculiar history which makes an experience and knowledge over and above the swing of atoms" (*L*, 6: 99). Although Eliot never argued that her writing was or could be an unmediated representation of the world, all her fiction and all her pronouncements on aesthetics were designed to persuade her readers that her art was dedicated to preserving the phenomenological neutrality of "experience," rendering it in a cultural form that would represent an impartial, unprejudiced, classless, transhistorical view of things.

Within the discourse to which Eliot's writing belongs, which may be typified by the discourse on education in her age, ideology is that which deviates from experience. It diverts individuals from their natural relations with each other and the world. Ideology is fought against by those people, like Eliot, who are given to believe that alienating differences between people of various classes would disappear if they only could meet each other as individuals apart from their social classes. In this situation, it is believed, they would discover the truth of experience apart from the distorted perspectives that displace it into a multiplicity of trivializing, confusing, or threatening allegories—such as Eliot represents in the plots of her novels. Contrasted to ideology in this way, experience becomes the supreme allegory of Eliot's realism.

The allegory of experience is the progressive design of Eliot's conception of rational discourse. To put it another way: because Eliot's fiction suggests that universal truth must emerge from experience even if this eventuality may be approached only very gradually, as in an infinite halving of the distance to perfection, experience is the allegory of allegories in Eliot's fiction. However, unlike the figure of the individual that is the basis of her fiction, experience is an allegory suppressed by realism. This is so because experience represents a formal necessity of deferring judgment, and yet it acts as a source of judgment in Eliot's novels. It is the representational subject of judgment, and yet it leads her characters to "grow" and to "develop" according to middle-class psychology while it shows them the short-sightedness or hastiness of their perceptions. Just as the figure of the individual is divided in the paradox that its independence from society is also the source of its attachment to society as a whole, the conception of experience in her writing is divided against itself. It represents the transcendent resolution of all allegories and the principle productive of all allegorical displacement. What the individual is in the space of Eliot's fiction, experience is in its temporal dimension.

For Eliot, then, there is no conflict with her doctrine of realism in those parts of her writing where the representation of character appears as a marked kind of allegory.[17] This happens especially at those points where the continuity of the philosophical, psychological, and social analysis of human nature is most dramatically marked and so turned more toward abstraction; but the plots of her novels in their entirety also tend to take on this appearance. For instance, one may think of the fact that Eliot's translator first thought of titling *The Mill on the Floss* "Amour et Devoir" (although Eliot was appalled at this idea) and of the way Tom and Maggie Tulliver in that novel may be crudely but not unfairly seen as exemplars of contrasting virtues reconciled only in the apocalyptic finale. Or there is the substitution of golden-haired Eppie for Silas Marner's gold as the key opening the plot of *Silas Marner*, the invocation of Dorothea as a type of St. Theresa in *Middlemarch*, the inheritance plot in *Felix Holt* that makes its drama an allegory of class history, and a wide variety of related features in all her novels. Eliot's characters are always being drawn into allegorical plots, moments, and imagery by the way Eliot drew her intellectual conception of society within the individual, taking humanity rather than the Bible as a scripture to be scanned for its *sensus spiritualis*. Because Eliot's goal was to make her discourse seem as one with its object, to make the drama of every individual life appear to be constituted of this brand of intellectual discourse, her self-consciousness turned the consciousnesses of others into a unified social mind. This social mind is an allegorical scripture meant to be all the more divine because all the more realistic for its imperfection.

This is the allegory of Eliot's allegories, the allegory of her realism: the definition of experience in the form of the discourse of the liberal intellectual. Following this definition, she could fill the vacancy of the abstract individual with the nature of ideas or signs. As she wrote in reference to Hetty's appearance in *Adam Bede*, "Nature has her language, and she is not unveracious; but we don't know all the intricacies of her syntax just yet, and in a hasty reading we may happen to extract the very opposite of her real meaning" (*AB*, 158).[18] So Will and Naumann read Dorothea as a work of art, and the error of their reading is presented to be experienced and then corrected in the reader's mind as well as in theirs. In this way one can see how the end of her writing is to establish a cultural instrument that would make her literary consciousness emerge as the mediation of conflicting interpretations. One notes that it is a "hasty" reading that goes wrong and that we do not "yet" know all the intricacies of nature's syntax.

The ironic consciousness signified by these words is Eliot's scheme of mediation. As she wrote elsewhere, "Attempts at description are stupid: who can all at once describe a human being? even when he is presented to us we only begin that knowledge of his appearance which must be completed by innumerable impressions under differing circumstances. We recognize the alphabet; we are not sure of the language" (*DD*, 1: 111). The difficulty of the text is noted, as is the difficulty of reading the individual. In this case as in the other, though, a way of transcending the difficulty is indicated; quite simply, it is the way of Eliot's liberal intellectual discourse. In this respect Eliot's surety for the accuracy of her language was the self-consciousness with which it was presented and made to represent neutrality, impartiality, gentility, and all the other qualities assumed to mantle the shoulders of those who were enlightened in her day. So Eliot could describe Dorothea's misreading of Casaubon's face and conversation and then proceed to say, "Signs are small measurable things, but interpretations are illimitable, and in girls of sweet, ardent nature, every sign is apt to conjure up wonder, hope, belief, vast as a sky, and colored by a diffuse thimbleful of matter in the shape of knowledge" (*M*, 1: 14). Truth is made to exist in the illimitability of interpretations, in the abstract ground of their production, and thus in the supervision of a text that resolves conflicts by continuously rediscovering individuals as abstractions, individual lives as allegories, and experience as the magic term uniting the worst tragedy and the highest elevation, the utmost simplicity and the highest cultivation.

Of course, these distinctions drawn among various means of describing characters in Eliot's work are not hard and fast. Ultimately, there is no way to distinguish among the stylistic devices that represent a character as a type and those that describe him as an instance of humanity or of philosophical truth. But this is just the point: that Eliot's characters, as individuals, are made to be her system of discourse. Her realism was not intended to mirror life but to make life appear to possess the nature of her text. And in her descriptions of her characters, Eliot's text emerges as the discourse of the liberal intellectual.

Eliot's realism is a network of affinities held secret by interiority or temporality but revealed by the experience unfolded within her narratives. Separate characters, events, scenes, places, and things appear as such only if one's eyes are directed to the interstices of the netting and not to the continuous thread that is projected as her narrative. So she directed her novels to be read by her audience just as she directed the characters within her novels to come to terms with themselves. As she wrote in reference to the family, "Nature, that great tragic dramatist, knits us together by bone and muscle, and divides us by the subtler webs of our brains; blends yearning and repulsion; and ties us by our heart-strings to the beings that jar us at every moment" (*AB*, 39). The emphasis here as throughout her fiction is on the essentially undifferentiated totality that composes all conflicts, while the Olympian recognition of tragedy in this passage sets the tone of the middle-class morality derived from this denomination of society as a whole. Unlike Thomas Hardy, who was to make of a similar image of nature a very dissimilar conclusion, as when the young Jude Fawley learned a lesson quite opposite to Adam Smith's when he saw that "mercy towards one set of creatures was cruelty towards another,"[19] Eliot made her irony a style of transcendence.

Moreover, this unifying totality that constitutes Eliot's style also accounts for the conception of causality in her novels. As she describes this conception in relation to Mr. Tulliver's bankruptcy in *The Mill on the Floss*, "So deeply inherent is it in this life of ours that men have to suffer for each other's sins, so inevitably diffusive is suffering, that even justice makes its victims and we can conceive no retribution that does not spread beyond its mark in pulsations of unmerited pain" (*MF*, 260). It accounts as well for her Wordsworthian belief that human life "should be well rooted in some spot of native land, where it may get the love of tender kinship for the face of the earth, for the labors men go forth to, for the sounds and accents that haunt it, for whatever will give that early home a familiar unmistakable difference amidst the future widening of knowledge" (*DD*, 1: 18). This nostalgia for home and childhood is meant to place in the individual's character the continuous thread that saves "widening knowledge" from degenerating into sterile incoherence or fragmented opinion.

This figuration of totality is also found in Eliot's use of parable. Since "there never was a true story which could not be told in parables," she wrote in reference to the introduction of Joshua Rigg in *Middlemarch*, "whatever has been or is to be narrated by me about low people, may be ennobled by being considered a parable" (*M*, 1: 353). In this passage Eliot was joshing in her most elephantine manner, but the point she was making has great significance for her novels. Ultimately they *are* parables, or allegories, of the individual. This is why, as she says, "you might put a monkey for a margrave, or *vice versa*." Both are taken to be individuals, mere ripples on the ocean, marks on the mirror, units of meaning in the undifferentiated continuity of the plane of rational discourse. And the goal of Eliot's style is to figure society so that one sees the secret continuity of individuality, even if this continuity can be touched on in the actual course of life only through imperfect thought and feeling.

Eliot interpreted all other texts and all human experience, in fact, in the style of her own text. Reality for her was of the nature of her art. It was the figuration of an ideal rationality. As the nature of the figure in Eliot's text is simultaneously to reveal and to dissimulate this idea, to present and to defer it, reality can be maintained only by the continuous extension of the figure so that no aspect of revelation or of dissimulation may be mistaken for its entire truth. This is the problem noted when Eliot described, in *Middlemarch*, how apparently random scratches on a mirror appear to be arranged in concentric circles when a candle is brought near: "These things are a parable. The scratches are events, and the candle is the egoism of any person now absent" (*M*, 1: 275). One must not be misled by partial perspectives but must turn to the figurative basis of these visions: the surface of the mirror itself. This undifferentiated surface is the style of her art, the allegorical basis of all figuration in this art, and the image of the liberal intellectual's mediating consciousness. It is the utopian surface of reason, and it is the provoking vacancy of the individual that this reason endlessly, tragically, tries to fill.

Chapter 4
Genteel Image and Democratic Example

Fiction, with its graphic delineation and appeals to the familiar emotions, is adapted to the crowd—for it is the oratory of literature.

Edward Lytton Bulwer, *England and the English*

In the beginning of "The Sad Fortunes of the Reverend Amos Barton," Eliot brushes against a social situation that would prove crucial to the design of all her fiction. When describing Shepperton Church, she notes that "in certain less eligible corners, less directly under the fire of the clergyman's eye, there are pews reserved for the Shepperton gentility" ("AB," 3). The crucial question is whether the gentility deserves its greater freedom from religious supervision. This question becomes more pronounced when one learns that the Reverend Barton's teaching is controversial because it is provocatively " 'familiar,' " as Mr. Pilgrim says ("AB," 12), in its evangelical appeal to the laboring and poorer sections of the community. "A troublesome district for a clergyman," Eliot writes, "at least to one who, like Amos Barton, understood the 'cure of souls' in something more than an official sense; for over and above the rustic stupidity furnished by the farm-laborers, the miners brought obstreperous animalism, and the weavers an acrid Radicalism and Dissent" ("AB," 23).

The situation is that of an upper class that takes itself in some measure to be exempt from supervision whereas the commonalty beneath it threatens to be unresponsive to the conventional forms of moral indoctrination. What has been put in question is the power of a traditional form of discourse once the administration of its form is extended to the ministry of the "soul": a term that took on a more demanding significance, at once religious and political, during the nineteenth century. In Eliot's telling, this communication problem was the modern "condition of England" question. It is for this reason that one of the set-pieces of the story is Reverend Barton's confrontation with a number of hard cases in the local workhouse, with Eliot commenting that he had neither the "flexible imagination" nor the "adroit tongue" ("AB," 26) necessary to the educated soul who desired to communicate with them. The protagonist of the story is trapped by the gentility he is offending and slighted by the class of people to which he is appealing, so he is threatened on either side. He appears to be on a debatable ground in history belonging neither to the past nor to the present, which leaves him, properly speaking, nowhere. In trying to make "official sense" speak to ignorant or violent nonsense, he falls into the possibility of a complete loss of vocation and significance as a human being.

This is the vision of class differences controlling Eliot's aesthetics: on the one hand, a perception of a genteel class with no warrant for its assumption of superiority and, on the other, of a lower class that increasingly demanded moral attention but was impossible to reach through forms of discourse identified with the traditional power of the upper classes. Such was Eliot's outline of the modern scene described by Mill in *The Spirit of the Age* as one of "intellectual anarchy."[1] Gentility of the traditional sort was demeaned in Eliot's fiction because she identified her art with the common people, who were garnering more attention as England gradually became more democratic in its political system and in its public values. However, the construction of a form of art in which these people could be given a new moral franchise clearly was no easy matter. It was this paralyzing situation that Eliot had described in "The Progress of the Intellect":

> We are in bondage to terms and conceptions which, having had their root in conditions of thought no longer existing, have ceased to possess any vitality, and are for us as spells which have lost their virtue. The endeavour to spread enlightened ideas is perpetually counteracted by these *idola theatri*, which have allied themselves, on the one hand with men's better sentiments, and on the other with institutions in whose defence are arrayed the passions and the interests of the dominant classes. (*E*, 28-29)

"Educate your Masters!" Robert Lowe was quoted as having said after the passage of the 1870 Reform Bill.[2] However, by that time it was not the need for education that was in question so much as it was the manner in which it ought to be assuaged. For example, for a long time Carlyle had been arguing that the aristocracy had become a "Phantom-Aristocracy, no longer able to do its work, not in the least conscious that it has any work longer to do,"[3] while also pointing out that democracy was "the grand, alarming, imminent and indisputable Reality";[4] but he did not think the education called for by these new conditions could be disseminated easily. People such as Thomas Arnold, Carlyle, Charles Kingsley, and the Tractarians in their various ways might seek to renovate Christian discipline within society; but even though Eliot might use religious language as a form of discipline or "as a means of giving dignity to human action,"[5] she did not find this language by itself to be a sufficient call to order.

To Eliot's mind, a radically new standard of belief was called for as the basis of her art. This new standard would shape the language of the contemporary preacher, teacher, and artist (these roles being virtually identical in her mind), and it would do so by accounting for its own necessity. In other words, it would be rational. Her art would begin at the point where more conventional forms of belief and understanding could no longer be administered effectively, would analyze the reasons for their slide toward decrepitude, and in its own nature would take over the supervision of human life that no longer could accrue to a superior social class. Therefore, to analyze Eliot's art as a representation of social history, one must try to understand how its transfiguration of the old *idola theatri* was meant to give birth to a power of communication appropriate to a society moving toward a democratic age.

For its context, as one can see in *Scenes of Clerical Life* and all her other works, this art emphasized the putative stability and coherence of the past. Despite her comment upon Radicalism in "Amos Barton" and her portrayal of popular agitation in *Felix Holt*, in which society is disturbed by a "brawny and many-breeding pauperism" (*FH*, 3), Eliot was more inclined to linger upon the deference paid to gentility in the times prior to her own. "For in those days," she wrote in *Adam Bede*, "the keenest of bucolic minds felt a whispering awe at the sight of the gentry, such as of old men felt when they stood on tiptoe to watch the gods passing by in tall human shape" (*AB*, 81). Although the historical accuracy of this characterization is very questionable, what is important in the present context is the way Eliot assumed the existence of this deference so she could proceed systematically to dramatize its lack of any foundation except in unthinking tradition.

Thus, when Adam Bede is allowed to discover the illicit relationship between the girl he loves and the gentle Arthur Donnithorne, he finds his world illuminated by "a terrible scorching light" that reveals to him "the hidden letters that changed the meaning of the past" (*AB*, 307). In effect, these letters are those composing the novel of which Adam is a part. He discovers what sort of literary figure he is, he comes face to face with the text that bears his name, in their revelation. They represent a change not only in his individual past but also in the meaning of the past in Eliot's art. In this scene, insofar as Adam was born a character "very susceptible to the influence of rank, and quite ready to give an extra amount of respect to every one who had more advantages than himself, not being a philosopher, or a proletaire with democratic ideas" (*AB*, 168), he *is* the past, waning before his own eyes.

Formally divided by this narrative into the character who is the protagonist in its events and the older man who is a friend of the narrator's in the modern world, Adam is also split between a deferential state and one more aligned with a modern morality. (In this respect, it is interesting to consider that Adam's character appears to have been based in part on Samuel Smiles's biography of the railway engineer George Stephenson and so, in terms of this ancestry, too, might be said to be oriented toward the modern world.)[6] Eliot took pains to note that Adam "was in his prime half a century" before the novel's 1859 publication date, remarking that the reader had to "expect some of his characteristics to be obsolete" (*AB*, 169); but this obsolescence was explicated just as well by the awakening to which Eliot brought him.[7] In this awakening, the traditional power of gentility is shown to be rationally groundless, historically outmoded, and, consequently, humanly destructive. This peripeteia represents the awakening of the system of all Eliot's fiction. For instance, it is in following this reasoning in *Middlemarch* that Eliot takes note of Fred Vincy's jolly belief "that the universal order of things would necessarily be agreeable to an agreeable young gentleman" (*M*, 1: 239) and then gradually dismantles this order, imaginary stone by imaginary stone, with the same excruciating deliberation that Dickens used to undermine the optimistic calculations of Richard Carstairs in *Bleak House*.

Still, Eliot was concerned about analyzing the standard of gentility in the society of the past, for an understanding of its effects would contribute to her reasoning as to the standard that ought to be the modern world's. In Eliot's account, as in literary history in general, one of the more important effects involves the attraction between individuals of different stations in life. It was in *Adam Bede*, when Eliot described Hetty Sorrell's attraction to Arthur Donnithorne, that she first gave this lesson a comprehensive statement.

In this novel, even though the sturdy Adam loves Hetty with such purity that she recognizes his virtues as a suitor and wants to keep him in this role, he "could no more stir in her the emotions that would make the sweet intoxication of young love, than the mere picture of a sun can stir the spring sap in the subtle fibres of the plant" (*AB*, 156). In this fantasy she is somewhat like Moll Flanders; her dreams are "all of luxuries" (*AB*, 102). However, she is different from this more robustly drawn figure in that her attraction to Arthur appears to have virtually nothing physical about it. "Hers was a luxurious and rash nature," Eliot writes, "not a passionate one" (*AB*, 346). Although she, too, looks to her lover as to a god, she is not like Hardy's Tess. When Arthur gives earrings to Hetty, Eliot notes that Hetty is more entranced with the ornaments than she is with their donor. This aspect of Hetty's character is further represented by her "peculiar form of worship": namely, her vanity when she tries to make herself look like "that picture of a lady in Miss Lydia Donnithorne's dressing-room" while she sits before the candlelit shrine of her bedside mirror (*AB*, 154).

Hetty's relationship to Arthur is described in pagan terms—"It was as if she had been wooed by a river-god, who might at any time take her to his wondrous halls beneath a watery heaven" (*AB*, 134)—but the pointedly literary figures in this description of pagan nature are significant. In fashioning this imagery as an artifice upon which Hetty and Arthur can recline, Eliot appears intent on showing that whereas Adam cannot produce a stir in Hetty's being,

Arthur can because of his social position and what it represents to her. Much more than Adam, he is a "picture of a sun" in place of the real thing. Because she is so impressed by social tradition that Arthur is indeed divine nature to her, Hetty fails to recognize the artificiality of his image. She is trapped by the power of metonymy.

As Eliot points out in her description of Arthur kissing Hetty, he, too, is entranced by the imagery associated with his position: "He may be a shepherd in Arcadia for aught he knows, he may be the first youth kissing the first maiden, he may be Eros himself, sipping the lips of Psyche—it is all one" (*AB*, 141).[8] Of course, this passage is meant to describe the erotic disordering of his consciousness. Nevertheless, the images in which this disorder takes form—these figures proper to a gentleman's classical education—have further significance. The formal, superficial, and, as it were, atmospheric gentility represented by Arthur is not simply demeaned through the consequences of his liaison with Hetty. It is also undercut through its more immediate nature as a condition given over to "a light and graceful irony" distanced from "a wide and arduous national life" (*MF*, 309-10). Arthur's education has clearly been of the unreformed type; thus Eliot works to demystify him much as Meredith in *The Egoist* analyzes Sir Willoughby Patterne, that " 'picture of an English gentleman,' " in the words of Mrs. Monstuart Jenkinson.[9]

In Eliot's analysis characters in a deferential society are always tempted to see themselves in terms of a "picture of a sun." Experience in this situation is merely a rhetoric designed to appeal to, or take the heat from, the image of gentility. Wholly taken over by the structure of social reflexiveness meant to put everyone in his or her place in relation to everyone else, this experience has no reality aside from this binding context. Eliot's analysis shows how the reflexiveness of society turns into a hard, cold mirror in which the deferential system of flattery appears stripped to its surface of naked power. The mirror meant to confirm identity instead proves alienating, like a glass in a nightmare. As the metonymies of gentility begin to appear baseless, gentility itself appears as a repulsive surface, a mirror exactly opposite to Eliot's mirror of reason.

Like the *corpus* of traditional romance to which Eliot opposes her own conception of literature, Hetty's entire body is preoccupied with gentility to the exclusion of physical reality. Hence her lack of sexual passion. In fact, Hetty celebrates her decision against suicide by turning up her sleeves and kissing her arms "with the passionate love of life" (*AB*, 399), as if to demonstrate a saving attachment to her body, no matter how imperfectly it may match the picture of the lady in Miss Lydia's dressing room. Having grown up with an image of beauty wholly defined by the order of gentility, and then having gone through a period of despair after Arthur's betrayal in which "even her own beauty was indifferent to her" (*AB*, 346), she succeeds in finding a new significance in her appearance that goes beyond the limits of the imagery with which she had been preoccupied. In this clarification of her confusion over the difference between the real sun and a picture of it, Hetty traces in miniature the clarification of the source of meaning in English society that Eliot saw in its progress away from aristocratic and toward middle-class values. Moreover, she traces the process embodied in Eliot's aesthetics, in which her "strongest effort" was to "avoid any . . . arbitrary picture" (*AB*, 181).[10]

Eliot was not intent upon the death of romance in her demeaning of gentility. Rather, she wanted to show that poetry and romance "exist very well in the same room with the microscope and even in railway carriages: what banishes them is the vacuum in gentlemen and lady passengers" (*DD*, 1: 209). She was devoted to showing that the "hard unaccommodating Actual . . .has never consulted our taste and is entirely unselect" (*DD*, 1: 393) and therefore should be made the universal basis of poetry and romance.

In contrast to Hetty, Dinah possesses a gentility wholly adapted to the laboring life of ordinary human beings and entirely superior to the misleading distinctions of social rank, as Hetty, Arthur, and Reverend Irwine gradually acknowledge. Hers is the very nature of Eliot's art. For the traditional world of gentility—represented by Arthur's dreadfully mistaken confidence that he "would be the model of an English gentleman" supervising "a prosperous, contented tenantry, adoring their landlord" (*AB*, 127)—this art substitutes a world of democratic sympathy in which desire is turned from fashionable image to moral example. The new sort of text that Adam discovers when he learns of Arthur's dalliance with Hetty, and which he is led to read in its most tragic implications through the course of Hetty's flight, arrest, and trial, shows its potential for transfiguring redemption in the character of Dinah. Presumably, it is for this reason that Eliot called the prison scene, in which Dinah brings Hetty to confess and repent, "the climax towards which I worked" (*L*, 2: 503). Once this scene has ritualized the thematic relation between Hetty and Dinah, Adam's reconciliation with Arthur in the Grove where they had fought and his engagement and marriage to Dinah can follow in short order.

A similar demeaning of the relationship between desire and gentility is an important part of all Eliot's novels. In *Middlemarch*, for example, Rosamond Vincy's attraction to Tertius Lydgate is so thoroughly dependent upon his upper-class connections that when he refuses to exploit them on her behalf, she is stimulated to the chilling simplicity of the thought that "if she had known how Lydgate would behave, she would never have married him" (*M*, 2: 176). In the overbearing attitude in which she continues to indulge herself, Rosamond is contrasted to her brother, Fred. He assumes a gentlemanly future for himself just as Arthur Donnithorne does and wreaks almost as much havoc on those around him because of it, but he saves himself through his decision to wholeheartedly adopt a life of virtuous though common labor and a bride of common but resolutely moral stock. Fred Vincy learns to discard his belief in the Providential world traditionally associated with gentility, as this is symbolized by his capricious Uncle Featherstone, and to rely instead on his own exertions. Dorothea, in her parallel experience, is forced to stop approaching

Casaubon "as if he were a Protestant Pope" and to cease "interpreting him as she interpreted the works of Providence" (*M*, 1: 51, 76). So, too, is Esther Lyon in *Felix Holt* turned from her assumption that romance lies in such refinement as is associated with a superior social position. In fact, she is brought to reject a providential award of such a position in favor of a marriage with Felix, who is characterized in part by his general disdain for the upper classes and even for such petty signs of gentility as " 'a house with a high door-step and a brass knocker' " (*FH*, 67). This drama of class-crossed lovers is less marked in *The Mill on the Floss*, but it is still played out in the way Maggie Tulliver rejects respectability—the narrow middle-class version of traditional gentility—in favor of morality, returning to St. Ogg's without marrying Stephen Guest after having floated down the river with him in so suggestive a manner. The case is somewhat different in *Romola*, too, in which the gentleman in question is the thoroughly corrupt Tito who gets married to a peasant girl in a mock ceremony and to the ladylike Romola in a legitimate one. Again, however, the development of the novel shows that both the peasant's blind adoration of Tito and Romola's more refined response to him are turned upon an illusory image of gentility and that true superiority can be found only in such moralized forms as the peasant's simple faith before all things and Romola's sacrificial commitment to the suffering of ordinary humanity. This lesson is further examined in *Daniel Deronda*, for Deronda finds Mirah to be like " 'a beggar by the wayside,' " treats her like " 'a king's daughter' " (*DD*, 2: 202), and then willingly surrenders his social position to devote his life to her and to their people. Even *Silas Marner* had a version of this plot in the pathetic end of the woman secretly married to Godfrey Cass, the local squire's son, when she dies outside Marner's house. Clearly, she, too, has had a mistaken attraction to gentility. In this respect, the relation between Silas and Eppie, the woman's daughter, may be seen as a moralized revision of this woman's relationship to Godfrey. Formally and thematically, the order of the societal family and of ordinary human life supplants the order of romance and gentility.

Eliot's transfiguration of gentility went beyond the sort of critique Jane Austen used in turning Catherine Morland from "the alarms of romance" to "the anxieties of common life."[11] As can be seen from the foregoing examples, it entailed the dismantling of a long-reigning worldview and an adaptation to a new form of society as well as a disciplined adjustment of perception, aesthetics, and other orders of representation. And it went even further. Gentility did indeed represent to Eliot the past she believed had been outgrown through the history of England in the nineteenth century, but she also thought it represented a continuing and universal aspect of human nature. It was this that she pointed to in Hetty's vanity and more commonly referred to as egoism or egoistic desire. Ultimately, the past was interpreted by Eliot as a system of representation that objectified in the structure of society and all its associated figures an impulse to self-assertion inherent in human nature. Therefore, to evaluate her picture of the past of "nearly sixty years ago" in *Adam Bede* and the past as it appears in her other fiction, one needs to analyze how she interpreted this past as a part of the present. One must analyze how those characters most entranced by the traditional order of gentility in Eliot's novels are also those who are most egoistic. Moreover, one must ask why this is the case especially, although by no means exclusively, with women.

Eliot dated the downfall of the traditional system of deference from the time of England's reform in the 1830s. However, she argued that in the absence of a more important reform in consciousness, the old values would continue to survive, and so she looked back at this time with a good measure of irony. "Will became an ardent public man," she writes near the end of *Middlemarch*, "working well in those times when reforms were begun with a young hopefulness of immediate good which has been much checked in our days" (*M*, 2: 424). The liberal intellectual who could not believe that truth lay in "machinery," in the nuts and bolts of opinions in any sort of immediate political context, would certainly not concede that historical change was to be found merely in the alteration of social systems, as one might guess from Eliot's decision not to commit herself fully to Positivism as it was adopted in England by such friends of hers as Frederic Harrison or to feminism as it was practiced by other friends such as Barbara Bodichon.

As far as Eliot was concerned, if it was to mean anything, social change would have to be a symbol of a deeper teleology. "That doctrine which we accept rather loftily as a commonplace when we are quite young," she wrote to a friend, "—namely, that our happiness lies entirely within, in our own mental and bodily state which determines for us the influence of everything outward—becomes a daily lesson to be learned, and learned with much stumbling, as we get older" (*L*, 3: 445). The downfall of the old notion of gentility would make sense only if one could look inward, within individuals, to find its redemptive transfiguration and, in it, an image of human progress and hope for the future. The "peculiar stamp of culture," Eliot wrote in reference to Felix Holt, is a "look of habitual meditative abstraction from objects of mere personal vanity or desire" that makes "a very roughly cut face worthy to be called 'the human face divine' " (*FH*, 303-4); and she aspired to bear this stamp on her own roughly cut face through her role as an author.

As Eliot perceived it, the fault of a morality caught up in social reflexivity, in the gaze of others, was that it might float free of actual social conditions. It could allow one to play with one's image and that of others as if they could be arranged artistically, independent of these conditions. One would then be slighting the real price of one's behavior in society, ignoring the "very expensive production" of irony (*MF*, 309-10). Unlike the independence from social conditions that the liberal intellectual would claim as necessary in the development of an enlightened vision of society over the course of its history, this freedom is pictured as factitious and limiting and therefore destined to produce error. It represents aristocratic power rather than middle-class reason, arbitrary privilege rather than deserved opportunity, and an exclusive rather than a universal perspective on society. So Hetty disastrously gives herself to Arthur, Arthur imagines he can engage in and then flee from the relationship as if it were a pretty story of gods and maidens, Rosamond becomes to Lydgate the basil plant that grows from his own murdered brains, and Fred mistakes the deference given him on account of his expectations as a surety instead of the tricky social reflection it really is.

According to Eliot, egoism unites all these cases and others like them in her fiction. This egoism knows no difference between image and reality and therefore is bound to mistake social distinctions for actual life. It is sure to choose the more perfectly composed genteel image, which is the purely imaginary reflexiveness of society, over the roughly hewn moral example, which comes from material labor and human commitment and thus is more difficult and painful to grasp.

In egoism individuals see their self-images and the images of others as fixed representations rather than the potentially ever-changing effects of individuals' actions in their relations with others in society. For instance, it is by this assumption of self-prepossession that Mr. Bulstrode meets disaster. It enables him to ignore the shady history by which he achieved his prosperity in favor of the pious image of himself he has managed to establish in the network of relations constituting the society of *Middlemarch*. He does not belong to the gentry—quite the contrary—yet in this respect is misled by precisely the same process that leads Arthur astray. He, too, is trapped by the egoism objectified in the deferential structure of society. When Raffles reappears in his life as a "loud red figure . . . in unmanageable solidity—an incorporate past which had not entered into his imagination of chastisements" (*M*, 2: 102), he is Eliot's figure of the Actual made horrible and intractable through repression.

In this portrayal society lived on its traditional basis is entirely a visual effect. It is a collective representation, an ideal, suspended within the relations of a community and continuously referred to by individuals as the most meaningful standard of their lives. All of society is turned to a picture of a sun. Hetty's imaginary enshrinement of the picture of the lady from Miss Lydia's dressing room is a pathetic microcosm of this metonymic system of collective representation that provides the terms of a society based on the traditional order of gentility. Her relationship to this picture is the drama in miniature of the downfall to which this system was doomed in Eliot's fiction. To Eliot, because all the world of traditional gentility was a picture of the sun toward which all individuals were turned by egoism, these individuals were destined to be scorched by the real light of day when they found this picture no longer sustained by the united gaze of the community. And there is no question that it could be sustained forever, the way Eliot presented it. This was a world of interdependence; everyone would look to the eyes of others for his or her own definition.

However, it was an imaginary and extremely fragile interdependence because it could not guarantee that the regard one gained from the eyes of others and granted through one's own eyes had a sanction outside the imagination. However well it might have served in more ignorant centuries, immaterial tradition was not sufficient insurance as far as the modern intellectual was concerned.

In modern times, this tradition would amount only to idle imagination. It was never meant to be rational and so could be destroyed when a single violation, such as Arthur's seduction of Hetty, turned characters like Adam and Mr. Garth and the Poysers and even Arthur himself into protorationalists. It might require only one gaze to be turned askew for the entire fabric of sociality to collapse if social institutions and life had no firmer ground than this. And this point held true for the institution of culture as well, as Eliot indicated by having Arthur hopelessly misconstrue classical literature when he kissed Hetty. This world of traditional gentility could never have had more substance than the world of polite literature, which was devoted to its images; Eliot's literature appealed for its basis to the ordinary human life consumed in the manufacture of this genteel art. From the perspective of Eliot's art, the traditional society of the past was wholly imaginary in its nature because unconscious of its system of representational order, knowing it only as blind tradition or as apologies for this. Therefore, according to her reasoning, it was destined to fall into errors that would either spur the development of a higher consciousness or the events of unredeemed tragedy.

As one might gather from the fact that the type of genteel literature Eliot mocked is especially identified with a female readership not only in her descriptions but in her age in general, or from the different fates of Adam and Hetty or Deronda and Gwendolen, the system of the past in Eliot's fiction does have a special effect upon women. It is for this reason that so awfully vain a creature as Rosamond is granted an extenuating understanding specifically on account of her sex, in addition to the broad human sympathy with which Eliot portrayed all her characters. Rosamond is not the simply ignorant victim that Hetty is, but still she is a victim of the way gentility was denominated a particularly feminine virtue. "For Rosamond never showed any unbecoming knowledge," Eliot writes, "and was always that combination of correct sentiments, music, dancing, drawing, elegant note-writing, private album for extracted verse, and perfect blond loveliness, which made the irresistible woman for the doomed man of that date" (*M*, 1: 279). Rosamond is treated as a formulaic construction of metonymies, a rhetoric of social reflexiveness. Therefore, it is only natural that the plotting of her life should be carried out so that an exotic stranger is "absolutely necessary to Rosamond's social romance" (*M*, 1: 122). It is only natural, too, that "the piquant fact about Lydgate" is "his good birth" (*M*, 1: 173) and that Rosamond proves to be adamantine in her power of self-prepossession, which is really her possession as a formulaic image within the vision of society. Rosamond is nothing without the society that regards her and, in so regarding her, constitutes her. Because Lydgate desires this variety of female gentility after having been burned by his encounter with the unconventional Laure, he asks for the despair Rosamond eventually visits upon him.

In Eliot's portrayal, women are indeed the sacred guardians of the collective shrine of gentility. Consequently, it is only to be expected that when someone like Felix Holt seeks to change the world, he says, " 'That's what makes women a curse: all life is stunted to suit their littleness' " (*FH*, 131), and believes he must never marry lest he be lured away from his purpose. His misogyny, like that of Bartle Massey in *Adam Bede*, receives the same apology that Rosamond's vanity does: that it is a natural outcome of the traditional nature of society. It requires a mind as sharp as Mrs. Poyser's to point out the contradiction in Massey's caviling at the feminine character: the fact that male desires encourage a women to be " 'a poor soft, as 'ud simper at 'em like the pictur o' the sun, whether they did right or wrong, an' say thank you for a kick, an' pretend she didna know what end she stood uppermost, till her husband told her' " (*AB*, 543). Although egoism is always made to be universal in Eliot's fiction, this construction still allows for the detailing of the control over its social expression. This expression is made to appear a special attribute of women precisely because real power is held by men. Here, again, one sees how Hetty's confusingly polarized vision is only an individual effect of a more general social operation that displaces everyone from the true source of illumination and meaning.

Still, having made such qualifications about the special effects created by egoism in past society and in the character of women under any society mentioned in Eliot's fiction, it is important to reiterate that Eliot turned this issue, along with all the others in her writing, into a universal form. In this case, the form is egoism. This point is important because the turn to this form could only diminish any will for reform (or any Will for Reform) that otherwise might be represented in her writing. The change from the 1871-72 to the 1874 version of the "Finale" of *Middlemarch* perfectly exemplifies the significance of this turn to universality, as this involved the discarding of specific criticisms of women's social position in favor of a more abstract commentary on the human condition.[12]

On a larger scale, the character of Gwendolen Harleth is especially interesting in regard to this issue because the novel in which she appears was the only one to which Eliot gave a contemporary setting. Therefore, it may serve to show how the egoism she described as the basis of the traditional order of gentility was a continuing problem even in a society in which gentility was being transfigured. In Gwendolen Eliot created a character who takes herself to be completely extraordinary and so illustrates the pure logic of Eliot's formulation of egoism. All Eliot's characters show themselves in their desires to be akin to Gwendolen, and one, Tito in *Romola*, pursues his desires even more single-mindedly than Gwendolen, who had decided early in life "that in this confused world it signified nothing what any one did, so that they amused themselves" (*DD*, 1: 159). Gwendolen is an especially dramatic example because she is so wholly a creature of egoism and yet, unlike Tito, is brought to feel the profound error of her disposition. Whereas Tito probably comes closer to being a devil incarnate than any other character in Eliot's fiction, Gwendolen is the character who most fully confronts, suffers, and overcomes her own devilry. The rest of Eliot's characters are ranged between these two in various compounds of egoism and renunciation, all more or less like one another but none representing as purely as Gwendolen the birth of a new figure of gentility.

Gwendolen's nature, like Hetty's, is not really sexual. Eliot writes, "With all her imaginative delight in being adored, there was a certain fierceness of maidenhood in her" (*DD*, 1: 70). If there is any sexuality at all in Gwendolen, it is in egoistic fantasies of power, as in the amusing meditation she has while considering whether she should marry Grandcourt: "Gwendolen wished to mount the chariot and drive the plunging horses herself, with a spouse by her side who would fold his arms and give her his countenance without looking ridiculous" (*DD*, 1: 138). This aspect of Gwendolen's character is certainly of interest in relation to many issues raised by Eliot's fiction, but its importance in the present context is in showing how completely Eliot made desire an egoistic and thus imaginary inclination. This is what Eliot's critique of the traditional order of gentility proved to her: that in the absence of an educated enlightenment, the true sun of the liberal intellectual in the nineteenth century, the object of individual desire would be an illusory image of self-gratification. It would be an image in which individuals were bound to be most alienated when they felt themselves most fulfilled, as Eliot has Maggie realize in her decision to return home without marrying Stephen despite her desire for him. As in her descriptions of Hetty before her bedroom shrine, in the luscious bower of Mrs. Poyser's dairy, or in the pagan reaches of the Chase where Hetty meets Arthur, Eliot characteristically attributed the most overpowering sensuality to the occasion of individuals preoccupied with themselves or, more precisely, with the imaginary consciousness of themselves through which society would dominate them.

What is important to keep in mind when reading Eliot, then, is this consideration: that despite her systematic demeaning of the world of traditional gentility, this world still made sense to her as an expression of universal human nature. Her psychology turns history into morality. Because of this psychology, the vestiges of irrational historical tradition—class privileges and the like—become relatively unimportant. By the reasoning typical of liberal intellectuals, once one can imagine history to have been transcended by reason, it is taken to be so.

Feeling "well equipped for the mastery of life," always feeling herself to be "the princess in exile" (*DD*, 1: 38-39), Gwendolen perfectly represents the conflation of the democratic and the aristocratic individual that occurs within this psychological scheme. The gentility of her heritage is by no means unclouded, and soon after the commencement of the novel, she finds her family poverty-stricken and dependent upon the largess of relatives. Nonetheless, Gwendolen has a firm conception of herself as being entirely a lady—but a lady unbound by any traditions or rules foreign to her own desires. Therefore, she appears as the anarchy implicit in the traditional order of gentility and explicit in a nation moving toward democracy. In her figure, the potential madness of the claim to gentility is revealed. In Eliot's picture, an age whose tendency is to allow self-assertion to be freed from its traditional class restraints will reveal to us that the assertion of gentility, rationally speaking, was never more than an unwarranted self-assertion. This is "the undefinable stinging quality—as it were a trace of demon ancestry—which made some beholders hestitate in their admiration of Gwendolen" (*DD*, 1: 67).

Gwendolen serves to illustrate the judgment that enabled Eliot to seem to comprehend all perspectives, all opinions, within the rationalized method of her art: "The most obstinate beliefs that mortals entertain about themselves are such as they have no evidence for beyond a constant, spontaneous pulsing of their self-satisfaction—as it were a hidden seed of madness, a confidence that they can move the world without a precise notion of standing-place or lever" (*DD*, 1: 258). Because it displaces all characters from their proper selves to a greater or lesser extent, egoism is the lever of Eliot's fiction. In a letter to a friend, she stated, "The test of a higher religion might be, that it should enable the believer to do without the consolations which his egoism would demand" (*L*, 5: 69). As oppressive and destructive as they may be, this is what genteel images amount to in Eliot's fiction—consolation; the democratic example of her art is dedicated to the truth even though this must always lead, in Eliot's conception, to an inevitable comprehension of tragedy.

According to Eliot's argument, in a society in which all impediments to ambition may be taken over by the homogeneous term of circumstances while the strictures of tradition and class lose their force, there is virtually no reason why anyone may not conceive himself or herself to be deserving of mastery. As Eliot demeaned the traditional order of gentility by arguing that egoism had been its essential meaning, the difference of the advancing from the retreating world came to be defined in terms of the way this egoism now could appear to be entirely "common." This is the advancing age of the "restlessly aspiring discontented me" of *Great Expectations*.[13] It is an age in which upper-class status is losing its traditional ideological justification and yet may win a new sort of deference insofar as it may be contrasted to unregulated middle-class drives. Eliot's assault on egoism, like Thackeray's and Meredith's universalizing metaphors of vanity, is the product of this age in which the demeaning of the traditional order of society is necessary to the rising middle classes and yet leaves these classes vulnerable to the implications of their new version of power. Her assault represents the issue of ambition, which is the most problematic phenomenon in the process that transfigures gentility in the modern world. Hardy recognized this in the plot he made of "the modern vice of unrest" in *Jude the Obscure*.[14] To the middle classes, ambition represented the progressive psychology of reason. Therefore, it appeared in need of the social regulation gained through such forms as the institution of education and the disciplines of natural science. Lacking this, it might appear to represent all the destructive tendencies traditionalists were still attributing to the progress of the intellect: violent competition, an inhumane disregard for others, an overthrow of all domestic and social ties, and an absence of all authority.

The reviewer of *Daniel Deronda* in *The Academy* in 1876 gave paradigmatic expression to this problem:

> Without wishing the objective rigour of the author's imaginative creations to be clouded by a transparent didactic purpose, her readers may not unnaturally look for an imaged solution of the logical dilemma— If the desires of A are not a trustworthy guide for A's conduct, how can they be a safe moral rule for B; and, conversely, how is A to be more secure in following B's desires than his own? Or, if the strength of moral ties lies rather in their association with the permanent as opposed to the ephemeral experiences of life, than in their association with altruistic as opposed to egoistic impulses, it will still have to be shown—though not of course proved—how and wherein the permanent conditions of life are more respectable than its accidents.[15]

Eliot had allowed herself an escape from this problem in *Adam Bede* by having the transfiguration of gentility remain within a time still governed by the old order, even though one of its representatives, Arthur, had to absent himself from the locality in question to remain at its center. In the time of *Daniel Deronda*, this gesture could not apply. The individuals freed from tradition and embracing ambition in the society of this novel might well appear, in the image Esmé Wingfield-Stratford suggested for Victorian competition, like the inhabitants of the Black Hole of Calcutta fighting for breath at a tiny window.[16] The problem of order that might have appeared merely amusing to a reader when Wordsworth wrote a querulous letter to the *Morning Post* in 1844, speaking against the proposed intrusion of the railway in the Lake Country on the grounds that one should not tempt "artisans and labourers, and the humbler class of shopkeepers, to ramble at a distance,"[17] would appear of the utmost seriousness to those who saw the willful rambling of ordinary people as the historical drift of the time. In this respect Eliot was in agreement not only with the aforementioned writers but also with Robert Owen, of all people. Both saw individual egoism or selfishness as the greatest problem of modern society. The crucial difference between them, of course, was that Owen blamed this quality on the reigning social structure and middle-class ideology, whereas Eliot understood it to be a psychological given. The term of egoism marks the point in her writing where its analysis of society terminates and where it begins: in the middle-class definition of nature.

Eliot assumes as the setting of her novel a milieu whose tendency is not to discard the traditional order of gentility but to destroy it by allowing its motivation to move everyone. In this respect, it is not so much her refusal to be a governess that shows Gwendolen to differ from a character like Jane Eyre; it is the fact that she regards superiority as being only adventitiously a matter of formal social position while she essentially takes it to be a matter of self-gratification. The world depicted in Eliot's description of Gwendolen's consciousness, with its ignorance of fetters on individual desires beyond "circumstances," is a world in which the social structure that used to measure gentility has lost all effective significance in relation to the individual. In it one sees the nightmare of enlightenment, the madness of reason, because the figure of individuality appears to be liberated from all arbitrary limitations and yet shows itself narrowed rather than broadened and increasingly frustrated rather than progressively fulfilled. The rhetoric composing Eliot's conception of reason is bared as rhetoric, as in the evisceration of a lovely body, or as in the revelation that a body is comprised of viscera and parts that do not add up to a coherent whole. This is not Sam Smiles's world, but Victor Frankenstein's, as one can see in Eliot's description of Gwendolen's condition after Grandcourt has died:

> All that brief experience of a quiet home which had once seemed a dulness to be fled from, now came back to her as a restful escape, a station where she found the breath of morning and the unreproaching voice of birds, after following a lure through a long Satanic masquerade, which she had entered on with an intoxicated belief in its disguises, and had seen the end of in shrieking fear lest she herself had become one of the evil spirits who were dropping their human mummery and hissing around her with serpent tongues. (*DD*, 2: 378)

It is precisely because Gwendolen is cast into a world of ordinary human life that her desires are allowed to take on such an extreme form and thus to represent the fears about democracy expressed by writers such as de Tocqueville in the late eighteenth century and Arnold in the nineteenth. Such a world makes it possible for Gwendolen to aspire to a superior status, but it fails to give any form to that status which would involve responsibility toward or attachment to others. Gwendolen's ego can be imaged variously in the terms of gentility, aristocracy, monarchy, and even divinity because all forms of superiority may be flattened onto one conceptual plane in this world, just as all strictures upon the ego may be summed up in a single word: the rationalized term of circumstances. (It is no accident that the period of this novel is also that in which a modern, rationalized, empiricist social science and psychology saw the light of day.) In Eliot's portrayal, these modes of language logically follow the loss of a differentiating social structure and of superstitious reverence for authority *qua* authority.

To Eliot the danger of democracy is that every self may become a godhead. The unruly and perversely inclined pantheon with which society is threatened is perfectly analogous to literature and to opinion in general, as Eliot viewed them in her day, when she feared the proliferation of trashy pieces of art and of sectarian opinions in place of a harmonious and humanizing culture. Gwendolen's self-assertion as an individual is opposed to Eliot's duty/right as an author, just as the demonic is opposed to the liberating potential of democracy. In the first place, one finds that when Gwendolen's ambitions begin to be disturbed, she may have "a vision of herself on the common level" and may lose "the innate sense that there were reasons why she should not be slighted, elbowed, jostled—treated like a passenger with a third-class ticket" (*DD*, 1: 271). However, one also finds that her innate conception of herself would not have been so high in the first place if her society had not lacked systematic constraints upon the assertion of individual desire.

Facing the prospect of life as a governess, Gwendolen has "a world-nausea upon her" (*DD*, 1: 282)—the obverse of Dorothea Brooke's equally dangerous "soul-hunger" (*M*, 1: 28)—because there are no monuments breaking the horizon between herself and the farthest edge of the world. She disregards religion, the traditional bases of social position, and in fact any authority except that which may come from her own standard of personal beauty—that most uncivilized of measures within the culture represented by Eliot's writings. She finds no impediments to her spirit or at least feels there ought to be none. In this way one sees that the Humpty-Dumpty of gentility has suffered an irreversible fall but that its scattered fragments now compose the world, each a little Humpty-Dumpty all the more eager on account of its littleness to assert a Napoleonic claim to sublimity. The horizon of Gwendolen's world is the horizon of literacy and enlightenment that was meant to sweep away all artificial barriers to individual accomplishment, but this operation appears to have taken place and to have discovered that no natural order would emerge from this initiation into reason. Instead there appears only the disorder of universal egoism. Therefore, Gwendolen appears in every feature of her situation—including the simple feature of her superficial beauty—opposed to the position Eliot wanted to constitute for herself as an author.

In *Daniel Deronda*, Eliot dramatically evoked the values of the liberal intellectual through Deronda's quest for a culture broader than a merely English one and through the contrast between this quest and Gwendolen's experience, in which the spirit of the liberal intellectual is represented at every step as it would appear if it were fully realized and yet realized to represent the evils its fiercest critics attributed to it. It is interesting in this respect that many critics of this novel have greatly preferred Gwendolen's section to Deronda's, just as many critics have responded similarly to the satanic sections of *Paradise Lost*. Eliot was also dealing with good and evil spirits—spirits that in her handling were turned from the scales of the epic and the romance to that of the novel.

On this scale, it is proper that Gwendolen should remain anxiety-ridden when she is redeemed, and it is proper that Deronda's righteousness should be imaged in an attachment to a cause hopelessly eccentric to the interests of most of the characters in the novel and of the vast majority of Eliot's contemporary readers.[18] These destinies are proper because in Eliot's telling the genre of the novel is defined as that in which salvation comes from a commitment to uncertainty. This is the nature of the democratic example as it is opposed to the absolute figuring of the genteel image. Within the conception of the liberal intellectual, truth does not lie in absolute doctrine of any sort but instead in a circulation of ideas that is supposed to eventuate in the gradual progression of intellectual revelation. It is for this reason that both Adam and Dinah in Eliot's first novel were turned from the rigidity of the positions they initially assumed: so they might step over the threshold of the traditional image and into a democratic life.

This is not to say the society of Eliot's time was anything like a completely democratic one or that she set out to portray such a society even in *Daniel Deronda*, the one novel to which she gave a contemporary setting. In terms of its system of political representation and especially of the values entrenched in its institutions and its people, with their "sneaking kindness for a Lord," as Gladstone put it,[19] this was certainly not true of Eliot's society. Similarly, it is clear in *Daniel Deronda* that Eliot could see the existing upper classes of her time still giving form to the aspirations of those beneath them. The point is that Eliot portrayed this society as being so oriented toward what she considered to be the spirit of democracy as to allow an individual like Gwendolen to take her inner valuation of herself, no matter whence this may have come, to be proof enough that she deserves a corresponding outward recognition.

On this point one can compare Gwendolen to Rosamond in *Middlemarch*. Rosamond has a similar vanity and desire to have it petted and yet directs that desire entirely toward the established forms of social superiority, as they are represented to her by Lydgate's upper-class relatives and by London society. She would never dream of being an actress, as Gwendolen does at one point. She would feel the same repugnance for such an idea as Deronda did when he was a small boy uncertain of the gentility of his birth and feeling this impugned when his guardian casually suggested he might wish to be a performer when he grew up. (This is the first incident in *Daniel Deronda* that prepares the reader for its transfiguration of traditional gentility into the terms of Eliot's artistic vocation.) As Eliot described it, this is the difference between the early 1830s and the 1860s: that the desire for social superiority in the latter years might be conceived entirely in terms of the vagaries of the individual's fancy.

By emphasizing the fascination of this "witch," as Eliot, like Gwendolen's mother, calls her (*DD*, 1: 97), with "her inborn energy of egoistic desire, and her power of inspiring fear as to what she might say or do" (*DD*, 1: 40), Eliot made her a kind of test-case for the state of modern society. In "what may be called the iridescence of her character—the play of various, nay, contrary tendencies" (*DD*, 1: 40), Gwendolen is both exceptional and common, beautiful and not beautiful (as the question that opens the novel indicates),[20] and in fact the elementary form of ordinary human life. She is the vacancy of the individual tasting what it believes to be its freedom and the recognition due it and in this experience learning that its anarchic diversity must be turned to a new order of consciousness if it is not to eventuate in the sort of subjection Gwendolen faces at Grandcourt's hands. Gwendolen's error is not so much in thinking she deserves a superior social status as it is in thinking anyone deserves this status.

In accordance with Carlyle's idea of narrative, Gwendolen's biography thus appears to be the biography of Eliot's own age. In Eliot's telling, the psychology of this age is one of desires seemingly set free from constraining laws but then experiencing the surprising shock of "circumstances." They experience the sacrifices demanded of individuals by their common membership in society. This is the aspect of her fiction in which Eliot most closely resembles Austen, who also emphasized the necessity for submission under this term of "circumstances."

Since it is art that comes to the rescue—in particular, Eliot's conception of a tragic art—Gwendolen's plans before she takes the step of marrying Grandcourt are significant. In the attempt to find support for her desires, she briefly entertains the thought that she might avoid the necessity of becoming a governess by becoming a singer or actress instead. She is discouraged in this project by Klesmer, the musician and composer to whom she goes for advice. As a result, she finds herself in the "bitter" experience "of being taken on some other ground than that of her social rank and beauty" (*DD*, 1: 265). Klesmer destroys her genteel image of art, saying, " 'Ladies and gentlemen think that when they have made their toilet and drawn on their gloves they are as presentable on the stage as in a drawing-room' " (*DD*, 1: 265). In place of such an image, he describes to her " 'a life of arduous, unceasing work, and uncertain praise' " (*DD*, 1: 263). In short, he offers himself as a democratic example of a novel sort of gentility, which he conceives to be an interiorized quality, one that " 'comes from the inward vocation and the hard-won achievement' " (*DD*, 1: 263).

Neither Deronda nor Klesmer is Eliot, of course. Still, the reader of Eliot's fiction and of her other writings on art will recognize their dictates as her own.[21] What Gwendolen faces in this lacerating situation, in these words that "had really bitten into her self-confidence and turned it into the pain of a bleeding wound" (*DD*, 1: 270), is the discovery of the art to which she belongs. As its implications are developed through her marriage to Grandcourt and her discovery of his relationship to Lydia Glasher, this passage in her life corresponds to that in which Adam Bede discovers Arthur's breach of faith with him, Hetty, and his whole community. Earlier, Gwendolen had appeared to belong to an art of a different era and had felt confident in this appearance, as in the scene at the archery contest when "the hour was enough for her, and she was not obliged to think about what she should do next to keep her life at the due pitch" (DD, 1: 105). Eliot had described her in similar terms before a dance: "Sir Joshua would have been glad to take her portrait; and he would have had an easier task than the historian at least in this, that he would not have had to represent the truth of change—only to give stability to one precious moment" (DD, 1: 116).[22] But in her meeting with Klesmer, Gwendolen has impressed upon her the fact that it is to Eliot's art that she belongs and that this art is very different from the idealizing portraiture of the past. It is an art that takes change into account and so comes to demand an entirely new kind of gentility from that which preoccupied artists like Reynolds. This novel gentility might pass over images of gentlemen and ladies and instead be found among microscopes or railway carriages. It might be found in works like those of the Flemish painters (to use the comparison Eliot used for her art in *Adam Bede* and that Scott had used in the *Quarterly Review* in 1821 to describe Austen's work). Or it might even be found in ministers who try, and fail, to communicate the word of God to the inmates of a workhouse.

Chapter 5
Imperfection and Compensation

*From George Eliot to her dear husband, this thirteenth year of
their united life, in which deepening sense of her own
imperfections has the consolation of their deepening love.*

Dedication in *Felix Holt, the Radical*

Eliot's discourse demands that the character of artists always be implicated in
their work, and she made the assertion of this demand a systematic feature of
her style of representation. Therefore, the moral commitment represented
within Eliot's writing is also a linguistic key. It can be used to translate
representations of social life into a theory of representation and vice-versa. No
wonder Eliot wrote to some of her friends, "Talking about my books, I find,
has much the same malign effect on me as talking of my feelings or my
religion" (*L*, 3: 99). The nineteenth-century custom of sprinkling allusions to
literary characters and their expressions into letters, conversations, and other
modes of casual intercourse is given a foundation in Eliot's writing by this
union of form and content, which is designed to make it embody the nature of
social life.

Even if one accepts for the moment the terms in which Eliot makes this
union appear so vital, a question about the nature of her aesthetics still remains. To put this as simply as possible: why is the discovery of ordinary
human life as the basis of society represented by an art even more exclusive
than that practiced within the world of traditional gentility? For this is how
Eliot presents modern culture, just as Deronda and Klesmer do. It would seem
this culture must appear open to all, but for that very reason, it must be truly
open only to a very small number of souls in society. Eliot's art was conceived
to be one that could tell directly only upon a few, as she once emphasized in a
letter to Harriet Beecher Stowe (*L*, 5: 30-31), and one that could be produced
by even fewer, as Eliot emphasized in her desire to institutionalize authorship.

But how can this conception be understood in relation to the "democratic" transfiguration of gentility with which it is identified?

One might begin to consider this question by analyzing the description of ordinary human life that is one of the most widely quoted passages in Eliot's fiction and yet one of the most curious. "That element of tragedy which lies in the very fact of frequency," Eliot writes,

> has not yet wrought itself into the coarse emotion of mankind; and perhaps our frames could hardly bear much of it. If we had a keen vision and feeling of all ordinary life, it would be like hearing the grass grow and the squirrel's heart beat, and we should die of that roar which lies on the other side of silence. As it is, the quickest of us walk about well wadded with stupidity. (*M*, 1: 203)

This passage is often interpreted as a particularly exquisite expression of the sympathy for "all ordinary human life" that was the basis of Eliot's art. What is curious about it is how dangerous the revelation of this life is imagined to be. According to Eliot's description, this life is so hidden and silent that it can be revealed, at least in the present stage of human development, only through images of occult and life-threatening power. A consciousness of ordinary human life would be the destruction of consciousness. Although Eliot's fiction appears dedicated to this life on the other side of silence, it also implies that this life is roaring death.

To be sure, in this paraphrase the passage sounds much more overwrought than it does in Eliot's rendering, which contrasts a rudely figured imperceptiveness ("well wadded with stupidity") to Eliot's delicate simile for sensitivity. However, the extremity of the paraphrase is justified by the extraordinary nature of Eliot's conception of ordinary human life throughout her fiction, in which she always insists on its existence beyond representation.

In Eliot's fiction the discovery of ordinary human life is the discovery of the fact of its concealment and also of the fact that it must be concealed, lest the appearance and the voice it assumes should prove destructive. Even though Eliot's writing is dedicated to raising it out of silence, as if the author were a Christ consorting with the weak, the halt, and the dumb and curing them of their infirmities, ordinary human life is silenced by Eliot. What this passage seems to regret as stupidity is in fact a demand integral to Eliot's consciousness as an artist: that even the more perceptive of us are unable to see and to represent ordinary human life with any exactness. Exception is made only for those few, like this artist and intellectual, who recognize the imperfection and make this recognition a sign of their intellectual status and the means of furthering the dissemination of their culture. Hence the curious fact that Eliot believed she must articulate the weakness she and her readers share: "You and I, too, reader, have our weakness, have we not?" ("AB," 33). If it were indeed a weakness obvious to everyone, there would be no need to call attention to it.

Eliot distanced herself from her readers by the very way she included herself among them, expressing her confidence in their mutual understanding through the form of condescension.

Because Eliot identified her art with ordinary human life, she had to refuse the possibility of its adequate representation so that it would be read for its *sensus spiritualis* and not for some other meaning that would be merely superficial, by her lights, as it bore reference to specific political interests or such like concerns. Moreover, this refusal would symbolically serve to assert the power of those who were in a position to act as interpreters of superficial appearances. What this attitude indicates, then, is the extent to which Eliot's writing leans on cultural resources that are taken for granted as the threshold of meaning. Eliot did not make representation a mystery because she had to confess its difficulties before the project of accurately representing ordinary human life but rather because she needed a technique for controlling the significance that would be allowed to that life.

The egoism that throws every social mechanism off kilter in Eliot's system of things is the psychological term for this hermeneutical turn of mystery. Politically this mystery represents the power of the middle classes in the distribution of knowledge in society. It represents the rationalized professional expertise that Eliot assumed to be hers as an author and that she took to be a provision for social order, in accordance with the growing demand for meritocracy in her age. What is at issue is her demand that the power of interpretation be given to liberal intellectuals such as herself because they alone are deemed capable of peering through the object and beyond present circumstances to the interiorized and proleptic conception of meaning that is the only one allowed to be true in her telling. And, as one might expect in a postromantic age, art is the discipline superior to all others in its capacity for this sort of interpretation: in this discipline of mystery. So Eliot commented, "I only wish I could write something that would contribute to heighten men's reverence before the secrets of each other's souls, that there might be less assumption of entire knowingness, as a datum from which inferences are to be drawn" (*L*, 3: 164).

Life does not appear so obscure and so threatening in this obscurity simply because it is ordinary. As in her general heralding of this life, what is at issue in this definition is the symbolic control Eliot would exercise over it to fashion it in accordance with the values of her art. Eliot's writing was indeed adapted to the crowd, in the phrase Bulwer suggested was true of all fiction, but adapted in a mode of symbolic control. The values of her art are those of a writer experiencing the entrance of England into a more democratic age, approving of the status this change gave to the middle classes to which she belonged and for which she wrote, yet fearing the representation of ordinary human life to which this change might lend power.

The key question to Eliot was what would signify. Her overriding concern was with what would be allowed to be meaningful within the modern system of literary production and consumption. It is for this reason that her art deliberately was designed to limit the power of signification to its scheme of values, which defines the liberal intellectual. In terms of society at large, her art was not designed to open human consciousness to its potential but rather to invent and regulate a discipline of communication, feeling, and mystery. This design is articulated in a kind of writing that had a relatively tiny readership even in the society of Eliot's day, but it is not insignificant for that reason. Even within Eliot's conception its power was never considered to be direct but was meant to lean on the power of the culture to which it contributed, along with the works of other contemporaries as various as Ruskin and Mill.

True, the relation between the power Eliot's writing was designed to assert and the development of law, science, schooling, medicine, economics, and other institutions of English social life was mediated so thoroughly that her works might seem to be extremely exclusive products irrelevant to most people going about their business in society. However, this beleaguered appearance, which Eliot actually helped to foster, is itself a technique of power. One need not see all works of art simply as consumer goods to see that in this aspect one is dealing with the fetishism of a commodity. The more its accessibility is questionable even for those apparently educated enough to read it—the more indefinable and invisible the terms of its understanding—the more precious art may seem. Such is the political logic of elitism and the philosophical logic of idealism within Eliot's description of the relation between true artists and society.

Even though Eliot's writing was never what she conceived it to be (if only because her conception of aesthetic truth ignored the material conditions of its birth), this duplicity does not represent a failure of understanding or execution. It is a powerful technique. It is the technique of aesthetic purity and exclusivity that was further developed after her death and, ironically, often in seeming rebellion against the nature of her art.[1]

Although Eliot's is an art of a society becoming more democratic, of a society in which ordinary human life is beginning to take on a new significance as its institutionalization within society alters, it is not for that reason an art of democratic values. Eliot took care to suggest this consideration when she described Daniel Deronda's "innate balance" by saying he was "fervidly democratic in his feeling for the multitude, and yet, through his affections and imagination, intensely conservative" (*DD*, 1: 376). Her art is never democratic; it is an attempt to take what she saw as the effect of democracy on the figure of ordinary human life and to silence it so that the nature of her art itself might appear as the nature of humankind. It is an attempt to recognize the shift of attention to democratic life that occurred when values based on the genteel few were losing power in society but, in this recognition, to control the shift of attention so this life would not appear to be what it was threatening to be, an all too perceptible and large-scale desertion of such values and of art like Eliot's that depended on them even while transfiguring them. So those who have understood Eliot's passage about a keen vision and feeling of all ordinary human life as an exquisite expression of sympathy have understood her only too well. They have understood her desire to make her idea of sympathy appear to be ordinary human life and so have understood how an art meant to identify with ordinary human life could be even more exclusive than art within an aristocratic conception.

Eliot's development of a necessary change from genteel image to democratic example may serve to represent this control over what may signify in the modern world, but this aspect of her fiction is represented most invisibly and powerfully by the premise in all her fiction that the significance of things is largely secret and noiseless. This is one of the aspects in which her writing at times may appear conventionally ironic, as writing will in any case in which a system of values that has enjoyed popularity is being depreciated. Thus it is that in her fiction as in her correspondence about her writing Eliot frequently contrasted it to an art based on the "ideal or exceptional" ("AB," 44-45). However, Eliot's irony goes beyond that represented in such passages. It goes so far as to appear a principle of consciousness that forbids any perception—even the perception of the ordinary—from being understood as reality.

Ordinary human life undercuts the confident assurance of genteel images, but then this life itself appears extraordinary. Its significance is systematically other than what its appearance may suggest. To take the appearance of ordinary human life for its reality is, then, equivalent to mistaking a drama of "ermine tippets, adultery, and murder" for an adequate representation of the society in which Amos Barton's "far from remarkable" character appears ("AB," 44-45). Significance lies elsewhere, in the silence that Eliot was determined to make the true subject of her fiction and of her society. As she wrote in *Romola*, "It is the way with half the truth amidst which we live, that it only haunts us and makes dull pulsations that are never born into sound" (*R*, 1: 338).

For this reason, Eliot refused to denigrate the Reverend Tryan's belief in the Divine Will: because "the profoundest philosophy" could hardly do a better job of filling up "the margin of ignorance which surrounds all our knowledge with the feelings of trust and resignation" ("JR," 357). This is why she notes her refusal to rationalize the superstitious effect of the rapping Adam Bede heard on his door at the time of his father's death (even though her self-consciousness about this incident effectively serves to rationalize it): "I tell it as he told it, not attempting to restore it to its natural elements: in our eagerness to explain impressions, we often lose our hold of the sympathy that comprehends them" (*AB*, 50). It is for this reason, too, that she comments as she does on Adam's sight of Hetty in court: "Why did they say she was so changed? In the corpse we love, it is the *likeness* we see—it is the likeness which makes itself felt the more keenly because something else *was* and *is not*" (*AB*, 446). Identity appears most strongly through the appearance of difference (as Eliot emphasizes with the metaphorical corpse that takes Hetty's place in this passage) because Eliot's discourse is founded on an idealization of alienation.

According to Eliot, the novelist must have recourse to figural representation because no positive science can accurately render the irrational vagaries of experience and the imperfections of knowledge within a community—not to mention the inability of such science to muster sufficient persuasion over society merely through the exercise of its own terms. Recognizing this necessity, the novelist who would rationalize her art will make the margin of ignorance around knowledge, formerly the domain of religious or superstitious deference, the mystery at the center of her art. The margin for error in the language of art, like the dullness of all our perceptions and the inevitable imperfections in our attempts to act, communicate, and construct a just society with our fellows, will be made to provide a systematic basis for understanding society. The role of art will be that of mediating all differences and thus squeezing sympathy from conflict.

Consider this role of art in the following passage from *The Mill on the Floss*, which is written in reference to an educational system by which the Reverend Stelling tries to teach Tom Tulliver:

> It is astonishing what a different result one gets by changing the metaphor! . . . O Aristotle! if you had had the advantage of being "the freshest modern" instead of the greatest ancient, would you not have mingled your praise of metaphorical speech, as a sign of high intelligence, with a lamentation that intelligence so rarely shows itself in speech without metaphor,—that we can so seldom declare what a thing is, except by saying it is something else? (*MF*, 148-49)

A regulating community is called for in Eliot's fiction, as in Wordsworth's "A Narrow Girdle of Rough Stones," to stop the mutual displacements of nature and language that would otherwise render them meaningless. So Mrs. Cadwallader advises Dorothea Brooke in *Middlemarch*, " 'We have all got to exert ourselves a little to keep sane, and call things by the same names as other people call them by' " (*M*, 2: 113). In contrast, Eliot describes how the hopelessly egoistic Rosamond is unable to understand Lydgate's description of the way she acts behind his back: "We are not obliged to identify our own acts according to a strict classification, any more than the materials of our grocery and clothes" (*M*, 2: 251). Taking the opposite stance, in *Daniel Deronda* Gwendolen responds to her mother's criticism of her for calling her sister " 'ignorant' " by saying, " 'I don't see why it is hard to call things by their right names and put them in their proper places' " (*DD*, 1: 27). In Eliot's system of things, both characters' arguments are misguided. Gwendolen identifies her egoism with an overly strict idea of linguistic signification, whereas Rosamond identifies hers with one that is too loose. As Mrs. Cadwallader indicates, as the course of Dorothea's and Gwendolen's lives goes to show, and as Eliot's educated familiarity with the problems of metaphor also shows, the more correct position is one that takes account of the social nature of language without idealizing it so as to believe it an absolute, in the manner of genteel images. In accordance with the democratic example committed equally to progress and to a conserving morality, exertion is necessary for one who would assume a positive role in language. One must suffer language toward the end of its gradual refinement.

In place of dreams of instantaneous transformation and absolute self-possession, such as those encouraged by the stimulus of genteel images working their magic on characters like Rosamond and Gwendolen, one finds the mediated reality of historical evolution and of the development of character. So Eliot wrote in "The Spanish Gypsy" that "in various catalogues/Objects stand variously" (*P*, 73) and committed herself to the liberal intellectual view of history. According to this view, history is essentially an endless series of figural changes played on the theme of universal human nature striving for its expression, which finally is comprehended within a rationality that allows all figures to express a common truth. (It is within this comprehension that "freedom" and "determinism" are reconciled within the philosophical idiom of Eliot's fiction and other writings.) In its rationalized form, Eliot's fiction is committed to an understanding of the process of figuration in history in general as well as in the particular society it represents. Because it acts across all social divisions and across all the centuries of human history, so that Eliot could read the problems of contemporary England in the time of Savonarola's Italy or in the time of *Antigone*, morality is supported on the basis of this conception in which meaning exists largely in secrecy and silence, beyond the coarse perceptions of human beings except as they are fine-tuned by an appreciation of the kind of universal culture Eliot believed herself to represent. As she wrote in "The Antigone and its Moral": "The struggle between Antigone and Creon represents that struggle between elemental tendencies and established laws by which the outer life of man is gradually and painfully being brought into harmony with his inward needs" (*E,* 264).

To enforce this conception, just as she made the reality of ordinary human life akin to the soundless throbbing of nature, so did she emphasize that nature in general was largely barred from perception by secrecy and silence. "Nature," Eliot wrote, "has the deep cunning which hides itself under the appearance of openness, so that simple people think they can see through her quite well, and all the while she is secretly preparing a refutation of their confident prophecies" (*MF*, 32). The characterization is of a kind with that which Eliot used to punish Fred Vincy for his trust in Providence, gentility, and his Uncle Featherstone. Nature, like Featherstone and ordinary human life, proves to be obscure and threatening in this obscurity within Eliot's art, despite the comment in her journal that "the mere fact of naming an object tends to give definiteness to our conception of it" (*L*, 2: 251).

According to Eliot's reasoning, any appearance of significance in any aspect of life—in any text—must be regarded as an index to reality that is imperfect at best. As Eliot wrote, "Signs are small measurable things, but interpretations are illimitable" (*M*, 1: 24). Or, as she put it in terms of perception, "By dint of looking at a dubious object with a constructive imagination, one can give it twenty different shapes" (*DD*, 1: 306). This condition means that the representation of human life should be an arrangement of signs adjusted to the consciousness that any such arrangement, natural or artificial, is most significant in what it cannot express. Therefore, corresponding to Eliot's emphasis on the imperfections of ordinary human beings—"My artistic bent is directed not at all to the presentation of eminently irreproachable characters, but to the presentation of mixed human beings in such a way as to call forth tolerant judgment, pity, and sympathy" (*L*, 2: 299)—is an emphasis on the limits of her artistic powers. As she wrote,

> The subtly varied drama between man and woman is often such as can hardly be rendered in words put together like dominos, according to obvious fixed marks. The word of all words Love will no more express the myriad modes of mutual attraction, than the word Thought can inform you what is passing through your neighbor's mind.
> (*DD*, 1: 311)

Thus she wrote ironically of the "round, general, gentlemanly epithets" commonly applied to young men like Arthur Donnithorne. She placed examples of these epithets within quotation marks—" 'nice' " and " 'good fellow' "—so as to indicate the imperfection devouring their apparent wholeness from within (*AB*, 128). Similarly, she wrote in *Daniel Deronda*, "Goodness is a large, often a prospective word; like harvest. . . . Each stage has its peculiar blight, and may have the healthy life choked out of it by a particular action of the foul land which rears or neighbors it, or by damage brought from foulness afar" (*DD*, 1: 68). So strong is this consciousness of imperfection that words may be granted value according to the extent to which they escape perception, approaching the condition of secrecy and silence that characterizes the greater world of significance. In this way words may become linguistic counterparts to the humble subjects of Eliot's fiction—and thus remind us that these subjects *are* words arranged within a specific discourse. As Eliot wrote in reference to the ways love is shown:

> Those slight words and looks and touches are part of the soul's language; and the finest language, I believe, is chiefly made up of unimposing words, such as "light," "sound," "stars," "music,"—words really not worth looking at, or hearing, in themselves, any more than "chips" or "sawdust": it is only that they happen to be the signs of something unspeakably great and beautiful.
> (*AB*, 510)

In effect, as Eliot's emphasis on variant perspectives also serves to indicate, all the words of her fiction are placed within the quotation marks of invisibility and silence.

According to Eliot's reasoning, in the representation of human life, one should try to approach the nature of silence and the silence of nature. One should try to represent the nature of consciousness as this is now found to involve the perception of all signs apart from any fixed and systematic relation to reality. Eliot's conclusion was that consciousness had to make itself the correct system by its "tolerant" adjustment to the idea of imperfect perception, since where system once seemed to exist—in nature and in society as it was ruled by the traditional images of gentility—it was no longer apparent. In this way imperfection would be turned to compensation for imperfection: by its recognition as the systematic basis of all consciousness. This adjustment is the education conceived by the liberal intellectual to belong to culture. It was this education that enabled Eliot to comment on the tragically deceptive appearance of life by transfiguring to her philosophical idiom a metaphor from the past: "No wonder man's religion has so much sorrow in it: no wonder he needs a suffering God" (*AB*, 375).

Hence the irony that an art conceived to be that of democratic experience proves to be so exclusive. The "pressure of that unaccommodating Actual, which has never consulted our taste and is entirely unselect," is made the reason for understanding the tragedy of all meaning: that we always must be beside ourselves with it. It can take place only in a situation sytematically other than that of social life. Therefore, it can be comprehended in anything like a satisfactory form only by those few in society able to absent themselves systematically from their own identities: the liberal intellectuals. Thus it is that the supposed weakness of the artist's and of the liberal intellectual's position in the modern world—its marginality—is actually conceived to be its strength, just as imperfection is described as being the general condition of phenomena to maintain a conception of ideal compensation. And thus it is that an art devoted to criticizing any sort of purely idealist metaphysics turns upon the purely idealist metaphysics of language. If Eliot's writing has any systematic meaning, it is a meaning that arcs the gap between figures of imperfection and compensation and between the figures of duty and right in her vocation as an author, so as to turn language into an ideal cultural form.

Again, one sees how Eliot was concerned above all else with establishing the type of interpretation to which she had dedicated herself and the type of interpreter she considered herself to be, just as Carlyle was so concerned when he discoursed upon nature in "The Present Time" (1850):

Half a century ago, and down from Father Adam's time till then, the Universe, wherever I could hear tell of it, was wont to be of somewhat abstruse nature; by no means carrying its secret written on its face, legible to every passer-by; on the contrary, obstinately hiding its secret from all foolish, slavish, wicked, insincere persons, and partially disclosing it to the wise and noble-minded alone, whose number was not the majority in my time![2]

It is helpful to remember this point when considering arguments such as that made by J. Hillis Miller about *Middlemarch*, which concludes that "for those who have eyes to see it" this novel "is an example of a work of fiction which not only exposes the metaphysical system of history but also proposes an alternative consonant with those of Nietzsche and Benjamin."[3] This is not a subversive reading of the novel; rather, it falls in line with the understanding Eliot depicted herself as sharing with such *illuminati* as Harriet Beecher Stowe, even if she did not foresee the day when Miller, along with Nietzsche and Benjamin, would join her crowd. Readers may understand *Middlemarch* as Miller has but in this understanding will show themselves to be subject to Eliot's text, which was indeed designed to depreciate metaphysical systems in favor of a system of interpretation that would allow "those who have eyes to see" to consider themselves to be more perceptive than others. Regarding *Middlemarch* and her other works, such as *Daniel Deronda*—in which Eliot commented, "And to judge wisely I suppose we must know how things appear to the unwise; that kind of appearance making the larger part of the world's history" (*DD*, 1: 343)—wide understanding depends on an assumption of superiority typically figured in Eliot's writing by a trope of inclusion and exclusion—a trope of social difference—which in this instance is represented by the function of the first person plural in her narrative address. Thus, when Miller makes a similar argument from a negative stance, writing that the "webs of interpretative figures cast by the narrator [of *Middlemarch*] over the characters of the story become a net in which the narrator himself is entangled and trapped, his sovereign vision blinded,"[4] his reading is blinded by the sovereignty of the figure of imperfection that Eliot does indeed cast throughout her writing, just as Miller does throughout this essay. In other words, his reading is based on a misconception of the "totality" of truth with which Eliot was concerned. It is a philosophical rather than a rhetorical reading, and so in its failure to analyze the political nature of Eliot's art—the differences of power it institutes—this reading ends in duplicating, explicitly and implicitly, the rhetorical gestures of the liberal intellectual.

It is in this curious way that Eliot's is an art keyed to a democratic consciousness of its human subject. This subject appears wholly in the nature of consciousness. It is no longer furnished by nature or society or any other arrangement of signs, in accordance with the demeaning of fixed figures of all sorts, which Eliot attributed to the historical changes of her century. As Eliot saw it, the problem this democratic consciousness posed was that of a loss of authority over the definition of humanity. The certainty that appeared to have been lost in the broadening of consciousness in this Age of Intellect, in the shift of attention to the ordinary, had to be reconstructed within the nature of consciousness lest it be so dispersed in imperfect and transient signs that there would be no unifying appearance to humanity, which then would be an inchoate mob of individuals.

In other words, what Eliot feared was the individual under the aspect of freedom. Hence the devotion of her writing to the sympathetic understanding of the individual subjected to the determinism of natural law.[5] It was not her scientism that made her plot her novels and design her descriptions and commentary in deterministic terms. It was her need to control the individual, this figuration of her own social identity, that made her receptive to the portrayal of scientism as aesthetic truth.

Consider in this respect a comment Eliot made in reference to the bankruptcy Mr. Tulliver brings upon his family in *The Mill on the Floss*: "The pride and obstinacy of millers, and other insignificant people, whom you pass unnoticingly on the road every day, have their tragedy too; but it is of that unwept, hidden sort, that goes on from generation to generation, and leaves no record" (*MF*, 209). To whom else but this artist and those who take her to represent them (the "you" of this passage) has the life of such a figure as Mr. Tulliver been unwept, unperceived, and unrecorded? Who but those who think themselves to be in a position of superior control have considered ordinary human life to have been outside history? Certainly Eliot's own social origins were ordinary enough, she was not driven to claim a more distinguished origin in terms of social class, and the dramas of her novels represent her determination to show that life will exist even where it is not granted significance. But for whom has "significance" been so defined that it can take account of ordinary human life only in the form of negations? This "significance" is not a term for the production of meaning in general; rather it stands for its institutionalization within a specific culture, with all that this implies about rhetorical protocols (such as exclusion, denial, censorship, fabulation, and transfiguration) by which society is subjected to this institutionalization. Eliot's generous hand is that of a patron who demands, with the utmost sympathy, that her discovery appear in the form and act in the way she desires.

So Eliot would comment upon such "insignificant people" as Dorothea Brooke, "the growing good of the world is partly dependent on unhistoric acts; and that things are not so ill with you and me as they might have been, is half owing to the number who lived faithfully a hidden life, and rest in unvisited tombs" (*M*, 2: 427). To be sure, Eliot may be seen here as writing in relation to an audience whom she expects might not be accustomed to see significance in the kind of subject she has chosen for her art, and whom she consequently patronizes with such a commentary. Nonetheless, the implied audience is one of Eliot's own construction and one with whose consciousness she identified by continuing to use negative terms such as unhistoric when describing a figure like Dorothea, even at the conclusion of a novel as long as *Middlemarch*. What such a passage makes clear is that ordinary human life has to be excluded from the domain of art if it is to be art for Eliot. Eliot took ordinary life as the subject of her art and yet took it to exist in a negative relation to her art, as a subject that had to be transformed into art, because her consciousness as an artist was devoted to a position of control over this life. The silence that bars this life from perception in Eliot's figuring is the unspoken assertion of the values Eliot held as an artist in opposition to what she took to be the appearance of this life. The hidden, insignificant, unhistorical nature of this life was constituted in this form for a consciousness that could not accept what the appearance of this life meant to it, whereas Eliot's extension of this distrust of appearances to all nature and to representation itself is evidence of her fear that this appearance was only too perceptibly the nature of her age. In this way Eliot assumed her task as an artist to be that of transfiguring the historical appearance of democratic life into the unhistoric nature of her artistic consciousness. The drama of Eliot's writing represents the tensions of her aesthetics, not the tensions of her society or of recent English history.

This is the reason Eliot looked at life as a text whose significance was largely hidden and at desire as the impulse to neglect this hidden significance: because she believed she had to recognize a society threatening to go beyond her, producing significance that could not be art or idea in the terms of her estimation. Significance had to be largely beyond perception because what she did perceive of ordinary human life did not accord with the rules of her art except in a negative or ironic condition. And desire in ordinary human life had to be seen as a kind of aristocratic assertion of the individual because this figuration of the past in the present would make it appear that the system of the past was only a mistake of desire in no essential way different from the illusions to which one might be led by desire in her own age. This reasoning allowed the past to become a means of controlling the present even as it was figured to be lost to the present.

Eliot's democratic examples are a transfiguration of genteel images, to be sure, but they are not essentially different from this other order of figures. They are this order rationalized, as Eliot conceived the scheme of interpretation to which she had the clue capable of rationalizing the figures of Christ, Savonarola, Antigone, and all other characters, societies, and nations of history. Thereby, she made history into her conception of art: by psychologizing it as a process whose significance was buried in desire, which would never change in an essential way. It was in this way, too, that the nature of art was made into the nature of humanity. This scheme allowed Eliot to always reflect upon the hidden, unchanging, unhistoric continuity of human life throughout history. By systematically rejecting the possibility of representing ordinary human life even while she claimed to represent it, Eliot buried her fear of the dispersion of values in the assumption that all values secretly had a common tragic root. History is rationalized, psychologized, and sentimentalized to constitute the drama of Eliot's intellectual discourse.

The discovery of ordinary human life that makes significance an occult sound, then, is also the discovery of egoism as a sovereign power within individuals and a bar of stupidity or silence between them. Through these relations the nature of Eliot's discourse is drawn into a thematics of representation and a drama of social conflict. So long as it lacks the rationalized basis represented by Eliot's art, the world that egoistic desire reads into consciousness must be many different and ultimately irreconcilable worlds in reality: "For if it be true that Nature at certain moments seems charged with a presentiment of one individual lot, must it not also be true that she seems unmindful, unconscious of another? For there is no hour that has not its births of gladness and despair" (*AB*, 302). The consciousness of individuals is constructed on the basis of their unconsciousness of others; desire shows itself as this unconsciousness of others; and the result is that no fixed significance can be attributed to any appearance of the world, since this sort of attribution would privilege one individual's perspective over all others. Egoism uses the world as a screen for its own projections—as Romola looks in Tito's eyes and reads "her own pure thoughts in their dark depths, as we read letters in happy dreams" (*R*, 1: 190)—and it does so in a world without a systematic standard of significance (such as that which once existed in a rigid class structure and a deferential religious belief) where any interpretation and even any naming of an object of consciousness must fall into silence or stupidity. So Eliot commented in *Daniel Deronda*, toward the end of a career devoted in large part to describing characters in her fiction, "Attempts at description are stupid: who can all at once describe a human being? even when he is presented to us we only begin that knowledge of his appearance which must be completed in innumerable impressions under differing circumstances. We recognize the alphabet; we are not sure of the language" (*DD*, 1: 111).

Such is the doctrine of representation in the works of a writer for whom the idea of conventional signs was outmoded because society, as she saw it, no longer was guided by an understanding that could furnish them institutional support. Through this sense of alteration in social institutions, language is driven back into the silence of the alphabet, the expression of opinion back into the abstract conception of the discourse to which it belongs, and the outward signs of gentility back into inward character. What might appear to be representations of crisis, of a failure to achieve understanding—comments like "Attempts at description are stupid" and the dramatic events to which they are applied—actually serve to recuperate society from what Eliot perceived to be a crisis. They were meant to act in this fashion by raising an epistemological bar between cultural figures such as Eliot (with all that she intended to represent in terms of sympathy, duty/right, humanity, and so on) and the social life of her time. Just as conservatives during the 1840s would oppose the Chartist demand for universal male enfranchisement by arguing, on the theory of "virtual representation," that every individual in society was already represented through the mediate forms of his or her interests,[6] so, too, did Eliot oppose her scheme of indirect representation to the idea that representation should or could be materially systematized. Felix Holt's politics are perfectly analogous in this respect to Eliot's conception of aesthetics.

Eliot took this virtual harmony to be real—to be the true identity of humanity—precisely because it could not be realized in any individual perception or conventional image and so forced individuals to defer to society as a whole, to the humanity it was made to represent, and to the liberal intellectuals whom she expected to interpret this humanity. The reasoning follows rhetorical, not logical rules, as in the exchange of a child for gold that takes place when Silas Marner is seized by catalepsy. Nonetheless, it is represented to be the essence of logic and rationality as well as the symbolic goal of art. After all, as Mill had explained, what was most important to liberal intellectuals in this time was their rhetorical mastery. This mastery was the fable of culture to which both Mill and Eliot subscribed.

From this perspective, Eliot's relentless assault on egoism may be seen to typify the middle classes' need to deny their self-assurance, their capacity for symbolic mastery, in order to figure their bond of universal identity with all others in society. On a universal scale, Eliot's tragic sense of life corresponds to the self-deprecation an individual can use, paradoxically, to make herself more powerful in the eyes of others. Tragedy is the term in which Eliot transfigures social inequity into moral and metaphysical thematics just as egoism is the term in which the characteristic figure of the middle classes is transfigured into a saving, because universal, tragedy.

Secrecy and silence were essential to Eliot's conception of society as a whole because it was through these means—through these margins at the center of her art—that she was able to symbolically compose all the differences her discourse would allow to exist in society. Without the underlying premise of secrecy and silence, this imagery of the middle-classes' secreting of their will in nature, Eliot's harmonizing vision of society advancing throughout history could not have been composed. Hence the reigning paradox transfiguring the terms of Eliot's art: that the consciousness of imperfection may be construed as a consciousness of the ideal, just as an art of ordinary human life may be an art of the select few. When Eliot did find a language that could be read accurately— the language exemplified by her own art—it succeeded by making the most trivial signs into the universal soul-stuff of all time and humanity, so that the face of a rather stupid country girl, for instance, might recall the spirit of a nation. Such is the wonder of this transfiguration. As Eliot wrote in a remarkable passage in *Adam Bede*, discovering within the unconscious Hetty the discourse of universality upon which all her fiction was based,

> Hetty's face had a language that transcended her feelings. There are
> faces which nature charges with a meaning and pathos not belonging
> to the single human soul that flutters beneath them, but speaking the
> joys and sorrows of foregone generations—eyes that tell of deep love
> which doubtless has been and is somewhere, but not paired with these
> eyes—perhaps paired with pale eyes that can say nothing; just as a na-
> tional language may be instinct with poetry unfelt by the lips that use
> it. (*AB*, 294)

Critics over the years have been tempted to view Eliot's emphasis on imperfection and the displacement of significance within it, especially when considering some of the harsher comments Eliot made in regard to the beauty of characters like Hetty, as bearing some relation to her own ugliness, which, according to many contemporary accounts, was quite stunning. There may be a point to such conjecture, although not in the simple psychological terms in which it has usually been made. After all, a recognition of physical ugliness is an integral part of Eliot's recognition of the "dreary prose" ("JR," 237) of ordinary human life as opposed to the ideal figures of romance. E. S. Dallas noted this in his 1860 review of *The Mill on the Floss* when he suggested "an allusion to the supposed impossibility of making a silk purse out of a swine's ear" as a criticism of the novel.[7] And Eliot did write in *Adam Bede*, anticipating the criticism Dorothea would make of art in *Middlemarch*, "I am not at all sure that the majority of the human race have not been ugly" (*AB*, 183)—even if this remark is made subject to considerable irony in this novel just as Dorothea's is in *Middlemarch*.

As Eliot portrayed it in relation to genteel images, the value of beauty, like the value of refined manners and social position, is a conventional predicate of virtue all too often mistaken for its substance. As she wrote, dryly noting the displacement of significance wrought within her aesthetics, "One begins to suspect at length that there is no direct correlation between eyelashes and morals" (*AB*, 158). Even apart from a lover's imaginings, then, physical beauty is an imperfect text, its significance largely beyond perception. In this guise it is like all other phenomena but more bewitching because of its traditional association with genteel imagery. Given this association, in art and in real life signs of physical beauty are likely to float above society at the cost of the vulgar work and suffering that go into their production. As Eliot wrote in her last novel, characteristically allowing the cultured style of her writing to intervene between the genteel and the vulgar viewpoints,

> Perspective, as its inventor remarked, is a beautiful thing. What
> horrors of damp huts, where human beings languish, may not become
> picturesque through aerial distance! What hymning of cancerous vices
> may we not languish over as sublimest art in the safe remoteness of a
> strange language and artificial phrase! Yet we keep a repugnance to
> rheumatism and other painful effects when presented in our personal
> experience. (*DD*, 1: 158-59)

Not surprisingly, the heroine of this novel appears as a kind of antitype to the figure of the narrator, her beauty an ugliness that can be redeemed only by her growing comprehension of the nature of Eliot's art.

Of course, apart from what psychological interest there may be in this attitude toward beauty, it is a commonplace of Eliot's time, especially in the terms of Evangelical and Dissenting religion, and is occasionally introduced into Eliot's work in a direct connection with such influences, as in the portrayal of Dinah in *Adam Bede*. And it is certainly true that a good deal of Eliot's emphasis on imperfection is merely an ironic inversion of those values grouped with gentility that is paralleled in the works of Dickens, Thackeray, and many of her other contemporaries—even writers in whose work beauty is generally identified with virtue. This popular formula simply inverts the predicate and the substance, making beauty an internal rather than an external quality and then making this interiority appear as the greater significance of the subject.

However, of greater interest than Eliot's adoption of this formula is the decided preference for homeliness that she identified with her recognition of ordinary human life and with her opposition to the world of traditional gentility. This preference appears as a positive element in her art rather than as a merely negative or ironic contrast. So she writes of the extra pleasure she takes in mongrel dogs or in the majority of common men: "Nay, is there not pathos in their very insignificance—in our comparison of their dim and narrow existence with the glorious possibilities of that human nature which they share?" ("AB," 45). This passage shows that the type of sublimity Eliot associated with the outmoded world of gentility was still the standard for her art but now a standard that represented both difference and identity. One would still measure ordinary human life according to this standard, but the measurement would yield sympathy rather than depreciation and thus an implied identity between glorious possibility and inglorious reality. Thus is gentility turned from a superficial matter, as Eliot viewed it in its traditional form, to one of intellectual and emotional comprehension.

Eliot's democratic consciousness may appear to be a simple form of irony because it is dedicated to the representation of imperfect, flawed, ungenteel appearances. More importantly, however, it is based on a rule of interpretation for all appearances. This rule transfigures them into the emotion of the ideal from which they all must fall short and thus, in effect, shows them to be ugly.

So the democratic example does not show up in Eliot's art simply in ironic relation to the genteel image, as a form of life that has been ignored or slighted; it emerges as pressure for a gentility of a novel sort that would belong to intellectual enlightenment and emotional refinement rather than to social origins and polite conduct. This novel gentility—this gentility proper to the novel as Eliot conceived it—would comprehend the relation that ordinary human life had borne to the genteel in traditional art and would make the significance of this relation its subject. The real subject of art would be neither genteel image nor democratic example but rather the scheme of interpretation conceived to mediate their differences. This is the scheme Amos Barton failed to apprehend when he was caught between the gentry and the rough laborers in his parish but that Eliot symbolically mastered when she looked down on his situation or when she constructed all her democratic examples out of their differentiation from genteel prototypes or antitypes. Amos Barton has pathos lavished upon him whereas Eliot need not request such sympathy because her position as a narrator corresponds to his but is assumed to have the superior power of intellectual comprehension that Amos could show only in its more naive emotional form. His sentimentalization makes his narrator appear transcendent, according to the general rule for the production of meaning in Eliot's fiction.

In effect, the object of every representation in Eliot's work must be understood to be nothing less than the spirit of humanity throughout history. This alone is a concept adequate to adjust the correspondence between signifier and signified. It is a scheme of interpretation directed to this concept that is capable of seeing the highest intellectual culture in the appearance of a stupid character's face. If one fails to master pathos and tragedy by mastering this kind of interpretation, one becomes a character like Gwendolen, as she appears in the scene in which she has agreed to marry Grandcourt. Having made this decision, she glances over at his horses, pathetically and tragically believing there is no identity between their beauty and the ugliness she would shun. To this heroine, still dominated by an overly simplified notion of semiotics, the horses are "the symbols of command and luxury, in delightful contrast with the ugliness of poverty and humiliation at which she had lately been looking close" (*DD*, 1: 324).

Whatever interest Eliot's own appearance may have had in the theme she developed from the topic of imperfection, then, it has no significance apart from the universal sweep she gave this theme, since it in turn was made to fit the articulation of middle-class discourse in this age. But the question of Eliot's psychology may still be intriguing. For if one supposes there is more than a casual relation between the emphasis on imperfection in her fiction and her own ugliness, as her contemporaries denominated it, this relation would exemplify, as an aspect of her creative process, the cultural function her writing was intended to have for everyone it influenced. In assuming this relation, one would see Eliot transcending her "imperfection" as an individual by transfiguring it into a universal form—just as her readers, along with the characters in her fiction, were supposed to overcome the problems they faced as individuals by regarding them as aspects of the tragic fate of all humanity. Within her reasoning, by calling attention to her imperfection she would transfigure her perception of herself into a transcendent and thus culturally enriching form—just as Wordsworth and his friends could name a place Point Rash-Judgment and in so doing establish it as the ground of good judgment. It is thus that imperfection and compensation in Eliot's writing—the figures of the real and ideal, material and spiritual reality, romance and novel, and so on—may be seen to take on meaning only as their displacement of each other is ordered by the overriding scheme of rationality within Eliot's art that designates what shall be imperfection and what shall bandage the hurt.

It does not really matter what the case actually might have been with Eliot's psychology. In this case as in others, the error of psychologism is not so much its naive grasp of history (although this is certainly one of its characteristic features) but rather its failure to observe that power lies in the production of meaning—and that only in middle-class fabulation can the authority for this production be that of an autonomous subject recapitulating his or her history.

In any event, Eliot's art was conceived in a negative relation to society in its modern as well as in its traditional aspect; and it was so conceived because in Eliot's analysis the essence of society could never be found in the established surfaces of social, economic, and political conditions. Although Eliot was concerned to trace these conditions and their transformations in their trivial as well as their general manifestations and was further concerned to encourage what she took to be their more progressive variations, she would always find the essence of society within the nature of the individual and more particularly within the nature of individual desire. Egoism, characteristically turned to vanity under the conditions of traditional gentility and to ambition under more democratic conditions, is the essence so defined.

Eliot did tend to see society advancing in definite and progressive stages, as in Comtean and Saint-Simonian as well as Hegelian theories. She also made explicit what systematic theories of society of this sort always must assume: that human nature is a historical constant, varying only in the degree to which it is conscious of itself. Thus it is that art, which Eliot identified with the fulfillment of consciousness, would regard society under any conditions as being essentially unchanging. Whereas a character like Mrs. Transome would perceive the society of the 1830s as an object completely changed from the world of her youth, seeing that "what she had once regarded as her knowledge and accomplishments had become as valueless as old-fashioned straw ornaments of which the substance was never worth anything" (FH, 32), an artist such as Eliot would look beneath "that high-born imperious air which would have marked her as an object of hatred and reviling by a revolutionary mob" (FH, 32) to see "a woman's keen sensibility and dread, which lay screened beneath all her petty habits and narrow notions, as some quivering thing with eyes and throbbing heart may lie crouching behind withered rubbish" (FH, 32-33). Thus, strikingly, would Eliot sift through the superficial trash of differences and confound both the aristocrat and the mob, just as the gentleman and the common man may be confounded by, as they are conflated within, the individual. It is art alone that can penetrate to this kind of secret and silent truth, while "those who had glimpses of her outward life . . . never said anything like the full truth about" Mrs. Transome and never "divined what was hidden under that outward life" (FH, 32).

In this respect Eliot's aesthetic technique was precisely the technique by which rationality was conceived within the discourse on education among the middle classes of her age. However, the special significance of this technique in Eliot's work lies in the unprecedented way she systematized the difference between a democratic consciousness of human nature and democratic conditions in society. By taking the former to be the essence of aesthetic concern and the latter to be a mechanical matter different from and likely to be hostile to art, she developed with striking rigor an exemplary formulation of the middle-class sociology of art. Romantics such as Wordsworth had seen art as the soul of society or as its true religion, but no one prior to Eliot had so revealingly explicated this religion as the idealization of imperfection. This formulation might be said to have been implied in Defoe's realism, in Wordsworth's and Scott's primitivism, and more generally in all the literature of the eighteenth and nineteenth centuries that in one way or another represented a democratization of values. However, it was left for Eliot to make this implication coalesce as a tradition by developing an art so completely identified with democratic values that it could disjoin them completely from social conditions and in fact assert that they were pure only when they were so disjoined. In this respect Eliot's work is typical of this period in which the middle classes were consolidating their power and aspirations in the face of diminishing threats from the traditional upper classes and of encroaching demands from the lower. It was at this point that a democratic consciousness fully became a religion—a discipline—because the middle classes that had advanced democratic values now acutely felt the need to control them. They needed to make a soul for themselves distinct from the image of the lower classes that were now demanding an enfranchisement that threatened the middle-class theory of democracy. Therefore, it was fitting for art to be exalted as a religion that was extraordinarily exclusive even among the middle classes.

One can see this development throughout Eliot's fiction, but the inheritance plot of *Felix Holt* provides an especially good example of it. Although awkwardly convoluted in its details, in its basic outline this plot might be taken to represent a simple shifting of power from the genteel upper classes to the democratic middle and working classes. Thus it is that we find Mrs. Transome retaining her hold on her estate only through the machinations of her lawyer, Jermyn, who sees to it that one legitimate inheritor dies in jail and that another person vitally involved in the succession, the drunken Tommy Trounsam, remains an unknown relation. Eventually it is revealed that because of Tommy's death, the estate belongs to Esther Lyon, the daughter of the impoverished Evangelical minister; and to add to this degradation, Mrs. Transome finds herself compelled to tell her son that Jermyn is his real father, after Harold Transome has struck him. So the genteel family is systematically demeaned, with Harold Transome forced to learn a truly democratic (as well as Freudian) lesson in place of the superficial Radicalism with which he had alarmed his mother. The pretensions of the old family collapse into utter ruin—but there is more to the story. After helping to effect a reconciliation between Harold and his mother, Esther resigns all claims to their estate and, when Felix Holt gets a pardon from jail, marries this would-be working-class leader. By this means Eliot shifts the terms of the novel from the structure of society to the structure of morality—if in fact any reader of the novel until this point could have mistaken its focus. Both sets of players are rehabilitated, and by the same means: the lesson of middle-class familial sentimentality. Just as the Transomes are forced to reconstruct their lives on the basis of feeling, so too must Esther surrender her former attachment to dreams of gentility and Felix his monastic devotion to ostensibly political causes (although, again, these had been entirely moral from the beginning). The property and class relations that had been at stake throughout the novel are put out of the question, while the only lasting concern proves to be the affective relations among individuals. This is how the liberal intellectual seeks to control democracy: by defining it as a quality of feeling, of "sympathy." Thus Eliot makes democracy into art.

The clumsiness of this novel's process might be taken to indicate how unconcerned Eliot was with the actual plots of class conflict and change in the social life of nineteenth-century England. She was as attentive as Dickens or Trollope to the manners involved in these plots and to the massive facts of social changes, but the structure of relations in society and its economic and political order were subsumed for her entirely within the moral—or, as Eliot dignified it, the philosophical—consciousness of a hidden identity in all humanity and in fact in all the universe. (For instance, one would never guess from Eliot's novels that it was possible for a woman in her time to live a life like hers, or that it was even likely that a man might be able to rise as eccentrically in society as she had.) All else was demeaned in favor of this meaning, which appears as a controlling thought more important than any plot.

For instance, this is the case when Lydgate is involved in the vote for a chaplain of Bulstrode's hospital. Eliot writes, "For the first time Lydgate was feeling the hampering threadlike pressure of small social conditions, and their frustrating complexity" (*M*, 1: 188). What Eliot's analysis of society accomplishes in this description is the transformation of gross social terms into terms that appear neutral and even scientific (the "pressure of small social conditions") and so serve her purpose. Because they may seem to allow an equally disinterested analysis of people in any social situation—the dream of sociology—they give her a rhetorical base from which she can glide into her moral claim of universal sympathy and further into the religious aesthetics that makes this sympathy the qualification for art. Art then becomes the highest social truth and, through the reversal of this process, the premise for the deduction of all social thought.

It is in this way that Eliot's fiction was indeed designed to be adapted to the crowd, as Bulwer phrased it, but adapted to its controlling definition and manipulation. If Eliot was not like the Reverend Archibald Duke—"a very dyspeptic and evangelical man" whom she portrayed as thinking "the immense sale of the 'Pickwick Papers', recently completed, one of the strongest proofs of original sin" ("AB," 57)—she was still very concerned that literature not be identified with a democratic audience. She was intent on demeaning an art of genteel images, but she was just as intent on making the ordinary human life whose suffering went into the expensive production of such images continue to suffer for its appearance within her art. It would not be excluded arbitrarily: reason would not tolerate such a fate. Instead, this ordinary human life would be made silent and invisible. In other words, it would be made the tragic soul of the middle classes. It would be made the object of sentimentality, the preferred middle-class egoism.

Chapter 6
Realism and Romance

Man can do nothing without the make-believe of a beginning.

Eliot, *Daniel Deronda*

In all its features, Eliot's fiction is a commentary on an art antithetical to her own. At times this art is evoked through literary allusions, at other times Eliot makes reference to it through her reflections on the work she has in hand, and occasionally her characters' actions, attitudes, words, and thoughts suggest they would be happier in the world of this antithetical art than they are in hers.

This other art may be called romance to distinguish it from Eliot's realism. In thus distinguishing them, though, one should also note that each seems necessary to the articulation of the other. The argument between them is played out in every aspect of her narratives. The genres she pursues and against which she reacts are made to appear as stages of social development and levels of human consciousness as well as aesthetic modes more or less accurately representing reality. Each is implicated ironically in the other and is also dependent on the other for its own full expression.

In Eliot's conception, realism transcends romance. However, it does not do so by a simple rejection of the values or inversion of the stylistic characteristics of romance; it transcends romance as the liberal intellectual transcends society in general: by interpreting it, understanding it, and so gaining the power to patronize it. Unlike an intellectual such as Burke, who could feel free dogmatically to condemn certain historical events, situations, or representations, a liberal intellectual like Eliot would insist that nothing be lost from history. Even if they appeared to her to be misguided, all historical conflicts and the arts associated with them had to be recuperated within the understanding of her art so it could maintain its claim to comprehensive sympathy and disciplined understanding. Such was the rhetorical logic Eliot drew from her assumption of her position as a modern intellectual. Therefore, to understand the art she was pursuing, one must understand this antithetical art against which she was reacting.

In its broader terms, this situation is no news to students of the history of the novel. It is arguably contemporaneous with or even definitive of the beginning of the novel as a genre, whether one cares to locate this in the eighteenth century or as far back as the time of *Don Quixote*. Thus, it is less important to ask about the history of this situation than it is to ask how Eliot in particular used an antithetical art to set up the terms of her fiction—and then further to consider why the way she manipulated these terms was so popular in her own time and continues to seem so vital to any understanding of the Victorian period.[1] As the history of the realism versus romance distinction shows, with works shuffled back and forth between these pigeonholes depending on what person in what historical situation is doing the sorting, it is useful to the production of literature but only nominally relevant to its understanding unless this is directed to particular cases under specific social conditions. Like all formal generic distinctions, it requires historical analysis because it represents the procedures by which texts may be institutionalized, as if these depended upon properties intrinsic to the texts, and so gives history the form of idealism.

The articulation of realism versus romance seems especially problematic in this regard because it was so frequently imagined to be more than a formal distinction. Whether one was Hawthorne saluting the claims of romance or Eliot those of realism, the choice was likely to be made one of morality and knowledge as well as style. Eliot's great admiration for Hawthorne and the fact that her own realism has often been analyzed for its romance elements may serve to indicate just what a slippery customer this truth over which everyone was arguing really was. Even apart from a historical understanding of genres, this difficulty always found when rigorously classifying the features of an author's work ought to call into question our usual schemes of generic classification.

Furthermore, in Eliot's case the art against which she was reacting could be referred to without explicit mention of any titles at all, or with mention of only one or two, because she was writing against her own image of such an art more than she was against any material that actually might be said to belong to it. It is not the accuracy of her classification and interpretation of the genre of romance that is at issue in understanding her writing (even assuming that the notion of "accuracy" should enter into this situation) but the role her construction of this antithetical art plays within her writing. This is an image at least as much imagined as real, one called forth from the necessities of her own argument as much as it is the source of her argument.

True, Felix Holt might refer specifically to Chateaubriand's *Réné* when he says, " 'Your dunce who can't do his sums always has a taste for the infinite' " (*FH*, 130). Moreover, he might excoriate Byron in similar terms. However, as the nature of Felix's comments indicates, much more is at stake in these aesthetic judgments than formal aesthetic distinctions, just as one would expect in the work of a writer who conceived true art to be "a real instrument of culture" and, as such, a social vocation fueled by individual inspiration. For example, it is evident that one issue involved in Eliot's rejection of this antithetical art is the nature of her readership in an age when this was likely to appear much more mysterious to the author than it had previously been. The anxiety she expressed on this score through her running commentary on the dangerous appeal of this other art shows that the proper denomination of art within her writing raises issues involving the organization of all society.²

So romance is Eliot's "make-believe of a beginning." In her delineation of this art antithetical to her own, it is ultimately middle-class morality rather than literary or historical analysis that guides Eliot's pen, as is only to be expected from a writer who believed this morality to constitute the essence of literature and history. It is for all the foregoing reasons that the significance of romance in Eliot's writing does not lie in the similar function such an image plays in many other novels. It does not lie in literary history as defined within the tradition to which Eliot sought to contribute but in the history of a time and place, nineteenth-century England, when the way Eliot used this image could appear important enough to make her an exemplary novelist of the age. Therefore, a student of literary history needs to conceive of this antithetical art of romance as one needs to conceive of realism itself. It is not a generic term that has a potential for being definitive and universal if clarified theoretically; it is a term used historically within the configurations of a discourse without which it would be as empty as the figure of the individual is aside from the interventions of middle-class ideologies. Rather than being trapped in a hermeneutic circle of texts and theory like a Casaubon or a Borges, then, one needs to look to the discourse within which Eliot was institutionalized as an author to see the significance that such terms as realism and romance could have in her writing.

The problem in analyzing an antithetical art so thoroughly implicated in Eliot's aesthetics as to be coextensive with her realism is that its scope extends beyond any summary term. Probably the word Eliot most often associates with romance is egoism, but she occasionally identifies it as romance proper. The nature of this antithetical art is indicated in her writing by references to trashy literature, superstition, magic, gambling, unenlightened religious enthusiasm, aristocratic mastery, infant narcissism, and sensual pleasure, to name just a few. Although her statement that all people are "born in moral stupidity, taking the world as an udder to feed our supreme selves" (*M*, 1: 221) might serve as a summary description of the attitude informing romance, so might many others whose diction and imagery offer quite distinct cultural references. Thus, in *Adam Bede* she anticipates Felix Holt in a slightly different idiom by referring slightly to "that order of minds who pant after the ideal" (*AB*, 189). In an early story, she suggests that readers who find her works uninteresting may find others more to their tastes since, she writes, "I learn from the newspapers that many remarkable novels, full of striking situations, thrilling incidents, and eloquent writing, have appeared only within the last season" ("AB," 45-46). Elsewhere, she speaks ironically of the hero "who believes nothing but what is true, feels nothing but what is exalted, and does nothing but what is graceful" ("JR," 300). Or, to give another example, she criticizes Gwendolen Harleth for wanting to be "the heroine of an admired play without the pains of art" (*DD*, 1:368).

Although it is true that Felix Holt refers to this antithetical art under the summary name of "Byronism," even to Felix this poet's name is only a broadly generic label, because he thinks *Réné* the same claptrap as Byron's works.[3] The fact that it is not a particular author or even a specific tradition of writing at issue in Eliot's work becomes even more clear when the references in question do not bear upon art except in figurative terms. Otherwise disparate elements in Eliot's fiction such as superstition and magic become aesthetic references when they are made to suggest an artistic practice, a style of representing the world, contrary to her own. For instance, even though Gwendolen's gambling is not a conventional art form, it represents one in *Daniel Deronda*, which opens with the image of this heroine playing in a casino and asks the question, "Was she beautiful or not beautiful?" (*DD*, 1: 3).

Despite their differences, such passages in Eliot's writing are affiliated formally by their common opposition to her "own" art and related thematically by their cumulative evocation of a world opposed to Eliot's. As the quotations cited above indicate, this world is characterized by the separation of the individual from society at large, the exaltation of the individual above others within this separation, and the growth of luxurious feelings within this exalted transcendence. The argument of Eliot's fiction is always antagonistic toward this world of romance and yet vitally bound to it—as one can see in the relation between the narrator of *Daniel Deronda* and the character of Gwendolen. In fact, the terms of romance and realism in Eliot's writing are so closely bound to each other that her critical position cannot be embodied in her characters except as a form of masochism. They must take pains not only to improve themselves, as students must even in a conception of education like Rousseau's, but to cure themselves through the experience of sickness and to undergo extreme suffering to purge themselves of romance. It is this reasoning that suggests Gwendolen is not beautiful in the casino but appears much more attractive in the marriage in which she is sickeningly brutalized.

From examples like this one, it is evident that romance is not wrong, as far as Eliot was concerned—in fact, it is only too right. It represents as a desirable world one that everyone does indeed desire, and this is precisely the problem. This desire, this make-believe of a beginning, represents the figure of the individual freed from the objective constraints characterizing traditional society and not yet caught by the subjective discipline Eliot hoped to see in an educated and professionalized modern society. Therefore, everyone is made a figure of romance—and romance is made untenable. Like Eliot's realism, it is portrayed as an art guided by universality. But romance is depicted as taking universality for granted. It does not recognize the contradiction universality poses to the individual, as Eliot did in suffering the difference between Duty and Right in her conception of herself as an author.

In other words, in her image of romance Eliot displayed a paradox in the conception of the individual. In her telling, as desire makes romantics of everyone, it also individuates people according to their egoistic desires. Such is the democratic common ground romance gives to all human existence. People may make romantic claims for themselves on the romantic assumption that they are singular figures in relation to society even though all other individuals in society may make quite incompatible claims based on the same assumption. The paradox is that of a conviction of singularity that may be shared by all humanity.

According to Eliot, unless it is turned into culture, such a paradox must result in either of two basic plots. One possibility is that it will lead to a disabling self-consciousness. In this plot, egos inevitably collide and so realize their dreams are impossible because they are common and competitive, not unique and transcendental. The other plot ends in isolation, in a lonely entombment of the individual in a private world, and thus in a tragic fate of the most common sort imaginable. The former result may be represented by Gwendolen's fate before she is reclaimed by Deronda; examples of the latter are Silas Marner in his period of misanthropy or Reverend Casaubon in his burial in dusty scholarship.

In Eliot's presentation, the cultural solution to these plots is suffering. Suffering appears within the design of her art as the thematic equivalent to the formal difference between particular and universal, individual and society, text and genre, that tragically figures in her continually reiterated distinction between realism and romance. As she puts it, we are all "children of a large family and must learn, as such children do, not to expect that our hurts will be made much of—to be content with little nurture and caressing, and help each other the more" (*AB*, 322). We must not be led into "fancying our space wider than it is" (*AB*, 100) but instead must surrender the gossamer dream of transcendence to the unpleasant labor of life—and thus rediscover it in a form calculated to make the original dream look like the shoddiest of goods, in accordance with Eliot's humanized *felix culpa*.

Such is the moral thematics Eliot developed from the discourse in which she was implicated. This discourse demanded that the term of the individual be basic to society and yet be subject, along with all the other terms of social life, to the universality conceived to be proper to the middle-class will. Thus it is that another possible end to this paradox of individual desire is never used as a dramatic fate for Eliot's characters but only as a figurative description for their fate. Demonic evil acted out toward others is a fate suggested by works that might seem to fit Eliot's image of romance. However, to accept such a possibility would mean accepting the idea that society could actually be a margin to singularity rather than the source of an imperative normality. It would mean one could truly become exceptional, in corruption if not in virtue; and the rejection of this idea is precisely what constitutes the argument to which Eliot is committed in her idealization of imperfection. Eliot's villains, such as the weak but essentially good Arthur Donnithorne of *Adam Bede* or the merely craven Raffles and the pathetic Bulstrode of *Middlemarch*, exemplify this. Even the brutal, wife-beating Dempster in "Janet's Repentance" is allowed a full measure of humanity and is shown to be as much his own victim as is Mr. Featherstone in *Middlemarch*, Tito in *Romola*, and Grandcourt in *Daniel Deronda*—all of whom are made pitiable, if not positively sublime, through death.

For one of Eliot's intellectual persuasion, the first assumption of all understanding had to be that individuals are always social figures, however singular they may feel themselves to be in spirit or make themselves in body. It was on this assumption that any idea of what was human had to proceed because society within her conception had been given over to the middle classes, to which she owed the possibility of her social position and the universal reasoning that developed from and justified it. To have argued otherwise would have been to argue as a figure of romance. Within Eliot's reasoning, romance, like egoism, serves to signify the persistence of the past in the present. In this way, it represents the disturbance of the modern world by forces, such as the untutored lower classes, that may threaten the middle-class assumption of its power as much as the traditions of the past do.

In accordance with this scheme of representation, the fact that the extremes of demonic agency and of superlative heroism are absent from Eliot's fiction can be taken to show its comprehensiveness. Similarly, elements that this fiction may seem to ignore—the unrespectable lower classes and the immoralities she thought ought not to be represented in art[4]—are actually disqualified from meaning, as far as Eliot was concerned. They are excluded from representation for the same reason the more violent actions of characters such as Tito are disqualified from signifying anything except the loss of self. Violence or evil on the one hand and extraordinary heroism on the other are not allowed within her scheme of representation except in the absence of characters from the truth of their ordinary selves—that is, in the temporary appearance of Eliot's realism as romance. Such elements would imply that society might not be adequate to its own conception, might be blind to or mistaken in its elements, might not possess itself within a controlling comprehension, and so might show the alienation of Eliot's characters to be a transfiguration of her own intellectual condition.

This is the first place to note the complicity between the opposing arts that form the argument of Eliot's writing. One reason they can form a coherent narrative despite their antithetical relation is because both are based on the question of the individual's relation to society as a whole. So Eliot writes of Maggie Tulliver's discovery, by way of Thomas à Kempis, that this relation is a central dilemma of her life:

> It flashed through her like the suddenly apprehended solution of a problem, that all the miseries of her young life had come from fixing her heart on her own pleasure, as if that were the central necessity of the universe; and for the first time she saw the possibility of shifting the position from which she looked at the gratification of her own desires—of taking her stand out of herself, and looking at her own life as an insignificant part of a divinely guided whole. (*MF*, 308)[5]

For Eliot as for so many Victorians, the most problematic trope was that of synecdoche. What was the relationship of the part to the whole? In what ways might the part adequately represent the whole, and in what ways might such a representation be misleading, "merely" a trope, and hence dangerous? Although Eliot explicitly addressed this problem in terms of the broader issue of metaphor—"for we all of us, grave or light, get our thoughts entangled in metaphors, and act fatally on the strength of them" (*M*, 1: 87)—the problem identified in the omnipresence of metaphor is this problem of synecdoche. The problem is not metaphor as such but that people have so many different metaphors, which, in their irreconcilable diversity, are still taken as adequate approaches to the whole of life.

For this reason all figuration is an allegory of the individual in Eliot's writings. The individual is the phantasm of positivity she needed to pin down to feel secure in her own identity as a novelist and intellectual. Thus, the system of the past would not have been so invidious in Eliot's portrayal if it were not for the fact that every one of its collective representations was liable to become a mere "picture of a sun" that would lead individuals astray, or even make the concept of the individual incoherent, because it could be interpreted in any way one wished. In contrast, Eliot argued that a way was needed to relate all the parts of society to the whole without leaving any remainder and yet without reducing the idea of society to the anarchic lowest common denominator of its constituent parts. So Raymond Williams has written in reference to Eliot that "part of a crucial history in the development of the novel" occurs when "the knowable community—the extended and emphatic world of an actual rural and then industrial England—comes to be known primarily as a problem of relationship: of how the separated individual, with a divided consciousness of belonging and not belonging, makes his own moral history."[6]

That this was a problem characteristic of her age and not just of Eliot's work can be seen by examining other literary works of the period, by considering the religious, political, and scientific arguments that wracked it, and, most basically, by noting the changing circumstances of the production and reception of literature in the nineteenth century. Moreover, this problem of identifying a united audience under these changing conditions was impressed upon the consciousness of people like Eliot by the huge growth of urban populations in this period. As Asa Briggs has written,

> It was the question of the relation of the constituent parts to the whole which gave point to most of the other questions contemporaries were asking about London. What was the whole? Did its constituent parts have a real life of their own? Was there any real sense in which London was one? These were questions about society which were intimately bound up also with questions about government.[7]

But just because the question of social life was commonly and understandably posed in this form does not mean Eliot's attachment to the form was natural. To accept the question in this form would also mean accepting her assumption that there is a natural discontinuity between the individual and society that justifies giving them supreme importance as conceptual categories. Furthermore, one would accept the obverse assumption to this. There would seem to be no other category of equal importance to that of the individual in analyzing the problems of social life. And, finally, one would accept the assumption that what individuals most dramatically experience to be different from or in conflict with themselves, at least until such time as they may experience the reconciling growth of education, is a whole society. One would assume that the idea of society as a whole constitutes a reality specific and coherent enough so that one could rely upon it for guidance and trust it to guarantee the stability of values.

As they are shared equally by Eliot's image of romance and by the realism she develops against it, these assumptions can be seen to stake out some of the most important limits to her imagination. By analyzing the formation of these limits as an effect of the discourse to which she belonged, not as the "themes" or "ideas" she or her culture developed, one can try to avoid being lured into the same trap that locks Eliot's writing into such complicity with the very art whose image she seems to oppose. For these assumptions are not simply some elements among the others involved in Eliot's writing. Along with the other specifications of her discourse, such as the superiority of feeling to science, they mark the possibility of this writing in the form in which it comes to us. They are the frontiers of its intelligibility. To put it crudely, romance is the Maggie Tulliver to realism's Tom, and the argument between the two is as coherent as it is logically interminable because they share the same grounds in discourse, despite all their differences. It was not for nothing that Eliot insisted she had just as much sympathy for Tom as for Maggie (L, 3: 299): she indicated this within the novel by drawing each figure closer to the other's grounds until the two finally consummated their identity in death.

The argument is coherent and interminable because at every point of its articulation, on the side of romance as on that of realism, it is drawn from a society encouraging the idea of itself as a whole in contrast to the individual. This encouragement is a consequence of the organization of society into an increasingly urbanized and competitive capitalist order. When the economic order of an industrial society grows rapidly in scale and concentration, the desire for self-gratification is likely to appear privatized, narcissistic, culpable, and even illusory because the grounds of social commitments swell with this economic change to a scale incommensurate with any pleasures with which the generality of individuals can identify in their daily lives. In Eliot's words, the "local system" of life is supplanted by "the great circulating system of the nation" (*FH*, 50).

This categorical division makes the historical changes that occurred in England over the eighteenth and early nineteenth centuries appear as they were rationalized neatly after the fact. However, it remains true that these changes commonly had the effect of removing society from the horizon of the individual and that this removal had both material and ideological consequences. These effects make it possible to see fields such as those of education, charity, political science, and realist aesthetics as belonging to a common discourse in this age, just as they make it possible to understand the interdependence of romance and realism in Eliot's conception of her art.

This increasing abstraction of society may be epitomized by the gradual fading of local traditions, festivals, and folk holidays throughout the nineteenth century and their supersession by a pattern of work and play keyed to changing commercial and industrial demands—the change Hardy memorialized in the club-walking at the beginning of *Tess of the D'Urbervilles*, as well as in many other novels. As Marx noted, "Even the ideas of day and night, of rustic simplicity in the old statutes, became so confused that an English judge, as late as 1860, needed a quite Talmudic sagacity to explain 'judicially' what was day and what was night."[8] Or perhaps an even better example of this change may be taken from James Plumptre's popular revision of Shakespeare's songs, first published in 1805, in which he changed *As You Like It's* "Under the greenwood tree / Who loves to lie with me" to "Under the greenwood tree / Who loves to work with me."[9] Many historians have described the changing nature of time and life rhythms in this period; a major effect of these changes was that the economic theory and practice of the time were made to appear to be the power of nature.

Because people were likely to be increasingly divorced from the face of society, a need was created for a morality based on the rationalized idea of society as a whole. Rather than appearing in local figures like the church and the squire, as it was thought to have appeared in that memorialized past when streets were laid out "before inches of land had value, and when one-handed clocks sufficiently subdivided the day" (Hardy),[10] nature was being promoted as economic law and abstract commercial and industrial demand. In this situation, the middle classes "naturally" felt a need for new modes of figuration that would bring home this modern nature to everyone in society. This need was broadly satisfied by the modern conception of education brought forth by the middle classes, by the transfiguration of the traditional gentleman that accompanied it, and, on a more detailed scale, by the myriad ways middle-class ideology would independently or "naturally" seem to appear in the day-to-day social life of the time.

In practice as in universal educational theory, society came to be promoted by the governing classes as a moral idea opposed in its abstract nature to the daily experience, desires, and needs of individuals. This ideological change was especially embodied in the attitude of the middle toward the working and lower classes (no longer "the poor" within the eighteenth-century conception). Hence Andrew Ure's argument that every mill-owner should *"organize his moral machinery on equally sound principles with his mechanical"* so as to discipline laborers to see their work as " *'a pure act of virtue.'* "[11] For good reason, this argument sounds like the ethos of Adam Bede and of Mr. Garth in *Middlemarch*. It is recapitulated even more fully in the address Eliot had Felix Holt make to the workingmen of her own time, in which the claims of these people for redress as a class are made subordinate to their moral development as individuals. As far as Eliot and her class were concerned, such people were not allowed to understand their situation in society except in terms of a conflict between their culpable self-indulgence, on the one hand, and the order of society as a whole, on the other.

Consider Eliot's comment on Caleb Garth's attempt to "reason with" a laborer who, along with several others, interfered with the surveyors for the railroad that was being constructed through Middlemarch:

> Timothy was a wiry old laborer, of a type lingering in those
> times—who had his savings in a stocking-foot, lived in a lone cottage,
> and was not to be wrought on by any oratory, having as little of the
> feudal spirit, and believing as little, as if he had not been totally unac-
> quainted with the Age of Reason and the Rights of Man. Caleb was in
> a difficulty known to any person attempting in dark times, and
> unassisted by miracle, to reason with rustics who are in possession of
> an undeniable truth which they know through a hard process of feel-
> ing and can let it fall [sic] like a giant's club on your neatly carved
> argument for a social benefit which they do *not* feel. (*M*, 2: 137-38)

A figure of the transition from past to present, Timothy is not devoted to the duties of either and so perfectly represents the individual at odds with society—albeit in a vulgar and amusing form. His "hard process of feeling" is represented by his argument that the railroad and other such changes in his lifetime have done nothing to help him or others of his kind: such is the violent interference, the unmeaning irrationality, with which reason must contend. The references to Paine situate him on the far side of democracy against which the middle classes were consolidating their power in this age, but more significant in the present context is the sociological assurance with which Eliot can approach this situation as she generalizes from Caleb's position to that of "any person attempting in dark times, and unassisted by miracle, to reason with rustics." Otherwise so intent on making the rhetoric of feeling transcend even reasoned opinion by figuring the utopian fulfillment of reason, in this situation Eliot can denature Timothy's feeling. She makes it "hard" and as destructive as "a giant's club" demolishing a fine piece of rhetorical art, which belongs to her readers as well as to Caleb ("your neatly carved argument"), because this feeling represents the configuration of the individual opposed to society as a whole and ignorant of this whole to which he is opposed. Timothy's argument is granted no meaning whatsoever simply because it does not take form in relation to the whole society but rather in relation to himself and to others of his kind. Timothy can see only what Hawthorne saw of the railroad when he described the English countryside in 1857—that its line "is perfectly arbitrary, and puts all precedent things at sixes and sevens"[12]—whereas Caleb, the author who comments sociologically upon his case, and the reader formally placed into agreement with her would have Timothy recognize the modern miracle of reason that can make the advantages of the middle classes appear as benefits paid to—and thus duties owed by—such a one as Timothy. With his "hard" feeling for himself and his peers in their present situation, Timothy fails to appreciate the proper way to preserve the past, unlike a character such as Mary Garth, who shows her rationality when she explains why she will not break her attachment to Fred Vincy. " 'It would be too great a difference to us,' " she says, " 'like seeing all the old places altered, and changing the name for everything' " (M, 2: 417). What Mary understands is that the past is meant to be preserved in sentiment, the proof of cultured individuality, in relation to which the world and words alike are only figures. According to Eliot's sociology, instead of trying to preserve the landscape of his life, Timothy should convert that landscape into feeling. He should turn himself into an inwardness, a subjectivity, in which the rationality of society as a whole may be made plain in the form of a feeling beyond any direct representation. He should attend to Wordsworth, not Paine.

The point is that the individual is not conceived in the grasping terms of Eliot's image of romance until the power of society has been pictured as being more abstract than it has been in the past and yet still appears in the process of being accommodated to the disciplines—scientific, technological, sociological—of modern rationality. The conception of romance in this grasping form occurs when their perception of this transitional situation makes those who speak for the authority of law feel they must solicit people to their various duties by promoting a common idea of duty identified with the interests and manners of society as a whole. Thus, in Dickens's *Bleak House*, " 'Esther, Esther, Esther! Duty, my dear!' " says Esther Summerson, a character who might be regarded as the *reductio ad absurdum* of this premise if there were not so many other contenders for the title. Dickens's heroine literally calls herself into being by regarding herself in the third person, which is to say, from the standpoint of society as a whole.[13]

This solicitation to an abstract moral duty does not make sense except in opposition to a degraded sense of localized and spiritualized duties. Individuals do not appear as random atoms before society becomes an order removed from the horizon of their perceptions, materially and ideologically demanding its perception as an imperative ideal rationally opposed to the daily experiences, conditions, and relations of a people in a local environment. Hence Eliot's conception of the structure of duty. On the one hand, it is a "supremely hallowed motive" that transcends all society. On the other, it is a motive "which can have no inward constraining existence save through some form of believing love" (R, 2: 125)—that is, which cannot be effective unless its transcendence is also its immanence in feeling. Society is systematically made a whole while being displaced beyond and within the surface of its appearance in social life. It is made a cultural figure: a figure as imperative in relation to the actions of individuals as it is elusive in relation to the social satisfaction of individual desires.

This structure explains the significance of Eliot's attack on egoism. This attack serves to elevate rationalized procedures over the effects of personalities but also over local effects of social life of all sorts. This figure of egoism is not conceived in relation to society as a whole: it produces the imperative moral effect of society as a whole. It marks a boundary of discourse constitutive of that discourse. Although Eliot describes it as an unfortunate source of the deviation of truth into rhetorical figures, it is required to produce the appearance of truth within her art in the same way the unreality of romance is required for the articulation of realism within her art. In this respect as in others, the conception of error within Eliot's writing is implicated within its construction of truth. It may be seen to reveal the politics of that truth in the same way a historical analysis of generic distinctions may reveal the purposes applied to idealist schemes of reading. Thus, desire does not appear categorically egocentric—even though it may be represented as having had this quality all the while—until society insists on its own image as a whole that can be grasped only through the public mind.

Understandably, then, the first technique of the middle-class moralist is to establish the grounds of every argument in the domain of common experience. Through this procedure, the figure of the individual is defined as tending to exceed or deviate from the common interest. Insofar as this technique prevails, society will not be judged through its actual state, organizations, institutions, and practices, as these may be experienced by such figures as Timothy. It will be judged within the public mind, and individuals correspondingly judged according to the extent to which this mind dominates them and continuously translates their experience into cultural generalities. Individuals must be read by society just as Eliot's readers, within the self-conscious elaborations of her art, are read into their proper places—are even led to feel Timothy's hard feeling attacking their property. It is for this reason that parallel distinctions will be drawn between the educated and the general public, the respectable and the rough workers, and the deserving and the undeserving poor as the individuals in question do or do not show an adherence to the cultural ideal. One need not actually possess culture as long as one shows oneself submissive to its rule, which cuts across all classes as the reality of society. Just as realism and romance ultimately are not separate conceptions but the articulation of a single discourse, so are these divisions that culture observes in the various classes in society most significant for the identity they signify—the identity they demand—through their production of differences in society.

In the promotion of this cultural ideal, the surface of modern society must be turned to invisibility and inwardness. Its disturbing railroads must be transfigured into preserving sentimental figures. This is the solution commonly offered to the problem of synechdoche in the governing discourse of Eliot's time, and this is the solution in her novels. As Eliot puts it in *Adam Bede*, commenting on the relation of the individual part to the social whole,

> Desire is chastened into submission; and we are contented with our
> day when we have been able to bear our grief in silence, and act as if
> we were not suffering. For it is at such periods that the sense of our
> lives having visible and invisible relations beyond any of which either
> our present or prospective self is at the centre, grows like a muscle that
> we are obliged to lean on and exert. (*AB*, 504)

In contrast to her image of romance, in which people are typically extreme or ideal types, Eliot presents her work as a historical discovery of individuals in whatever state or condition they may be found. And yet, at the very moment when art thus comes to understand individuals, or rather to create individuals in the modern sense of the term, it does so by placing them in relations beyond their grasp. It defines their concrete individuality in terms of a mysterious sociality and identifies their true interests with the generality of social interest, in accordance with Adam Smith's brilliant myth. Individuals are discovered so that they may be disciplined in Eliot's fiction as in nineteenth-century English society, in which the individualistic doctrine of laissez-faire economics was used not only to deny workers recognition as a class and to resist class activity in unions and other working-class organizations but also to assert that any conflicts that may occur in a competitive society in reality are not conflicts at all. According to this fable of consensus, to take conflicts as such is to exalt one's self and one's local situation at the expense of society, whereas the proper course is to recognize that one's true interest lies in the ends of competition and thus in the future of society as a whole. From this perspective, one can see that the figure of the individual is invented so that all conflicts can be made individual and all truths social. Romance is the falsity of individual conflict which must be recognized so that realism may be recognized as this social truth.

In thus making knowledge of individuals a means of disciplining them, so that all the cognitive measures in her work are also supervisory and punitive, Eliot was following in the realm of the novel the measures taken by the mainstream of pedagogical thought. Factories were schools for a new discipline in this time, and the extension of education to the lower classes throughout the nineteenth century was conceived primarily as a means of controlling them. Historians have pointed out that the purpose of education was never at issue in the late eighteenth-century arguments over whether or not it should be extended to the lower classes, and this continued to be the case throughout the nineteenth century. As some working-class leaders recognized, people on both sides of this argument were in favor of disciplining the individual to serve the economic and political ends of society. The only question was whether education would serve this purpose or instead incite disorderly ambitions among its students.

In nineteenth-century educational policy and practice, as in Eliot's novels, the development of knowledge is the development of a social discipline oriented to the changing economic conditions of this age, especially as these concerned the lower classes. As the issue was put in 1834 by a writer for *Fraser's Magazine* who was arguing in favor of a government-sponsored education based on liberal principles, directed instruction is considered especially necessary for the poor "because they have not the advantages of parental assistance to enable them to turn the eye of inquiry into themselves."[14] Such is the nature of psychological analysis in this age as in Eliot's work: the demand for social supervision of the individual. In the dominant discourse of Victorian society as in Eliot's work, the very concept of knowledge, like the cognitive division between the individual and society as a whole, is constituted to promote the supervision of society over every aspect of the individual's behavior and beliefs. In this way it is designed to make discordant behavior and beliefs appear categorically ignorant or violent—or romantic. In this age whose modern social arrangements have been described by G. M. Young as eventually bringing "the entire range of ordinary life, from birth, or even before birth, to burial . . . within the audit of public interest and observation,"[15] Eliot's attention to ordinary human life within the novel also appears as a supervisory control over it in the guise of principled observation.

So one can understand how, for Eliot, the qualities of invisibility and inwardness that characterize the discovery of the individual were all-important. Given the assumptions of her discourse, Eliot could not accept any idea of the self that was not from the very beginning included within the category of society. Therefore, she had to invent a mystery—this invisibility and inwardness of social truth—because she needed it as a sponge with which to soak up such conflicts and contradictions as were evident within society. It is thus that she probed the problematic boundaries of the discourse in which she was involved and turned them into representations of social history. In a time in which "balloon views" of cities were popular as a way of seeking "a new and more ordered vision" of them,[16] the universal vision of the public mind was designed to control, even to efface, the more immediate panorama of society. Hence Felix Holt's trust in public opinion over political measures and Eliot's general antagonism to any rule except that of her own narrative supervision, which sees all characters in their circumstantial particularity and at the same time dissolves this particularity within the breadth of a mind beyond circumstantial constraints. That same supervision which identifies individuals as utterly unique subjects also pulverizes them into the most general of abstractions:

> The great problem of the shifting relation between passion and duty is clear to no man who is capable of apprehending it: the question whether the moment has come in which a man has fallen below the possibility of a renunciation that will carry an efficacy, and must accept the sway of a passion against which he had struggled as a trespass, is one for which we have no master-key that will fit all cases. The casuists have become a by-word of reproach; but their perverted spirit of minute discrimination was the shadow of a truth to which eyes and hearts are too often fatally sealed—the truth, that moral judgments must remain false and hollow, unless they are checked and enlightened by a perpetual reference to the special circumstances that mark the human lot.
>
> All people of broad, strong sense have an instinctive repugnance to the man of maxims; because such people early discern that the mysterious complexity of our life is not to be embraced by maxims, and that to lace ourselves up in formulas of that sort is to repress all the divine promptings and inspirations that spring from growing insight and sympathy. And the man of maxims is the popular representative of the minds that are guided in their moral judgment by a ready-made patent method, without the trouble of exerting patience, discrimination, impartiality—without any care to assure themselves whether they have the insight that comes from a hardly earned estimate of temptation, or from a life vivid and intense enough to have created a wide fellow-feeling with all that is human. (*MF*, 531-32)

Supervision is opposed to patent methods as discovery is to creation, passive understanding to active comprehension, inspired to imposed knowledge. Whereas patent methods might be put to use as analytic tools by the individual, this supervision is to be accepted as an unbreachable limit. One demonstrates one's wisdom by one's deference: the *professional* ignorance, marked by "patience, discrimination, impartiality," that causes the shifting relation between passion and duty to be unclear to anyone capable of apprehending it. (One should note, of course, that the existence of an opposition between passion and duty is taken for granted in this passage.) The limit defines the particular individual within society but, at the same time, establishes society as that which will not tolerate differences, particularities, or partialities. It is in this contradiction that the vacancy of the individual appears like a glimmering form on the horizon of Eliot's fiction, waiting to "grow," to be filled with ideological substance, and thus to be materialized as the realist image of a living and breathing human being. Its denomination as an "instinctive" component of good sense indicates that this supervision of the individual represents nature. Indeed, in the drag it places upon all actions, it is the tragic principle of nature that is nothing more or less than the rhetorical design of all Eliot's writing, the "logic" of its rationality, the "experience" of humanity. "Naturally" the same understanding that recognizes the individual also neutralizes this figure. Naturally, the form of Eliot's argument in this passage illustrates the understanding it recommends. It opposes itself to casuistry, and yet it draws truth from the shadows of this opposing method.

This supervision is prevalent throughout Eliot's writing. It appears in the distinction between the art she is pursuing and that against which she is re-acting, as well as in all the other differentiations productive of its meaning. According to this supervision, the individual is such only as long as this figure is a transfiguration of middle-class will. Thus, perpetual reference to special cir-cumstances may be demanded, but it will be contradicted by perpetual reference to the generality of "all that is human," which signifies the com-prehensiveness the liberal intellectual constructs through procedures such as the denial of classes, the exclusion of violence, and the protocols of taste. To put the matter crudely but not inaccurately, this contradiction is not represented as such within Eliot's fiction for the same reason that it was not thought to be a contradiction in her society to demand that workers offer themselves to employers as individuals and not as a class while supporting this demand with the argument that as a class workers were too unenlightened to know their own best interests. Although the versions of this contradiction played out in the legal, philosophical, economic, religious, and aesthetic doctrines of the time cannot simply be reduced to a common figure and thus comprehended in all their implications, in all these cases individuals are recognized so that they may be neutralized, or paternalized, within this discourse of rational and natural law structuring representation in Eliot's society. Because Eliot demands the recognition of individuality but refuses to allow any space to this recognition, individuals are so constituted in her writing that they must appear in conflict with themselves if they are in conflict with society. Regarding "self-satisfaction" as "an untaxed kind of property" (*M*, 1: 162), Eliot takes her mission to be that of socializing the self by taxing it with society.

Chapter 7
The Supervision of Art and the Culture of the Sickroom

The psychological profundity, metaphysical solidity, and moral breadth of English naturalism: all, to my mind, follows from this communication of sympathy.

Ferdinand Brunetière, *Le Roman naturaliste*

Eliot's society is made to be seamless and all-encompassing, so it appears natural that her individuals can find a private space for themselves only in an image of romance that is nothing but an empty reflection of themselves. It is "no wonder," Eliot would write, that the supervision of this situation should find its image in the scene of suffering. Given an aesthetics so deeply implicated in the mode of representation it opposes, a realism that takes the antithetical power of romance to be universal and unavoidable, and a writer who must forever find herself at a rhetorical impasse in trying to distinguish the "wretched falsity" of "unveracious attempts at universal consolation" from her own universal doctrine of "resignation to trial" (*L*, 4: 128), it seems only appropriate that Eliot's argument should be clarified most distinctly in the terms of a scene of suffering. As Eliot turns her rigorous intelligence on the structures of her discourse and thus on her own status as an author, it is in this scene that the truth of romance is made to feel its contradictory nature and thus to be transfigured to the greater truth of Eliot's art.

What one sees in this scene is the initiation of middle-class consciousness as this was mythologized, given a "make-believe of a beginning," in Eliot's writing as in her culture in general. So she wrote in *Adam Bede*, "Deep, unspeakable suffering may well be called a baptism, a regeneration, the initiation into a new state. . . . Doubtless great anguish may do the work of years, and we may come out of that baptism of fire with a soul full of new awe and new pity" (*AB*, 440-41). Or, as she put it in "Janet's Repentance" at the beginning of her career as a fiction writer,

No wonder the sick-room and the lazaretto have so often been a refuge from the tossings of intellectual doubt—a place of repose for the worn and wounded spirit. Here is a duty about which all creeds and philosophies are at one; here, at least, the conscience will not be dogged by doubt, the benign impulse will not be checked by adverse theory; here you may begin to act without settling one preliminary question. ("JR," 367)

Here—and only here, as far as Eliot was concerned—one can view individuals and act toward them as an individual. One can do so because the sufferer appears to be discovered, not artificially created; appears passive before one's understanding, not actively engaged in one's life; appears an inspiring, not a demanding figure. In this scene the individual caters to the supervision of art by lying helpless before it. It appears as a figure reduced to its ground and so puts the nurse outside "the form of argument" (R, 2: 187) and the "importunities of opinion" ("JR," 368) because it appears to be entirely vacant of ideology. It is in the state of ahistorical grace proper to the middle classes, which recognize no ideologies as such, recognizing only natural law and universal reason. In the sickroom "the moral relation of man to man is reduced to its utmost clearness and simplicity" ("JR," 368) because in this scene there is no danger of individuals arising and demanding gratifications that might place them in romantic opposition to other people and thus to the peace of society as a whole.[1] There is no problem with men of maxims because in the duty inspired by this scene one can feel but cannot think. In the utopia of this scene of medical supervision one goes beyond the imperfections of all signs,[2] one reaches the highest prospect of Eliot's art—that which goes beyond all analysis—and this pinnacle of the spirit is the suffering of the body.

This suffering is shared by the attending angel of duty, by the sympathetic reader, and by the writer who supervises the whole scene, suffering in the writing of it and yet feeling this suffering necessary to the therapeutics of literary art. As Eliot wrote in *The Mill on the Floss*, discussing her work as the problem of relating "the smallest things with the greatest" and contrasting its resolution of this synecdochic problem to the work of "romantic visions,"

It is a sordid life, you say, this of the Tullivers and Dodsons. . . . I share with you this sense of oppressive narrowness; but it is necessary that we should feel it, if we care to understand how it acted on the lives of Tom and Maggie—how it has acted on young natures in many generations . . . for does not science tell us that its highest striving is after the ascertainment of a unity which shall bind the smallest things with the greatest? In natural science, I have understood, there is nothing petty to the mind that has a large vision of relations, and to which every single object suggests a vast sum of conditions. It is surely the same with the observation of human life. (*MF*, 288-89)

No object and no individual can pass the supervision of art unless they can be related to the greatest of objects. In Eliot's reasoning, this is the cultural conception of society as a whole. The scene of suffering exemplifies Eliot's art as all those involved in it are bound to each other by the mysterious knowledge constituted by pain, which appears as the experience of humanity and thus as the truth of society embodied in culture. Eliot's approach turns outward while it turns inward, committing the self to the acceptance of its constitution as its suffering dissolution in the cultural ideal of society.

Eliot could make fun of that "favorite abstraction, called Society" to which the ladies of St. Ogg's adjust their consciences, such as they are (*MF*, 539); and in an essay for the *Westminster Review* she might refer to society as being "like 'matter', and Her Majesty's Government, and other lofty abstractions" (*E*, 323). Nevertheless, a remote ideal of society dominates the construction of her own writings. She was perfectly capable of turning on the terms of her own narrative argument because this irony is made to signify the refinement of her language toward the silence and invisibility beyond representation that represent her scheme of reason in all its social power. Even though Eliot might have Esther Lyon say, " 'I think half those priggish maxims about human nature in the lump are no more to be relied on than universal remedies' " (*FH*, 421), this evidence of her self-consciousness about her own universalizing habit did not inhibit her from evoking "human nature in the lump" at every turn. Rather, it creates an ironic differentiation within her writing between the "half" meant to be understood as shadow and the other half meant to comprehend this darkness and transfigure it to light—even though these halves cannot be separated radically or even formally. Similarly, Catherine Arrowpoint may say, " 'People can easily take the sacred word of duty as a name for what they desire any one else to do' " (*DD*, 1: 254), although she and Eliot still hold to the prescriptive sacredness of the word over its social usage. The rhetoric of Eliot's writing is always of this utopian variety because the premises of romance are her own, even though she exchanges the self-reflection of the individual glorified in her image of romance for the self-reflection of society glorified in the writing she designates as her own in opposition to this image.

The sickroom in which this glorification is represented most clearly is related throughout Victorian literature to the ideal of charity, as in the use made of Esther Summerson's nursing and suffering in *Bleak House*, or as in the rhetoric Thackeray applied to "hospital nurses without wages—sisters of Charity, if you like, without the romance and sentiment of sacrifice—who strive, fast, watch, and suffer, unpitied; and fade away ignobly and unknown."[3] So it is not surprising that Eliot's treatment of the individual parallels the Victorian theory and practice of charity, as well as its discourse on education. After all, it was not until the Education Act of 1870 that these fields were separated and popular education "was no longer a charity but a right."[4] In the discourse upon charity, too, truths were social and faults individual. Geoffrey Best has written,

The helping hand of charity, when it reached *de haut en bas*, almost always had a disciplinary and/or condescending glove on: disciplinary, in that the recipient had been adjudged 'deserving' (i.e. potentially if not actually respectable) and was expected to remain so (big, business-like charities often incorporated a system of surveillance); condescending, insofar as the recipient was pressed to make ample acknowledgment of his gratitude and dependence.[5]

Because Eliot shared the same discourse thus constituted as charity, she could offer her readers the following paradigm in the opening of *Adam Bede*: "The idle tramps always felt sure they could get a copper from Seth; they scarcely ever spoke to Adam" (*AB*, 5). For Eliot, charity is a means of signifying character, that fable of Victorian subjectivity, in the giver as well as in the recipient. Thus it is that the "idle tramps" of this description find a contrast later in the novel in the character of Hetty, who may be pregnant and in despair but still thinks that "the 'parish' " is "next to the prison in obloquy" and that begging from strangers lies "in the same far-off region of intolerable shame" (*AB*, 390). The point is not that any particular opinion about charity regulates the meaning of Eliot's writing, as one can see in the way Adam and Seth are contrasted but placed under no determinate judgment on account of their opposing attitudes toward charity, but that the form of the discourse given to charity, like that given to education and to Eliot's fiction, served to produce a subjectivity, a moralized interiority, in which the social adjudication of opinion could be represented as spiritual comportment and psychological law.

In effect, Eliot's perpetual reference to the special circumstances of ordinary life belongs to the same discourse as the plans for investigating the poor that were developed by the charitable Provident Societies set up in some of the large towns of England in the 1830s. Their reasoning, as one of their reports put it, was that "the artifices of hypocrisy and cunning can only be baffled by information obtained through long acquaintance and habits of confidential intercourse."[6] Eliot could have written that sentence—in fact, virtually did write it on several occasions—with hardly a word changed. Similarly, her supervision is of a piece with the proposal made in 1884 by an economist, Alfred Marshall, that people moving to London be inspected "in a rigorous, uncompromising way" to determine their nature. The result he hoped for was that "a good many shiftless people who now come to London would stay where they are, or be induced to go straight to the New World, where the shiftless become shiftful."[7]

To be sure, this proposal was rather eccentric. The point is that it was formulated in terms of a discourse that produced character as an interiority accountable to social discipline by conceiving of the individual as a figure divided from and yet comprehended within society as a whole. In this age in which charity was not distinguished clearly from government relief for the poor (as opposed to the situation of government sinecures for the genteel, as Radicals liked to point out), the discourse given over to this conception of character had been institutionalized in the New Poor Law of 1834. The "doctrine of least eligibility" in this law was specifically designed to make relief equivalent to penal judgment, and the poor recognized this fact by christening the new workhouses Bastilles. Similarly, one can compare Eliot's writing and the argument made in 1812 by William Allen, the Quaker philanthropist, that hospitals should not be open to all but rather should require fees or letters of introduction from the poor so that these creatures might be placed under "full inspection."[8] Like Bentham's plans for prisons and schools and, on the other side of the ideological spectrum, Robert Owen's "bug-hunting" practices in his model communities,[9] this demand for supervision is of a kind with that made by Eliot in the novels she wrote in the later years of the century.

To describe these configurations within the discourse of Eliot's age is not to identify charity with education or particular educational documents with the "themes" of Eliot's work, as amateur and professional sociologists alike are wont to do in studying literature, but to trace the related ways in which objects—including their own disciplines—were constituted for people within fields that seem so diverse. As an element in society, "literature" certainly cannot be treated as a category perfectly congruent with "charity," or "charity" with "education," as if these words were merely the effects of discourse and had nothing to do with people, institutions, and practices in society by no means equivalent in form, extent, and power. However, it is also true that the analysis of writing like Eliot's can only be mystified if one fails to recognize the discourse to which it is given over and the way the regulations of this discourse—such as the conception of the individual in relation to society as a whole—are important not only in Eliot's work but also in the social history of the time.

This treatment of the individual in relation to society was further elaborated in the opposition throughout the nineteenth century between the uses of voluntary and governmental organization. Of course, government intervention into social problems and organizations increased steadily from the 1830s until the end of the age; but such intervention always faced strong resistance from attachments to local government, voluntary service, and laissez-faire economic laws. Although government intervention and centralization greatly increased throughout the period in realms such as education, health, and sanitation, this government action generally developed in response to immediate pressures and public outcries, not as a result of a deliberate practice of state control. Middle-class ideologies did not really recognize or follow the fact of government practice, and those who were "disadvantaged" (to use a word of twentieth-century sociology) were still generally seen as being responsible for their own distress. (Thus, Young noted he could not find the word unemployment used earlier than the sixties; overpopulation was the preferred form.)[10] So in the most practical aspects of social affairs—the assignment of governing powers to bodies within the nation—one can see played out the contradiction between the middle-class commitment to universality, which implies a need for a kind of centralized regulation, and its equal commitment to individuality, which is liable to conflict with this.

As a narrator of this situation, Eliot is a kind of Mme. Beck. She runs a school maintained by a constant surveillance that in itself constitutes its conception of education. It appears that one must first submit the individual to the supervision figured in the conception of society as a whole. Then, and only then, can the thought of social change be entertained. By this principle radical social change and even radical social thought of any kind is outlawed categorically. They are characterized as the dreams of romance. One ends up in that territory to which Thackeray passively was led, he said, by "the destiny of his narrative": a territory in which one finds on one side "Self and Ambition and Advancement; and Right and Love on the other."[11] In a time when the new role of the inspector had become a focal point in the "condition of England" question, the call for supervision also appears in the form of this artistic practice, which may serve to reveal how the liberal humanitarianism of this Age of Reform was a rigorous social law, the promotion of sympathetic feeling an ideological construction, and the observation of individuals the rhetoric of this ideology.

It should be added that in Eliot's emphasis on the scene of suffering as the paradigm for all social discourse, there is a strong relationship to the Evangelical emphases on suffering conversion and sacrificial duty familiar to Eliot from her youthful religious attachments. Indeed, the early letters she wrote when she was still under this Evangelical influence are filled with adjurations against "this world of egotism" (L, 1: 145) and with discussions of the need for self-abasement, just as they are also filled with appeals to feeling that resemble those in her later writing. This relationship certainly enters into the topics of her fiction and into the imagery with which she described psychological development, yet Eliot's conception of suffering remains quite distinct from the Puritan or Dissenting.

First, there is the consideration that suffering as she defined it serves as a passage from the improper conception of the individual to that of the individual in society. Despite the religious idiom given it, the function of suffering in her work is opposed to any movement of the individual toward a spiritual transcendence of the world. It follows the general principle of humanization in her work that leads her to picture "human beings who never saw angels or heard perfectly clear messages" (R, 1: 343) and to image as romance representations contrary to this order of figuration.[12] What the experience of suffering brings is a social circumscription of the self, the translation of the self into a social figure, and thus the discovery—in what are represented to be the most minutely detailed and individual of circumstances—that every object of perception, everything given to Eliot's representation, is a figure turned to the ideal of society as a whole.

Moreover, it is important to remember that suffering is not only an expectation of the Evangelical conception of duty but also a characteristic of the feminine vocation in this age, and a characteristic as well of the capitalist imperative toward self-denial, which was being developed in various forms of communication the middle classes hoped would prove influential over the lower. These aspects of her society are transfigured within Eliot's conception of suffering, which turns them into a universal morality by way of natural philosophy and human psychology. For this reason, even though Eliot's emphasis on nursing as a sacred activity might seem to counter the values represented in the traditional invalid heroine of sentimental fiction, this "activity" proves to be no less a passivity before that which is represented to be experience within her writing.

Feeling, the universal figure Eliot represents as the redeeming outgrowth of suffering, is especially interesting when considering the relation of romance to realism in Eliot's fiction. It shows another aspect of their complicity. Eliot describes these arts as being antithetical, but they nevertheless agree in emphasizing feeling over the other conceptions of human faculties current in her time, just as they agree in stipulating the relation of the individual to society as a whole. An examination of this figure shows even more clearly the extent to which Eliot's images of realism and romance were formed by a discourse that by its very structure set the limits to the life imaginable within it. In addition, this examination can show from another angle the reason for the emphasis on the scene of suffering in her work.

As Eliot portrayed it, the antithesis to feeling is not reason as such but the calculating application of reason. "Not calculable by algebra, not deducible by logic, but mysterious, effective, mighty as the hidden process by which the tiny seed is quickened, and bursts forth into tall stem and broad leaf, and flowing tasselled flower" ("JR," 346), feeling operates her conception of society in ordinary human experience. It represents the domestic figuration of her art. At the same time it turns individuals to inwardness, feeling also turns them toward the invisible extension of themselves to the whole society. Opinions are a derivative and unreliable reality in relation to feeling because "naked feelings make haste to clothe themselves in propositions which lie at hand among our store of opinions" so that "to give a true account of what passes within us something else is necessary besides sincerity, even when sincerity is unmixed" (R, 2: 150). By eluding ideological analysis, feeling guarantees the order of Eliot's art even as it promises relief to her readers, who live in a time "when opinion has got far ahead of feeling" ("JR," 282).

As far as Eliot is concerned, feeling is an entirely positive term that serves to pin down the problematic figure of the individual. Feelings such as Timothy's that do not show the "breath of poetry" proper to "tenderly-nurtured unvitiated feeling" (SM, 364-65) simply are marked as "hard" perversions of the norm. Because it fills the vacancy of the individual, feeling is the ground given to all the figures of Eliot's art: characters, landscapes, societies, tropes, and so on.[13] It owes its positivity to the silent figuration of middle-class will as nature, which stands in opposition to the clamoring irrational violence all too common among individuals within Eliot's representations of everyday social life. Thematically and formally, feeling is the figure in Eliot's writing in which the vagrant tendencies inherent in rhetoric are steered to a reassuring identity. In feeling, various representations of opinion are reconciled so as to compose the interiority that produces truth within the sentimentalization of culture that constitutes humanity for the liberal intellectual. Feeling is the artistic substance given to the immaterial limits of Eliot's discourse. In its obscurity, fragility, and sensitivity, feeling represents Eliot's anxious comprehension of this immateriality and yet still serves to forcefully represent the power of supervision over society that Eliot assumed within the conception of her art.

As Eliot's art demands every individual be understood in terms of the circumscriptive ideal of society, so that the freedom of the individual is structured in accordance with social laws that appear as laws of the universe, feeling balks at reason only when it would stop short of this ultimate concern of validating society. Thus, when Eliot says emotion is "obstinately irrational: it insists on caring for the individual" ("JR," 356), it does so by dissolving individuals into the common figure of society while allowing the author to analyze the figure of the individual or of society. It is for its intensive inwardness and extensive mystery, for its transfiguration of society as a whole into individual experience, that feeling is recommended:

> Yet surely, the only true knowledge of our fellow-man is that which enables us to feel with him—which gives us a fine ear for the heart-pulses that are beating under the mere clothes of circumstance and opinion. Our subtlest analysis of schools and sects must miss the essential truth, unless it be lit up by the love that sees in all forms of human thought and work, the life and death struggles of separate human beings. ("JR," 30)

Feeling is individual experience that is not individual but essential and universal, just as individuals in general will be recognized as such only insofar as they recall the figure of society as a whole. Therefore, as previously noted, in her fiction Eliot can trust in an inevitable law of consequences for immoral actions: because this law represents her design for the individual. Feeling is the rhetorical figure in which is grounded this production of morality: "Without this fellow-feeling, how are we to get enough patience and charity towards our stumbling, falling companions in the long and changeful journey?" (AB, 215).

However she may dramatize discoveries of feeling in terms that may seem to appeal to human experience in general, the appeal to feeling in Eliot's writing is always to a framework of discourse and to the ideological points she gave to this in the form of social attitudes, political opinions, historical biases—and the conception of "human experience in general." It is not for nothing that Eliot wrote of "the spiritual police of sentiments or ideal feelings" in *Theophrastus Such*. Born of the scene of suffering, like the word of duty which is its often-times contentious but always complicitous sibling, this word, too, serves to define individuals by erasing the differences that make them stand out against the background of society as a whole:

> But it is not ignoble to feel that the fuller life which a sad experience
> has brought us is worth our own personal share of pain: surely it is
> not possible to feel otherwise, any more than it would be possible for
> a man with cataract to regret the painful process by which his dim
> blurred sight of men as trees walking had been exchanged for clear
> outline and effulgent day. The growth of higher feeling within us is
> like the growth of faculty, bringing with it a sense of added strength:
> we can no more wish to return to a narrower sympathy, than a painter
> or musician can wish to return to his cruder manner, or a philosopher
> to his less complete formula. (*AB*, 547)

Characteristically, in this passage Eliot's argument is suggested to be the physiological, natural, and inevitable end of culture.[14] It is "surely . . . not possible to feel otherwise" than one is led to "feel" within the representations of an artist who indicates the comprehensiveness of her powers by her assured use of the examples of the sophisticated painter or musician and the accomplished philosopher. The passage illustrates in an exemplary form this author arising from the sickroom scene of sad experience to the discovery of her own transcendent art of feeling, just as the sufferer of cataracts is brought to a cure to represent the higher ideals of cultural refinement.

Eliot knew there was fog in this language of feeling. She conceived it to be necessary—a pragmatic mystification. It is the humanistic equivalent to the appeal to authority by which the orthodox may be induced to cling to religious belief.[15] As such, it is comparable to Dickens's characteristic paradox that one sees most clearly through eyes blurred with tears, and indeed serves to manufacture a like sentimentality. As Eliot would say, "Thank heavens, then, that a little illusion is left to us, to enable us to be useful and agreeable" (*AB*, 15). This fog is the image of thought in process because the fable of improvement assumed within the liberal intellectual's conception of reason requires that any stipulation of meaning be blurred around the edges by a recognition of temporality that is also an acknowledgment of the social identity that must always lie hidden in interiority. Thus it is that Eliot would describe how all love "at its highest flood rushes beyond its object, and loses itself in the sense of divine mystery" (*AB*, 32). In this passage she converted a theological mystery to a humanistic idiom just as she did, for instance, when she made Felix Holt appear to Esther "as if he belonged to the solemn admonishing skies, checking her self-satisfied pettiness with the suggestion of a wider life" (*FH*, 366).

Still, there remains the question of why it is the language of analytic calculation that is opposed to the language of feeling. This was a conventional opposition in English writing at least since Burke's time, but the fact of this conventionality does not explain the way it was used in Eliot's fiction, in which this scientific vision is dramatically obscured by the mists that shroud the summit to which feeling is supposed to lead humankind. At the very time when "an increase in . . . methods of measuring, counting, and observing . . . may be taken as the most distinctive and original feature of the age,"[16] and in the writing of an author evidently committed to scientific reasoning and opinion in her fiction as in her other writing, why does feeling become a language so insistently opposed to this sort of measurement?

The reason may be found by observing what language is produced by this marking of difference between the languages of feeling and of science, and the first point to note in this regard is that the "arithmetical considerations" ("JR," 356) to which Eliot opposes the "irrationality" of feeling or emotion are not ultimately opposed to it. Eliot is clearly being ironic in saying feeling is irrational, so the first consequence of this opposition between feeling and science is just this: an ironic positioning of the author in relation to her material.

As previously noted, this deployment of the text is also accomplished in other ways. However, all of them may be seen to bear a relation to this calculated subordination of science to feeling, in which Eliot assumes a superior position in relation to her readership just as she does in relation to her image of romance. The effect of irony created by the opposition of these terms of feeling and science gives Eliot's writing the appearance of self-conscious control that she gains elsewhere by the device of reflecting on the incapacities of language. As science is opposed to feeling within Eliot's art only when its limited application is made to threaten the overawing reference of feeling, the judicious supervision of science thus marked serves to elevate Eliot even above her own sanctified language of feeling. Paradoxically, it serves to make that language appear all the more powerful.

So it is not science, analysis, or philosophy as such that opposes feeling. Opposition to the language of feeling is posed when such languages become the language of interest, whether that be narcissistic self-interest—as in Eliot's image of romantic feeling—or limited social or technical interest. In either case, the mysterious margins of life are blotted out by some variety of assertion that Eliot considers to be so much lumber in the eyes of individuals. For example, in Lydgate's case it is not his medical enthusiasm as such that is at fault but the fact that in his search for the fundamental tissue of life he takes his technical interest to be unlimited in its scope in his life, just as Casaubon does with his search for the "Key to All Mythologies." As far as Eliot was concerned, the failures of these figures are not so much epistemological or historical as they are moral. Their parallel quests would not have been given such significance in *Middlemarch* if it were not for their similar engrossment in these occupations at the expense of others' lives: at the expense of the space of sentimental feeling opposed to the space of competition, romantic or capitalistic.

The opposition in Eliot's writing between feeling and calculating reason, then, is rather more complex than the opposition developed along more traditional lines in Mill's *Autobiography* or Dickens's *Hard Times*. In Eliot's hands, this historical opposition is not interpreted in terms of a division of human faculties or of social interests, but in terms of the structuring of meaning in society, which Eliot took to be forever displaced from any specific social site. In Eliot's conception, it is displaced even from her own person as an author, as one can see in the ironic juxtaposition of her historical quest in *Middlemarch* to Lydgate's and Casaubon's projects. Epistemological and historical problems are allowed within her narrative project just as they are within the projects of these characters, but her moral consciousness appears quite different from theirs as a result of this cultured impression of irony given to her writing.

The opposition between feeling and science serves to produce the image of culture as the truth of society while also producing the appearance of Eliot as an author who transcends her own language. Therefore, the traditional opposition between feeling and science is used to nullify all marks of opposition within her writing. It even nullifies those marks that might be constituted by the emphasis of a particular language, such as that of feeling. Instead there is a structuring of meaning in which the absence of absolute regulation—theological, scientific, linguistic, or otherwise—forces meaning to return to the transfigurations of the individual into society and of society into the individual. Thus it is that meaning is turned away from all statements except the statement of Eliot's method of reason.

So the opposition between feeling and science does not assert a division in meaning. It establishes a supervision of meaning, or a process of interpretation, in which meaning is always ceded to the cultural ends of society. As science is made to defer to feeling, so are all the terms of Eliot's art—including "feeling"—subjected to the overriding form of that art figured in feeling. Feeling can be the ground of figuration in Eliot's art, the bottom to individuality, because it is opposed even to itself within its structuring as a figure. It is no accident that Eliot so often figures feeling in artistic terms and so allows her writing to be poised upon the boundary of its own birth.

To be sure, feeling is opposed to science so that science may be subordinated. More importantly, though, it is opposed so that a sense of irony may be produced that seems to situate the production of meaning in the continuous displacement of the text—and of society—into culture. It is by means of this irony that it seems only natural in Eliot's fiction that the feelings said to be within individuals are always found beyond them and can be made coincident with their consciousness only through the experience of suffering, which leads to individual "growth." To put it simply, this irony is a name for the necessity of the antithesis between romance and realism in the articulation of Eliot's realism. It is the groundless assumption necessary to the establishment of the grounds of her art. It is the assumption of form that marks Eliot's un-consciousness of herself and so it may seem to turn her writing into formless, transcendent feeling.

The significance of this opposition between feeling and science can be seen very well in *Felix Holt*. It has been noted that the real opposition to Felix is not posed by the social system he supposedly wants to reform, for he is able to analyze and measure its faults, but by the workers who want to pursue their claims against society, when he would have them first purge themselves of self-interest. Despite its lack of congruence with the history of working-class politics in the early nineteenth century, this situation makes perfect sense within Eliot's writing because the difference between Felix and the other workingmen, like the difference between Felix and the actual "Moral Force" Chartists with which the novel associates him, takes society as it may be conceived both within and without the novel and places it under the ironic displacement that is culture. In opposition to the "gossamer irony" of romance, which Eliot represents as being exerted within society to elevate certain individuals above it, an irony is forced upon all society to shake it loose from any semblance of ideology into culture's realm of universality. Thus, her own ideologies seem to be inward and invisible truth, or "feeling." The case is the same in the "Address to Working Men, by Felix Holt," which Eliot directed to the actual workingmen of her time, as they were conceived of by the genteel readers of *Blackwood's*. In Eliot's reasoning, Felix Holt is a proper representative of workingmen precisely because he does not represent them, just as feeling does not represent. There is nothing beyond Felix as there is nothing beyond "naked feeling" because these *are* culture as it appears in opposition to ideologies within the transcendent supervision of art. As experience is drawn into inward-ness and inwardness extended into invisibility, feeling is designed to show the limits of representation and to identify individuals with these unbreachable limits.

Feeling, then, is in a word the discourse with which Eliot identified. Within this discourse, individuals must not represent themselves or any limited part of society, as Timothy or the workmen opposed to Felix would. Instead, they must *be* culture. Hence the relation between Eliot's writing and the conservative theory of virtual representation, which opposed demands for the ballot on the grounds that those without the franchise were virtually, or figuratively, represented. In Felix's case in particular, this demand for a utopian transcendence of representation is obvious, as one can see in the way he turns the issue of political representation into a scientific figure dependent on feeling for its ultimate "bottom":

> Now, all the schemes about voting, and districts, and annual
> Parliaments, and the rest, are engines, and the water or steam—the
> force that is to work them—must come out of human nature—out of
> men's passions, feelings, desires. Whether the engines will do good

work or bad depends on these feelings; and if we have false expectations about men's characters, we are very much like the idiot who thinks he'll carry milk in a can without a bottom. (*FH*, 305)

What the language of feeling does not represent in Eliot's fiction, and what it is not meant to represent, are the affective relations consciously held among people. In effect, feeling is the unconsciousness Eliot imposes upon her characters and forces into consciousness in the select among them who are allowed to "grow." By this means she is able to remain unconscious of the power involved in her assumption of authorship.

From this description, feeling begins to sound like that sort of unfettered dream that Eliot rejects in turning away from the desire for transcendence characteristic of romance—and rightly so. It is the dream of culture, which was implicitly and explicitly transferred within Eliot's writing from its traditional identification with the manners and members of the upper classes to its modern identification with intellect and intellectuals. It is the implication of romance in realism, a make-believe of a beginning, a fiction of the origin of society. Culture in this modern sense of the word supervises the panorama of society by turning vision inward, to the impalpability of the self, so that this inwardness comes to dominate social reality. Whereas culture in the traditional sense of the term was a show put on by the aristocracy to affirm its own position while awing all outsiders into a position of deference, this modern culture, by a quite different technique of power, makes the outward show of the world vanish within the invisibility and inwardness of a universal identity. For Eliot, feeling is this human identity that is omnipresent but that still must be learned by individuals and drawn out of the *membra disjecta* of society. It must be a thing discovered as the identity of society, not imposed upon society.

This role of feeling is a further elaboration of the complicity between Eliot's art and that which she seems to oppose. Even though she rejects what she sees as the egoism in the way feeling is exalted in romance, her realism agrees with romance in rejecting the limited determinations of identity imposed on the individual in social life. Romance exalts exquisite feeling, and realism, suffering; but both agree in opposing feeling to more limited specifications of identity. Whereas Eliot rejects the notion of the outsider, the individual superior to society, she also rejects any social classifications of individuals in favor of her overriding assertion that the real individual, like the real society, is literally and figuratively in no place. True individuality and cultured feeling and society as a whole are as one in the utopia of culture—represented by her own writing and dramatized through the sickroom scene—in which one finds through the labor of the intellect the transcendence misleadingly conceived in the dreams of romance. In realism as in romance, the appearances and actions of individuals within social life are rejected as any sort of objective determination of their definition or of the definition of society. Society does not define culture or the individual; culture defines both society and the individual. It is thus that culture is the fullest development of the third term—the silent copula of invisibility and inwardness—that solves the problem of relating social parts to social wholes.

When Eliot criticizes feeling, then, it is never because it is excessive. It cannot be so. In the same way that she criticizes calculating reason, she criticizes it when it becomes too limited. Problems arise when it is egoistically focused on the individual—as in the early stages of Dorothea's religious conversion—or focused only on "the nearest" to the individual, so that one "is apt to be timid and sceptical towards the larger aims without which life cannot rise into religion" (*R*, 2: 126-27). Even when dealing with the most sublime aims, though, feeling must enter all and correct all: "There is no general doctrine which is not capable of eating out our morality if unchecked by the deep-seated habit of direct fellow-feeling with independent fellow men" (*M*, 2: 201). The effect is to force into nonexistence any social question that cannot be imaged in the terms of the crucial sickroom scene. Only this scene of suffering, constantly maintained as the end of feeling, can keep individuals from being at odds with one another.

Culture supervises the individual by personalizing society. As a narrator, Eliot is so concerned with the inner lives of her characters—she is a self-described psychological novelist—because to her psychology means the transcendence of social life and relationships. Eliot became such an exemplary novelist of this age because she would not allow individuals to appear except as cultural objects: persons whose consciousness would be defined solely by their relation to the dominant culture represented by her own narrative consciousness. Whereas she would show a Dissenting minister limited by his community or a miller by his parochial ignorance, she would always describe this kind of situation so the characters' identities were taken from their limited articulation within social life and displaced into the space of interiority. Eliot always made her culture the measure of her characters, and thus the source of their representation, even as she dedicated herself to measuring them in terms of their personal, social, and historical circumstances.

That this is so is never more clear than in her pictures of uneducated rural types, for whom—as Eliot would have it—all authority and all established institutions appear as nature. In "Mr. Gilfil's Love-Story," the Knebly farmers "would as soon have thought of criticizing the moon as their pastor," who "belonged to the course of nature, like markets and toll-gates and dirty bank-notes" ("MGL," 88). In *Adam Bede*, the illiterate Bill "would hardly have ventured to deny that the schoolmaster might have something to do in bringing about the regular return of daylight and the changes of the weather" (*AB*, 242), and Arthur Donnithorne appears to Hetty, as all aristocrats are said to have appeared to commoners in those times, as a god. Critics such as John Goode and John Bayley have indicated[17] that this is a cultural and not a historical subjectivity, despite Eliot's insinuation of fiction into the fields of history and sociology. Moreover, Eliot certainly knew culture was the source of the subjectivity given to her fiction in contrast to the evidence of social life. This awareness becomes clear in her letters and essays, in which her picture of the lower classes is much harsher than in most of her fiction, indicating middle-class fears rather than middle-class sentimentality.[18] Within her fiction, the difference in her picture of the laborers in *Felix Holt* from her picture of the peasants in *Middlemarch* or *Adam Bede* or elsewhere exemplifies this cultural split between fear and sentiment. It also exemplifies the way this difference was typically understood in terms of a parallel division between urban and agrarian life, despite the fact that many of the most striking working-class disturbances in the first half of the nineteenth century took place in the countryside.

Eliot's representation of peasants has everything to do with the law that inflicted death upon a nineteen-year-old boy because he knocked off the hat of a prominent financier during the agricultural uprisings of the 1830s but nothing to do with that boy as a historical being.[19] It is middle-class will and no other approach to peasant life that can represent peasants as creatures who regard law as nature and aristocrats as gods in an age that began with a series of widespread agricultural disturbances and continued to see disturbances in the cities—populated to a large extent by workers from the country—throughout the century. One need not conceive of the necessity, possibility, or desirability of "objectively" representing the sort of peasants Eliot undertook to represent to show the politics of her conception of culture. The popularity of Paine's and Cobbett's works early in the century, the lower classes' rumors that the cholera epidemics of 1831, 1848, and 1853 were deliberately spread among them by the upper classes so as to govern them better,[20] and the christening of workhouses as Bastilles all may serve as testimony to a range of consciousness unimaginable in works such as *Scenes of Clerical Life* and *Adam Bede* and even *Felix Holt,* in which the working classes are represented in a manner opposite to the pastoral and yet are just as bereft of intellectual consciousness as within the gentler mode. With her peasants as with all her characters, Eliot's representation comes from an imagination for which reality, announced as making an entrance in all its minute relations and petty details, is in fact supervised by the public mind in which all figures, living or literary, are made into social figures of cultured feeling, tropes of the middle-class intellect.

To grasp the power of this mind one need only turn to the criticism of Eliot's work, which overwhelmingly accepts her representations as telling pictures of social life, in accordance with Eliot's own formulations. Perhaps an even more interesting testimony to this power, though, is furnished by a modern historian, Dorothy Marshall, in one of her descriptions of traditional country squires. She writes, "Few people questioned their authority over their dependents but what the private reactions of the villagers were is more difficult to gauge. Trained to submission and living in a community where tradition was all powerful, it seems likely that they accepted the squire for good or evil in much the same way as country folk accept the weather.''[21] Although Marshall offers considerable qualifications to this statement, one can see resurfacing within it the same figure for peasant consciousness that Eliot used. In fact, the figure is all the more striking because of the extent to which Marshall's writing offers evidence that would lead one to question the assumption of mindlessness implied in it. It seems as if this historian, writing within the modern empirical tradition in which judgments are meant to be objective according to the standards of reasoned argumentation within one's profession, loses her balance when she raises the uncharacteristic question of the "private reactions" of the lower classes. She is drawn to literature, it seems, for a refuge from the implications this question might have for her method.

The point of this example is not simply to indicate the way nineteenth-century fiction may be adopted as nineteenth-century history even by a distinguished historian of our own day but to indicate the politics of representation, literary and historical, in which Eliot's liberal humanism gave her a power that still can appear very modern. There is no reason to fault Eliot's novels for not being history or even to fault history for being novelistic. But it is important to show how the psychological analysis to which Eliot devoted herself is entirely a matter of cultural representations manipulated in the service of middle-class ideologies. They have nothing to do with the analysis of "mind" or of "self" in a purely phenomenological sense (even assuming there is such a sense). They have everything to do with an author's promotion of a culture and with her blindness to her discourse. Questions about the nature of fiction and history as disciplines are implicated in this analysis, especially when one is dealing with the work of a writer who also conceived herself to be a historian in more than a casual sense of the word. However, it is the nature of consciousness within Eliot's writing that is most important in the present context.

This is not to say the "psychological depth" of Eliot's fiction is merely a formal effect. On the contrary, it is to assert that this effect represents a social discipline that may be traced in correlative forms in other fields such as education, charity, government, and academic psychology, such as that represented by Lewes's work on the mind. Moreover, because it is identified with Eliot's grasp of psychology, her conception of realism assumes a position superior to romance in the same way that she, as a narrator, assumes a position superior to her characters.[22] In this aspect of her art, one sees another way the opposition of these genres is designed to produce the effect of truth according to the specific social disciplines developed by the middle classes of Eliot's time.

One must consider, too, that implicit in this psychology of Eliot's realism is a distinction between the inner and the outer lives of human beings that is as radical as Eliot's distinction between individuals and society as a whole. This is another way Eliot's realism is complicitous with her image of romance, in which the drive is entirely to deny the outer world so as to exalt the inner; and here, too, one must understand this distinction as a boundary of Eliot's discourse. In some sense, a consciousness of the world as something radically at variance with and harshly opposed to consciousness may be figured throughout history; but only an idealist view of things can make this "consciousness" and "world" appear identical to themselves in all times and places. In any event, the estrangement of inner from outer reality with which Eliot was concerned is related to the massive economic changes of nineteenth-century English society.

To the middle and upper classes of the time, this separation resulted from the dilation of economic and social horizons to a national scale. This expansion forced an identification with one's family and immediate community to stand in stark contrast to a wider identification with society as a whole. The consequence was the development of a domestic culture that could appear to be an alternative to, or at least a refuge from, those aspects of the wider social life that did not fit the image and values of these classes. The home does not become a castle, and marriage does not become a haven of hypercathected sentimentality, until the impression is fostered by the structure of society that extrafamilial relationships and the work of industry and business no longer include the family and the domestic life of the individual as their basis. This is what nurtured the sentimental values developed in the eighteenth century to their mature flowering in the Victorian period: the fact that the changing nature of society forced out the old meanings of family and marriage and left them ripe for the reception of this new influx of values, which could be taken either to complement or to transcend the values of society in its larger sense. Although one was not compelled to experience this radical psychological division between an inner and an outer self, the popularity of this middle-class psychology is understandable. When adopted and presented as normative, this psychology brilliantly served to ensure that when conflict was felt between the individual and society, social challenge was averted by an emphasis upon the distinct, invisible, mysterious interiority of the self, the home, and—in Eliot's figuring—the sickroom.

This same psychology operates in Eliot's sentimentalization of labor. What matters to the workers whom Eliot lauds is that they do not " 'throw away their tools . . . the minute the clock begins to strike' " (*AB*, 9). Workers such as Adam Bede take their work personally, subjectively, as a source of pleasure and in fact as a metaphor for all behavior and order in life. In the workroom as in the sickroom, relations are simplified so that the individual may be threaded into the social fabric. The workroom, too, serves to create the dynamic interiority of character in Eliot's art as in her society, in which "the idea was still strong in the eighties that there was no way of separating the workers from the worthless, other than by test labour, that is, their reaction to arduous physical work in the stone yard, the parish saw pit, or even the tread mill."[23] As Eliot puts it in commenting on Felix Holt's characteristic fault of being easily angered, " 'Not to waste energy, to apply force where it would tell, to do small work close at hand, not waiting for speculative chances of heroism, but preparing for them'—these were the rules he had been constantly urging on himself" (*FH*, 299). One could instance, too, the case of Caleb Garth, whose "prince of darkness was a slack workman" (*M*, 1: 28) and who succeeds in turning Fred Vincy to the good by teaching him a sense of pride in honest labor.

This conception of work as a craft was already anachronistic even in the earlier times in which Eliot set most of her fiction—not to mention in her own day. The new reality was large-scale manufacture, not guildlike control over and pride in quality. In this respect, too, one sees the purpose of her psychology to be ideological. It is directed toward the consciousness of her characters so that it may be directed away from the organization and material reality of their occupations. Like masochistic feeling and burdensome duty, craft is merely culture in a different aspect. It is the presumption of self-discovery through self-sacrifice that constitutes the running argument of all Eliot's writing.

This is not to say Eliot was unaware of the problems posed by her claim to a subjective sympathy with all humankind that could not be allowed to appear in any form that was not basically subjective or literary. A culture that is all inwardness and invisibility is difficult to sustain in novels that must also claim a faithful and continuous attention to the details of the external world. One sees this difficulty expressed in Eliot's writing as the subjectivity whose recognition she demands is always imprisoned and suffering, in its inwardness and invisibility, against the appearance of the external world. But this is precisely the point: that the culture of the sickroom is not only the image of society as a whole but also the image of the individual soul. Here, again, is the discursive nexus where these two meet. Like the reality of society, the reality of the soul must be discerned within and projected beyond the appearance of outer circumstances. Individuals must be both patient and nurse, both suffering interiority and ministering ideal. It is in this entirely personal and yet entirely selfless relation that individuals must identify themselves and thus make themselves figures of society as a whole. All Eliot's heroes and heroines move toward this allegorical expansion: to incorporate the ends of society in their individual persons. It is significant in this regard that as a narrator Eliot assumes a role as a personal guide to her readers. Even though this evocation of herself as a personal guide does diminish when one moves from the *Scenes of Clerical Life* and *Adam Bede* to her later works, Eliot's omniscient view of things is always given with this tone. She personalizes society in the style as well as in the argument of its representation.

Eliot's understated comment on this state of affairs is that "the tragedy of our lives is not created entirely from within" (*MF*, 427). The elaborate coda at the end of *Middlemarch* presents the matter most complexly. As she writes of Dorothea in relation to her marriages,

> Certainly those determining acts of her life were not ideally beautiful. They were the mixed result of young and noble impulse struggling amidst the conditions of an imperfect social state, in which great feelings will often take the aspect of error, and great faith the aspect of illusion. For there is no creature whose inward being is so strong that

it is not greatly determined by what lies outside it. A new Theresa will hardly have the opportunity of reforming a conventual life, any more than a new Antigone will spend her heroic piety in daring all for the sake of a brother's burial: the medium in which their ardent deeds took shape is forever gone. But we insignificant people with our daily words and acts are preparing the lives of many Dorotheas, some of which may present a far sadder sacrifice than that of the Dorothea whose story we know.

Her finely touched spirit had still its fine issues, though they were not widely visible. Her full nature, like that river of which Cyrus broke the strength, spent itself in channels which had no great name on earth. But the effect of her being on those around her was incalculably diffusive: for the growing good of the world is partly dependent on unhistoric acts; and that things are not so ill with you and me as they might have been, is half owing to the number who lived faithfully a hidden life, and rest in unvisited tombs. (*M*, 2: 427)

Dorothea's is the history of culture, and thus her image is the very image of society. Hers is a history that is unhistoric, an outward pattern of circumstances and events that is inward, a visible life that is invisible, and so, in short, the very essence of a massively influential discourse that shows its repression within representation in this characterization of an isolated figure in an unknown sepulchre. Dorothea is indeed "many Dorotheas," just as the two young people in *The Mill on the Floss* are said to represent many young people, because she is an individual only insofar as she is a figure of society as a whole—even though this figuration must be hidden, the discourse from which it develops turned into unconsciousness. Eliot's novel is, then, a memorial of unknown memorials—"unvisited tombs"—because the cultural ideal of society, like cultured feelings and unlike aristocratic culture, must deny itself any public representation. It must be presented as something wholly inward and invisible even though it is being produced in Eliot's lengthy volumes. It must not be representable but rather the limit of representation itself. Society and feeling show their true selves in the scene of suffering as they do in the grave of this passage because it is there that they appear under the sign of death—beyond history and public representation—while to attempt their realization in the public world of society is to evoke the violence of death and of life.

So it is not surprising that the workingmen in *Felix Holt* who seek political representation for themselves must end up in a scene of rioting and death. On the positive side of the situation, it is not surprising that the Daniel Deronda who had "longed for either some external event, or some inward light, that would urge him into a definite line of action, and compress his wandering energy" (*DD*, 1: 376) should discover his true heritage and the vehicle for his cultural ideals through his rescue of a girl about to commit suicide—in other words, through a sickroom scene. Similarly, Romola finds herself floating on ocean waves and wishing "she could lie down to sleep on them and pass from sleep into death'' (*R*, 2: 127) just before she enters the scene that regenerates her: a plague-stricken village that she will nurse back to health. The scene in which Hetty is reborn in *Adam Bede* also occurs in a kind of sickroom: the prison cell in which she is nursed, literally and figuratively, by Dinah. Silas Marner's Eppie substitutes for his gold and regenerates him after crawling away from her dying mother and presenting herself to him as a creature to be nursed. And in a story written at the very beginning of Eliot's fiction-writing career, Janet Dempster is regenerated through massive overdetermination when she first overhears Reverend Tryan comforting a sick woman by referring to his own symptoms of approaching illness and then cares for him when he is dying after caring for her own dying husband, whose beatings she had previously suffered.

Of course, the most striking incident in this regard is the ending of *The Mill on the Floss*. In it one sees the two figures that may be taken to caricature the text and antitext of all Eliot's writing—the obdurately dutiful realist, Tom, and the transcendentally desiring romantic, Maggie—and one witnesses their entombment together, undivided as Eliot's discourse is meant to be undivided in the inwardness and invisibility of its cultural monumentality. Here is the ultimate complicity of realism and romance. They clasp each other in the grave, in their mutual identification with the ideal of culture that is beyond representation as it is beyond death. And once again this reconciliation and exaltation of culture is figured through a sickroom scene, a scene of suffering, which is prefigured in the novel by the incident in which Tom injures himself with a sword. In the end, Maggie becomes aware of her brother's physical distress and goes to his aid, under Eliot's supervision, and to the accompaniment of Eliot's assurance that ''we are all one with each other in primitive mortal needs'' (*MF*, 553).

Chapter 8
Private Fragments and Public Monuments

The human nature unto which I felt
That I belonged, and reverenced with love
Was not a punctual presence, but a spirit
Diffused through time and space, with aid derived
Of evidence from the monuments, erect,
Prostrate, or leaning towards their common rest
In earth, the widely scattered wreck sublime
Of vanished nations.

Wordsworth, *The Prelude*

In all the volumes of Eliot's collected correspondence, one letter appears radically different in style from the rest. Perhaps there were others as different that are now lost. In any case, in reading the volumes one is impressed by the uniformity of Eliot's style from the time when she was a young woman until the time of her death. Discounting relatively trifling variations, all her correspondence has the formal rigidity of a public monument burdened with that kind of heroic self-consciousness commonly found in park statuary. This aspect of her work might well call to mind J. Bronowski's description of Eliot and other Victorian moralists as persons suffering from "premature immortality."[1] In these letters, no matter what subject or person Eliot was addressing, it seems she might as well have been addressing the public at large.

The dramatic exception is a letter written in 1879 to Johnny Cross, after G. H. Lewes's death but before Eliot remarried Cross. There is no other passage either in her letters or in her fiction that appears so unmistakably personal as this letter. It reads, in part, as follows:

Best loved and loving one—the sun it shines so cold, so cold, when there are no eyes to look love on me. I cannot bear to sadden one moment when we are together, but wenn Du bist nicht da I have often a bad time. It *is* a solemn time, dearest. And why should I complain if it is a painful time? What I call my pain is almost a joy seen in the wide array of the world's cruel suffering. Thou seest I am grumbling today—got a chill yesterday and have a headache. All which, as a wise doctor would say, is not of the least consequence, my dear Madam.

Through everything else, dear tender one, there is the blessing of trusting in thy goodness. Thou dost not know anything of verbs in Hiphil and Hophal or the history of metaphysics or the position of Kepler in science, but thou knowest things of another sort, such as belong to the manly heart—secrets of lovingness and rectitude. O I am flattering. Consider what thou wast a little time ago in pantaloons and back hair. (*L*, 7: 211-12)

The formality of almost all Eliot's extent writing makes sense in terms of her strong concern to keep her personal life hidden from the public in her later years. It was for this reason that she refused to let a correspondent publish her answer to his inquiry about *Daniel Deronda*, arguing that "when anyone who can be called a public person makes a casual speech or writes a letter that gets into print, his words are copied, served up in a work of commentary, misinterpreted, misquoted, and made matters of gossip for the emptiest minds." Therefore, wrote Eliot, "any influence I may have as an author would be injured by the presentation of myself in print through any other medium than that of books" (*L*, 6: 289). Giving much the same reason, she declined to have her face become known through a portrait by an American artist living in London (*L*, 7: 207) and agreed with Mrs. Charles Bray, the wife of the philosopher, that burning "is the most reverential destination one can give to the relics which will not interest any one after we are gone," lest they be made light of or endure the "desecrating fate" of being looked upon "with hard curiosity" (*L*, 7: 340-41). As she wrote to another friend, "My writings are public property: it is only myself apart from my writings that I hold private and claim a veto about as a topic" (*L*, 6: 167). She typically gave this attitude a dogmatic formulation, at once moral and aesthetic, by arguing that "the rewards of the artist lie apart from everything that is narrow and personal" (*L*, 3: 226).

Even given her exacting formulation of this division between personal and public life, however, it is still remarkable that this formal presentation of herself to others—which observers in her later years described as her manner in company as well—was maintained in so much writing produced over such a great time span. One needs to read her correspondence from beginning to end to appreciate how startling this break in her formal style really is. To borrow a phrase Eliot employed in describing the sight of a human face "with all a heart's agony in it, uncontrolled by self-consciousness," the effect of this letter might be to make us feel "as if we had suddenly waked into the real world of which this every-day one is but a puppet-show copy" ("JR," 339). Read in the context of her other writing, this letter might seem a fragment of open feeling in a monument of impersonality.

One might then notice that a line of formal morality enters into even this fragment. "What I call my pain," Eliot writes, "is almost a joy seen in the wide array of the world's cruel suffering." This is a line typical of her other letters and of the enlightenment the characters in her novels are made to experience. Therefore, in this line one may see this fragment fractured, as it were, by the pressure of the monument in which it is embedded. It would seem that even in this most intimate of addresses, Eliot could not help but adjust her consciousness to the world at large, if only for a moment. And the fact that the world should be so much with her even in this private address may appear just as remarkable as the formal control she appears to have maintained over herself in her other letters and in her fiction, in which her transcendent supervision of her characters is constituted of such extremely rigorous rhetorical conditions.

Moreover, her address to Cross is made in the form of one of the most popular codes of Victorian romance: that of the male lover who dismisses his beloved's intellect while elevating the appeal of her sensibility. Although in this case the sexes are reversed, the code is adhered to. It is lifted whole from the culture of Eliot's time yet communicated as if it were unique to her private relationship with the "manly heart" of Cross. In itself this situation is perfectly ordinary, as language is always social and cannot be thought of as communication except in terms that exclude the notion of absolute originality; but still the recognition of this code will make the letter appear to be less exceptional than it otherwise might appear at first glance.

This sense of conventionality is reinforced if one realizes from a reading of Eliot's fiction and letters that she presented herself as one who believed in the code that made women especially gifted with spiritual refinement rather than intellect.[2] She wrote, quoting from *The Winter's Tale*, "as a fact of mere zoological evolution, woman seems to me to have the worse share in existence. But for that very reason I would the more contend that in the moral evolution we have 'an art which does mend nature'. It is the function of love in the largest sense, to mitigate the harshness of all fatalities" (*L*, 4: 364). Given this perspective, not only is the private feeling of Eliot's writing represented by the adoption of a public code but Eliot's sexual transformation of that code does not appear original. Apparently there would be no significance to this transformation greater than its indication of a calculated variation of a rule. There would seem to be no substantial transformation of the meaning of gender, as it was conceived within this cultural code, but at most a rhetorical reversal already well rehearsed in the culture at large, as one can see in the depiction of feminized characters like Dobbins in *Vanity Fair* and Joe in *Great Expectations*.

This recognition that Eliot was writing in the most public of voices in what otherwise might be the most private of communications is further reinforced if one considers how her personal feeling is indicated by the informal use of the "thou" form—as it was later used, for instance, in D. H. Lawrence's novels. Although this usage appears informal and is unexampled elsewhere in Eliot's letters, its service in the cause of expressing love was entirely conventional. This usage was a formal code for informality.

Again, there is nothing novel about this understanding of Eliot's language—unless one has been struck by the appearance of this letter within her work and so has been led to desire an understanding of just what it is that distinguishes this "personal" letter from Eliot's "public" writings. After all, Eliot did formulate this categorical difference as an important one throughout her writings. Moreover, readers and critics are forever making judgments about authors like Eliot on the basis of their impression of the difference of the individual author from the general culture.

Finally, since this letter does appear different from Eliot's public writings and yet does not reveal a meaning that differs from the culture with which she publicly identified herself, it would seem that it is the mixed and disjointed nature of the writing in this letter—its fragmentariness—that most strongly conveys the individual and the private occasion. Although none of the features of this letter would appear remarkable if they were to be interspersed within the rest of her correspondence, they give the impression of a private meaning because of the scattershot style with which they are flung together upon the page. They seem to reveal a haste and spontaneity that have overwhelmed all concern with the usual proprieties of writing. This impression suggests Eliot as a person is represented most directly by the faults or cracks in her writing, by the breaks between her lines and idioms, or by the division between this letter and the generality of her correspondence—a division in which the meaning of her writing appears discomposed. It is not in its substantial difference from the public world but in its fragmentation of this world that this letter—or any example of Eliot's writing—may be said to express the personal feeling of an individual human subject. In other words, in Eliot's writing desire shows itself as a monument in fragments.

There would be no point to these observations if Eliot had not committed herself as an author to such a strong distinction between private and public selves that desire cannot appear in her writing except as a disruption of communication and personal identity must seem a demolishment of public order. The fact that Eliot elevated this common contrast within the discourse of her time to such a level of strict necessity is one of the more important influences on her representations of social history, in which the appearance of human life is regulated by boundaries to discourses such as this one. This influence is evident in the way images of fragmentation in people and objects are frequent in her fiction and are related to expressions of personal desire like that which is obvious in the fragmentariness of this letter. This is the enlightenment her characters must suffer: that personal desires can be wholly satisfied only within the imagination, can find expression in the public world only in a fragmentary form. As Eliot conceived her role as an artist to be an eminently public one entrusted with a religious social responsibility, there was expressed in her conception of this role a consciousness of public life, or a demand on the part of public life in contrast to the category of private life, that would have to be brought home to her characters in the form of this fragmentation if they were to be allowed to function as moral agents. This contrast is another aspect of the figural grounds of her realism. It is another break in that surface of reflection to which she attributed the unbroken qualities—comprehensiveness, transcendence, harmonious power, and so on—of the liberal intellectual.

Although it occurs throughout Eliot's fiction, in *Middlemarch* the imagery of fragmentation raised by this division between the private and the public is especially pervasive. Lydgate quarrels with Rosamond and finds that thenceforth "life must be taken up on a lower stage of expectation, as it is by men who have lost their limbs" (*M*, 2: 235), as Eliot says in one of her better jokes. Similarly, having learned of her husband's secret shame, Mrs. Bulstrode "needed time to get used to her maimed consciousness, her poor lopped life, before she could walk steadily to the place allotted her" at his side (*M*, 2: 337). When he is surprised by Dorothea Brooke in a position that suggests a compromising attachment between himself and Rosamond, Will Ladislaw is described as having "no more foretaste of enjoyment in the life before him than if his limbs had been lopped off and he was making a fresh start on crutches" (*M*, 2: 392). Dorothea is first introduced to the reader as a fragment—"a fine quotation from the Bible,—or from one of our elder poets,—in a paragraph of to-day's newspaper" (*M*, 1: 5)—and because she does not show herself to be aware of this fragmentary condition she, too, must experience a ruin of her early hopes that does not appear completely recuperated even in her eventual marriage to Will. As Eliot wrote in *The Mill on the Floss*, in words that might apply to all her fiction, "To the eyes that have dwelt on the past, there can be no thorough repair" (*MF*, 557).

Eliot's eyes are always dwelling upon the past, and in doing so they observe for the benefit of her readers that a vision of the past must result in a consciousness of fragmentation in the present. Eliot seems compelled to this observation within her writing, in which desire looks as if it might have been perfectly satisfying in the individual or social past precisely because it finds itself shattered against the public world of the present. In other words, the past may don an ideal garb because its completed and emotionally distanced nature, in contrast to the yearning and pulsating nature of desire, leads the individual to resist the perception of any necessary form in the present.

This is the point of the contrast Eliot drew at the beginning of *Middlemarch* between St. Theresa and Dorothea and between the epic and the novel. In Eliot's scheme of things, the historical change she sketched in this contrast is really not a change at all. That it may appear as such is testimony to the naïveté of the sort of historical imagination that views fragments from the past as perfectly finished monuments. After all, it is important to remember that St. Theresa's reforms were ultimately in the service of a cause—Catholicism—that *Middlemarch* suggests was erroneously conceived, injuriously executed, and destined to become moribund. *Middlemarch* does not show Eliot conceiving that the epic represents a better reality than that found in the modern novel but rather thinking that this genre, like all works of romance, reveals a more satisfying world because it is inferior to the novel in its representation of reality.

Hence the import in *Middlemarch* of the pivotal image of Rome, "the city of visible history," a place of "stupendous fragmentariness," its "unintelligible" weight "a vast wreck of ambitious ideals, sensuous and spiritual, mixed confusedly with the signs of breathing forgetfulness and degradation" (*M*, 1: 201-2). This is the place where Dorothea learns that the sacred text she had imagined Casaubon to be is in fact such a fragmented manuscript as his own "Key to All Mythologies" turns out to be. Consequently, she finds that the fulfillment her desires had identified in the past was an illusion and that they are destined to appear in a state of suffering fragmentation. Rome is not Rome but a shattered image of itself, virtually an incoherent image of fragmentation pure and simple; and so are all the environments of Eliot's characters liable to appear transfigured into a meaningless jumble of objects when it becomes evident that they never could have been made to conform perfectly to the desires of any individual. Rome is exceptional only in the imaginary promise of monumental unity that it has held forth to all humankind in the past, a promise mocked by its modern appearance as by every situation in which Eliot's fictional characters find bits of their being eroded by the unresponsiveness of the world.

Nevertheless, because it is revealed to the individual in the form of a negation, this realization that the public world is always insufficient in relation to private desire impresses on the individual the imaginary appearance of a past in which the world was whole, in contrast to a present time of shattered prospects. In Eliot's writing this is the structure of individual memory as well as the structure of social history. It is the tortuous logic she teases from the romantic nostalgia of her age. Because of the negative relation in which Eliot's writing makes public stand to private life, this same recognition that exposes the illusions of the past still makes the naïveté of that past seem to have been more satisfying, however illusory that satisfaction may have been. It is thus that desire in Eliot's writing turns on the romantic figure of contrast between past and present.

Through this figure, fragmented scenes and characters alike appear in Eliot's writing as the stuff of her historical consciousness. In accordance with this figuring, Lisbeth Bede finds herself after her husband's death "like one who has been deposited sleeping among the ruins of a vast city" (*AB*, 107-8). Similarly, in *Middlemarch*, when Rosamond's desires are rebuffed by Lydgate she finds "her little world . . . in ruins" and feels herself "tottering in the midst of a lonely bewildered consciousness" (*M*, 2: 369). In effect, the Rome of *Middlemarch*, the desolate Lisbeth of *Adam Bede*, and a host of like characters and scenes throughout Eliot's fiction compose the same figure. They all represent this fragmentation of desire in the consciousness of history that resulted from the discourse Eliot adopted in her role as an author.

As Eliot presents it, this fragmentation is the figure of the present in her art from which she reflects upon the past and looks to the future. The sight of

Rome in its present condition is simply overwhelming, just as her characters in their shattered moments are so overwhelmed that they cannot grasp the unity of the past and yet cannot envision a different future, and it is Eliot's intention to evoke this figure of the present and then to reconstruct it into a modern monument. As Eliot once comforted a friend about the "shock" given her by Rome and advised her "to get to some point of view from which one can see the distant hills—the everlasting hills one may call them by comparison with that changing surface of man's creation" (*L*, 7: 155), it is indeed the aim of her art to figure its perspective as one that is everlasting and comprehensive.

One does not go far beyond Eliot's own imagery, then, and not at all beyond her constant themes, in saying that all her major characters must find themselves in a state of fragmentation. From the very beginning of her career in fiction, one of Eliot's favorite ways of describing the entrance of characters into maturity was to represent them in ruins. In "Janet's Repentance," she compared Janet to "a glorious Greek temple, which, for all the loss it has suffered from time and barbarous hands, has gained a solemn history, and fills our imagination the more because it is incomplete to the sense" ("JR," 320). The image is more conventionally picturesque than that of Rome in *Middlemarch*, but the impression is that the attainment of maturity—the self-consciousness that is also a consciousness of history—reduces one to the status of a monument in fragments. Hence the ending of *The Mill on the Floss*, in which "the complex, fragmentary, doubt-provoking knowledge which we call truth" (*MF*, 487) is figured in the deathly and yet culturally redeeming flood: "Huge fragments, clinging together in fatal fellowship, made one wide mass across the stream" (*MF*, 556).[3] Maggie and Tom Tulliver merely duplicate this description in their dying embrace, in which these fragmented characters reclaim an imaginary lost unity. It is not surprising, then, to find that in her early letters Eliot judged her own quest for maturity in this imagery: "I have been rather humbled in thinking that if I were thrown on an uncivilised island and had to form a literature for its inhabitants from my own mental stock how very fragmentary would be the information with which I could furnish them" (*L*, 1: 108). Just as the sickroom scene figures in her fiction as the locus of naked feeling and just as the consciousness of imperfection is made the measure of perfection in humankind throughout her writing, so, too, does this imagery of fragmentation figure as an indication of the comprehensiveness of one's sympathetic vision of things.

Of course, in Janet Dempster's case there is the fact that she physically suffers from the barbarous hands of her drunken husband. However, this sort of physical degradation is really beside the point of Eliot's imagery of suffering fragmentation. This imagery is directed to Eliot's overwhelming conviction that a mature consciousness must find in the present the shattering of monumental dreams raised by the past. It does not matter whether these dreams involved the egoism of a childhood in which "the outer world seemed only an extension of our own personality'' (*MF*, 162), the airy castles of a lover's imagination, or any kind of error into which one may be led because one's reasoning proves to have an admixture of personal desire. Whatever the particular circumstances may be, the images of fragmentation in Eliot's writing all suggest the fate of the modern world itself as those who belong to it look upon the past and find its temples defiled, its productions fallen to bits, its schemes of faith and order wrecked by the advance of time.

Ultimately, as far as Eliot was concerned, all these dreams are of a piece. All suggest the world could have the nature of a monument; all Eliot's writing suggests that even monuments which seem perfectly flawless are in reality composed of fragments. Living without this realization, people are likely to be conscious only of the present moment and are therefore likely to be shattered when they learn this moment is but a fleeting aspect of the structure of time, which decomposes the very perception of the moment. "The moment" in this phenomenological sense—as a perception of time in terms of the qualities of wholeness, coherence, and stability—is the temporal equivalent to Eliot's spatial imagery of monumentality and to her social imagery of consensus. It contains its fragmentation as a condition of its existence, or as a mark of a refractory human ignorance, and can be made real only through the recognition of this condition. Thus, a well-versed reader in Eliot's writing may know enough to beware when Don Silva in *The Spanish Gypsy*, in love with Fedalma, feels completely fulfilled in "each momentary Now" (*P*, 146).[4]

It was not exceptional—it was even characteristic—for a writer in Eliot's age to figure the present as a fragmentation of the past. One could take this to be a positive event, as material progress and a release from the shackles of class and religion and politics, a negative event, as a desecration of hallowed tradition, or some combination of the two. In any case, this consciousness of a peculiarly modern fragmentation of a timeless past was an assumption of the discourse of Eliot's time and had been so since the later years of the eighteenth century. One can instance Wordsworth's description of "the widely scattered wreck sublime / Of vanished nations" or Carlyle's "Characteristics," in which he wrote, "The Beginning of Inquiry is Disease: all Science, if one considers well, as it must have originated in the feeling of something being wrong, so it is and continues to be but Division, Dismemberment, and partial healing of the wrong."[5] Or there is the comment Hawthorne made in reference to the British Museum: "The fact is, the world is accumulating too many materials for knowledge. We do not recognize for rubbish what is really rubbish . . . and as each generation leaves its fragments and potsherds behind it, such will finally be the desperate conclusion of the learned."[6] Examples of the use of this sort of figure abound in the literature, social commentary, and casual documents of this age. What is of more interest in the present context is the way Eliot transfigured this common trope for historical consciousness into the very nature of her characters' lives.

Insofar as these characters are granted maturity—and insofar as Eliot's readers come to an understanding with her—what they learn is to see in their lives this figuration of the historical process. As Eliot wrote in a passage that epitomizes this process by which individuals suffer fragmentation in the world and recomposition by the author, "We see human heroism broken into units and say, this unit did little—might as well not have been. But in this way we might break up a great army into units; in this way we might break the sunlight into fragments" (FH, 191-92).

Eliot is writing in reference to Reverend Lyon, so one can see how she represents her consciousness of history while dwelling on the individual life. This representation is made whenever she reflects on the nature of the characters she depicts. She pauses in her narrative, as it were, to hold them up to the reader to show the universal history faintly but definitely illuminating their every action, gesture, and cell. For all their ordinariness, for all the precise description devoted to their appearances, manners, thoughts, attitudes, activities, and desires, they are this intellectual abstraction: Eliot's historical consciousness.

Eliot's representation of any character at any moment in time is always systematically subordinated in importance to the lesson that no such moment should be taken by her readers, whether in the novel or in parallel instances within their own lives, to be a conclusive index to character or to the truth of things in general. The distinction between private and public life that fragments the appearance of desire in Eliot's writing is made the stuff of human nature by way of this scheme of mediation in which all the features of Eliot's discourse appear as if they were born of reason. It is for this reason that she adds a "Finale" at the end of a novel already as expansive as *Middlemarch*, reminding her readers that "the fragment of a life, however typical, is not the sample of an even web" because "promises may not be kept, and an ardent outset may be followed by declension; latent powers may find their long-awaited opportunity; a past error may urge a grand retrieval" (M, 2: 420).

What Eliot wants to impress on her characters, as on her readers, is a historical consciousness that makes such an allowance for the past and the future as to suspend every judgment of the present in the ideal process of mediation that serves as her museum walls to the images, works, and events of the moment. To this author for whom "every single object suggests a vast sum of conditions," characters are composed in the same way: "it is surely the same with the observation of human life" (MF, 289). As she worded her conclusion about this situation in another passage, "It belongs to every large nature, when it is not under the immediate power of some strong unquestioning emotion, to suspect itself, and doubt the truth of its own impressions, conscious of possibilities beyond its own horizon" (R, 1: 257). It is thus that character is fragmented by the historical consciousness that regards it as "a process and an unfolding" (M, 1: 154). Its appearance at any particular moment is viewed only as the manifestation of "a possible self" (*DD*, 1: 138), and yet it is recomposed as an intellectual figure by the mediation enjoined on the observer by this consciousness. Individuals become the fragmented stuff of Eliot's art as well as its unifying spirit because their nature is that of her own historical consciousness. This consciousness is construed as universal and so may make the rhetorical features of Eliot's discourse—like this distinction between private and public life—seem only natural, according to a rational understanding. The physical, emotional, and spiritual wounds of Eliot's characters, like the fragmentation Eliot applies to Rome in *Middlemarch*, are the manifestations in the form of experience of this method of reasoning.

In the service of this historical consciousness, Eliot will subject her view of humanity to temporal correction: "I, at least, hardly ever look at a bent old man, or a wizened old woman, but I see also, with my mind's eye, that Past of which they are the shrunken remnant" ("MGL," 95). This view will also be submitted as a moral correction: "The trivial erring life which we visit with our harsh blame, may be but as the unsteady motion of a man whose best limb is withered" ("MGL," 217-18). Moreover, as the Finale to *Middlemarch* indicates, the same process of correction must be projected into the future. In all representations of character in Eliot's fiction, the result is the same. She wants to impress on her readers, and on her enlightened characters, that the world is neither a monumental image of perfection nor a mere chaos of fragmented desire but rather a monument of fragments to be composed within one's consciousness of history. Consequently, in Eliot's reasoning, one ought to take any judgment on circumstances as well as any desire felt in any circumstances and adjust their exercise to the consideration that the present is bound to be different from the past and the future.

Such a conclusion may seem unremarkable enough, even if one is aware of the hysterical extension of this line of thinking in the inability of Hardy's Little Father Time to enjoy the sight of flowers because he knows they will eventually wither. Even if it is a difficult lesson to learn, as Eliot maintains, it might seem only natural that a consciousness of time as a process of change should replace the "constant, spontaneous pulsing of . . . self-satisfaction" (*DD*, 1: 258) in individuals who are granted maturity. Even if one sees in this taxing approach to the present moment and to personal desire an idealized version of the temporality and ethics promoted by middle-class business and industry, this coincidence might be discounted by means of a common argument: that human beings are distinguished from animals because they have a consciousness of the past and so can gain perspective upon the present and take a calculating approach to the future. In this way Eliot's writing would seem to embody universal human truths, just as she would have hoped. Her conception of culture as the leading distinction of humanity would actually appear to be the imperative basis of education on every level, from that of the most trivial manners to that of the highest intellectual scholarship.

The problem with such an approach to Eliot's writing is that at this abstract level—precisely the level to which Eliot's own formulations lead the reader—there is no accounting for the motivation of the argument. If what she dramatizes in her writing is in fact the very nature of humanity, why should the revelation of this nature be such a shattering experience to her characters? Why should it be necessary to demonstrate that desire is fragmented by a consciousness of history if in fact this consciousness is definitive of humanity? One might reply that "humanity" to Eliot is always a relative term forever subject to improvement, to a greater consciousness of itself; but in so doing one would make clear how this term finally appears purely technical. It emerges as a "god-term" inserted into her writing so as to make it seem to have the coherence it cannot possess. It obscures the fact that the line her writing draws between consciousness and unconsciousness, like the line it draws between public and private life, is always arbitrary and unsystematic.

Even if one accepted Eliot's community so far as to accept this term of humanity as a heuristic mystification, the question remains why her intellectual consciousness should take on this specific imagery of fragmentation and monumentality, private desire and public mutilation, rather than any of the other thematic patterns one could imagine being applied to her method of reasoning. Therefore, one could reformulate this same question recalling Eliot's letter to Cross, that fragment so dramatically isolated in the monument of her correspondence, so private and yet so public in its every line: what could be the meaning of this?

A biographer might account for the interminable mediation of judgment in Eliot's conception of historical consciousness by characterizing it as a result of the break from strict Evangelical religion that formed such an "epoch" in her life, to use her own terminology. Or, more subtly, a biographer might perceive in her early life a pattern of commitment and apostasy in relation to various ends that gave way in her later years to a compensatory manner of tentative or conservative judgment. Certainly Eliot's letters and her fiction show a great aversion to the "narrow" judgments typical of Evangelical religion in her time, and one might broaden the relevance of this consideration with the fact that Herbert Spencer, among others, described Eliot's temperament as an almost too " 'quickly forgiving' " one resolutely opposed to " 'harsh judgments'."[7]

Just as the humanistic explanation is too broad, this one is too narrow. Whatever the evidence may be for such a biographical interpretation, by itself it cannot account for the fact that Eliot's conception of character in terms of this historical consciousness proved so influential among her readers and can be seen by the student of this period as an exemplary formulation of the ideals of the liberal intellectuals of this time. Whatever the biographical interest of Eliot's writings may be, to understand them it is necessary to consider why this novel presentation of character should make sense in nineteenth-century England. For it *is* novel, at least in appearance, and therefore in some respect must have been received in terms of other codes already established in the culture of her day. Although Scott popularized the novel based on historical event and informed with a theory of historical change, there is nothing in his novels or in any English novels prior to Eliot's like this systematic construction of character as a theory of history and of historical epistemology. One must look beyond purely literary effects to find the implications this representation of things could have had for Eliot and her readers.

Of course, even in regard to her completed novels Eliot was humble, seeing within them a fragmentary form. In reference to *Romola*, she wrote, "my predominant feeling is,—not that I have achieved anything, but—that great, great facts have struggled to find a voice through me, and have only been able to speak brokenly" (*L*, 4: 97). The modesty illustrates the lesson about the fragmentation of desire embodied in her fiction and also shows the tension between Duty and Right, imperative morality and personal will or desire, drawn through her conception of authorship. What needs to be analyzed is why Eliot should believe "a religious and moral sympathy with the historical life of man" is "the larger half of culture" (*L*, 4: 97) and what she could possibly mean in expressing such a sentiment. The question is why a historical consciousness was so sacred to Eliot that she made it the very nature of the characters in her fiction.

Take the example of the very first line of Eliot's first story, "The Sad Fortunes of the Reverend Amos Barton," which advises her readers that "Shepperton Church was a very different-looking building five-and-twenty years ago" ("AB," 3). All her writing is informed with this kind of attention to historical change, but it is not change in the abstract or even changes in appearance that most preoccupy it; as Eliot describes it, what most separates her modern world from the world of the past is precisely the consciousness of history as such. She does not present this consciousness merely as the leading aspect of culture but as a novel aspect of society as a whole. According to Eliot, history simply did not exist as a part of the life of most people in society before the changes that came to England in the nineteenth century. The dividing line may not be exact and not precisely the same for every part of England, but sometime in the first third of the nineteenth century a change took place. Before this time men were conscious only of nature or of the phenomena of social life as aspects of nature, while temporality was absorbed by tradition. It is only with the modern world that change becomes recognized as a dynamic force in society so that history may take the place of nature in the minds of men: such is the import of the opening sentence of "Amos Barton," once one reads it in the light of the rest of the story. It is only with modernity that the world becomes intellectual.

Thus Eliot describes the Knebly farmers who "would as soon have thought of criticizing the moon as their pastor" and contrasts to a more modern town "the Boeotian Knebly," where "men's minds and wagons alike moved in the deepest of ruts, and the landlord was only grumbled at as a necessary and unalterable evil, like the weather, the weevils, and the turnip-fly" ("MGL," 88, 90). Similarly, Adam Bede, "not being a philosopher, or a proletaire with democratic ideas," responds to rank as to a dispensation of nature, regards craftsmanlike work as a natural duty, and in general is inclined "to admit all established claims" unless he sees "very clear grounds for questioning them" (AB, 168). Even those in the past whom Eliot describes as being in the middle classes, such as Mr. Deane in The Mill on the Floss, belong to the traditional rather than the progressive face of this class and are as suspicious of novelties as the peasants around them. Eliot is always making the point that these times were in a transitional period between an age governed by tradition, in which the established laws, institutions, and practices of society were as nature to the generality of the population, and the modern society contemporary with Eliot, in which people have become conscious of historical change and are no longer willing to regard society as an unquestionable aspect of nature. It needs to be accounted for, or moralized, in a completely new way.

This picture of the division between the past and the present does bear some relation to history. For instance, historians have remarked that visitors from Elizabethan England would have found little in the lives of people in the early eighteenth century that was essentially changed from what it had been in their own day, whereas if they visited England in the middle of the nineteenth century, they would have found the entire landscape of the country as well as the way of life of its inhabitants radically transformed. Looked at in the broadest perspective, as the hundred and fifty years before Eliot's time had seen a change from a traditional and predominantly agricultural society to a progressive industrial society in which the majority of the population lived in cities, this change certainly had an effect on the conceptions of nature and of time among the English people. However, it is only in these broadest of terms that Eliot's characterization of this change is unprovocative. Any analysis more specific shows it to be a fable of her own time rather than an objective account of the experience of the people about whom she appears to be writing. It is a fable that appears triumphantly to reconcile the present to the past, whereas it has in fact manufactured this division and thus prescribed the form of its resolution. In other words, it is a narrative rationalizing the form of the discourse given to the middle classes of this time as a result of their material position and ideological heritage within society.

It is this fable that accounts for the significance of Eliot's depiction of character in terms of historical consciousness. The way Eliot makes this consciousness the nature of her characters is understandable only in terms of this class in nineteenth-century English society whose interest it was to identify with that society as if its essential nature was a progressive differentiation from the past. Thus her description is an elaborate way of naming this class with which she identified herself and her readership. It is a way of rationalizing its existence, as it were, by sheer linguistic force. Given this recognition, what remains to be analyzed is the significance of the details she gave to her interpretation of the difference between a devotion to natural phenomena and the development of a historical consciousness.

In itself this conception of change did not pose a problem for Eliot. Although the nostalgic form of her novels can be seen in the Tory idealism with which she pictured the attitudes of the common people of the past, she could admit her fondness for this lost image of society without arguing merely on the basis of this loss that her own society was inferior. She found a problem in this change, and a great danger to morality and to the structure of society as a whole, in her conclusion that too many people do not realize historical consciousness has come to replace nature. Eliot's reasoning is that people need a new truth to replace the vanished assumption of nature if society is to have any stability and individual life any meaning, or that nature must be transfigured into this new semblance of truth; but she fears the modern world may have only opinion in the place where this truth should be.

So Eliot contrasts "the Boeotian Knebley" to the "Attic" Shepperton, which "had turnpike roads and a public opinion" ("MGL," 90). And she writes of "these days," her own time, "when opinion has got far ahead of feeling" ("JR," 282). To Eliot, what is most characteristic of modern times is opinion of all sorts: political, economic, religious, scientific, and so on. Sometimes she uses the words "theory" or "philosophy" in this regard, but the significance is similar because she sees particular judgments on individuals or society as a proliferating division and vitiation of the relations that ought to bind humanity together. These opinions sprout like weeds in the landscape cleared of the cultivated nature of the past and then proceed to choke one another off from their essential nutrients. The monumental unity of nature loses place to this fragmentation of opinion. "Free-thinkers are scarcely wider than the orthodox in this matter—they all want to see themselves and their own opinions held up as the true and the lovely" (L, 3: 111).

Again, it is fair to say "opinions" were of a qualitatively different nature in Eliot's time because the huge growth of journalism, of cheaper publishing, and of an increasingly large audience for such productions spurred their development and gave them a material distribution they had never before possessed. However, it is not the mere fact of multiplying opinions that so bothered Eliot but what this proliferation meant to her: self-assertion among multiplying masses of people freed from the deference traditionally paid to rank, religion, and natural moral law. Although she was an intellectual participant in movements like biblical criticism of the "higher" sort that indirectly helped to weaken the bonds of deference, by no means was she such a radical in social matters as to think that liberated humanity should be allowed to take its course without some assurance of rigid control to keep it from running wild. This is exactly what the lower classes threatened to do, in the eyes of Eliot's class, which associated undisciplined thought with lower-class violence from the time of the French Revolution until well beyond Eliot's own day.

Therefore, what Eliot needed was to reconstitute society on a fresh basis by discovering within reason a new sort of nature. She needed to provide a fable of consensus as stable as that she gave to the world of the past by describing it as existing under the timeless and unquestioned sway of nature. She found this in the discovery of a historical consciousness, as in her commitment to education, her transfiguration of the traditional notion of gentility, her opposition of feeling to science, and her ideas of psychology and sympathy.

All these aspects of the modern nature Eliot sought to construct are opposed not only to her imagery of fragmentation but also to the imagery of gambling that similarly serves to indicate moral surrender to wayward opinion, desire, and action. Thus, at one point in *The Mill on the Floss* Dr. Kenn says to Maggie, who has gone to him for moral advice, " 'At present everything seems tending towards the relaxation of ties—towards the substitution of wayward choice for the adherence to obligation, which has its roots in the past' " (*MF*, 528). Similarly, Eliot describes Bulstrode watching over the sick Raffles in *Middlemarch* and generalizes about "the common trick of desire—which avails itself of any irrelevant scepticism, finding larger room for itself in all uncertainty about effects, in every obscurity that looks like the absence of law" (*M*, 2: 291). To Eliot, the loss of the old law of nature opened up wider areas of obscurity in experience in which desire, freed of supervision, might run wild. Once society was no longer accepted deferentially as nature, once one became conscious of it, every aspect of it was liable to appear threateningly obscure in this way. And, as Eliot comments, "By looking at a dubious object with a constructive imagination, one can give it twenty different shapes" (*DD*, 1: 306). The loss of nature might be said to create subjectivity but one that in the absence of Eliot's historical consciousness would have no law to guide it. It would appear as Mr. Hyde rather than as Dr. Jekyll.

Arthur Donnithorne in *Adam Bede* falls prey to this new system of things, toying with his conscience as Dickens's Dick Skimpole plays with his finances. As Eliot comments on the old tradition of confession in the course of presenting a scene in which Arthur fails in his intention to submit his conscience to Reverend Irwine, "Still, there was this advantage in the old rigid forms, that they committed you to the fulfillment of a resolution by some outward deed" (*AB*, 167). (Ironically, gambling is Reverend Irwine's vice, too, although his is a much more venial sort.) Similarly, Godfrey Cass in *Silas Marner* tragically gambles that "some throw of fortune's dice" will relieve him of the difficulties involved in his secret marriage, leading Eliot to comment that "Favorable Chance is the god of all men who follow their own devices instead of obeying a law they believe in" (*SM*, 289). Moreover, when Silas was precipitated into his period of despairing misanthropy by his Dissenting congregation's misguided accusation that he was a thief, this accusation was made on the basis of bibliomancy, or a chance reading of the Bible. There is also the case of Fred Vincy in *Middlemarch*, who relies on "the favor of Providence in the shape of an old gentleman's caprice" (*M*, 1: 355)—whereas one of the ways he reclaims himself is by rescuing Lydgate from gambling when his brother-in-law is first overcome with shock as a result of his debts and his problems with Rosamond. And, for Tito in *Romola*, who betrays his stepfather and is ultimately murdered by him, this imagery is driven to its logical end as all life takes on "the aspect of a game" in which there is "an agreeable mingling of skill and chance" (*R*, 1: 330).

However, the character in whom this substitution of waywardness for law is developed most fully is Gwendolen Harleth in *Daniel Deronda*. "This problematic sylph," as Eliot describes her, is found at the beginning of the novel gambling in a casino, leading Eliot to comment, "She had begun to believe in her own luck, others had begun to believe in it: she had visions of being followed by a *cortege* who would worship her as a goddess of luck and watch her play as a directing augury" (*DD*, 1: 7). She believes she can conduct her entire life as she conducts herself in the casino, trusting that the dubiety of the laws and objects opposed to her desires will not take any form so definite as to dethrone her from her imaginary sovereignty in life and, of course, finding herself miserably disappointed in this expectation. She suffers from the uncertainty of the modern world, like so many characters in Eliot's novels; however, she suffers more profoundly because she has trusted in that uncertainty more than most. Nevertheless, the fact that she *is* relatively lucky is illustrated by the way Mr. Lapidoth, Mirah's father, appears on the scene when Gwendolen is beginning to reform as if to show the depths to which she might have sunk if not for the influence of Deronda. As Eliot comments on this degenerate case, one sees the global image that gambling always implies in her writing and its categorical opposition to the human faculties she prizes:

> The gambling appetite is more absolutely dominant than bodily
> hunger, which can be neutralized by an emotional or intellectual
> excitation; but the passion for watching chances—the habitual suspen-
> sive poise of the mind in actual or imaginary play—nullifies the
> susceptibility to other excitation. In its final, imperious stage, it seems
> the unjoyous dissipation of demons, seeking diversion on the burning
> marl of perdition. (*DD*, 2: 390)

Three major points may be made about this representation of fragmentation in the modern world through the imagery of gambling. First, as the genteel status of Arthur, Fred, Godfrey, Tito, Lydgate, and Gwendolen indicates, and as is further indicated by the sovereign or aristocratic imagery with which their hopes are described, it marks Eliot's recognition that the law embodied in the traditional system of deference has fallen. One cannot trust individuals solely on account of their rank in society any more than these individuals can trust their position to confer on them an innate guidance in moral and social affairs. This is the most conventional aspect of Eliot's imagery, as gambling had long been represented in her culture as the characteristic vice of the upper classes. Hence her description of an anonymous gambler: "In his bearing there might be something of the tradesman, but in his pleasures he was fit to rank with the owners of the oldest titles" (*DD*, 1: 5). Gambling in this respect serves mainly to reinforce the demeaning of traditional social rank, which Eliot manages more directly in other ways.

Second, as Eliot's characterization of gambling as trusting in fortune or Providence indicates, her use of this imagery marks her recognition that the world of her novels is no longer that of the eighteenth-century novel. One cannot trust in a teleology innate to the world any more than one can trust in the innate virtues of the established ranks in society. This recognition corresponds to her own religious and philosophical beliefs but more importantly to a demand for some sort of intellectual consciousness to replace the law that had been thought to reside in nature. In Eliot's description, gambling is still an unconscious deference to nature, but it is a perverted deference, an illusory semblance of consciousness, a homage paid to the obscurity of nature rather than to its enlightenment. In this respect her image of gambling resembles its presentation in *The Return of the Native* and others of Hardy's works, in which it figures as a satire of the lawlessness of the universe in relation to human ends.

Third, again as in Hardy's works, this gambling serves as an image of the economic practice of Eliot's own time. At least from the time of Locke there had been a conventional association between commerce and gambling.[8] By Eliot's time this association was a well-established metaphor, as one can see in the way Tom builds his fortune in *The Mill on the Floss* by taking the "chances" offered to him by Bob Jakins—and by the way this commerce leads him astray from traditional human ties. What one sees in Eliot's image of gambling in this respect is the nightmare underside of the laissez-faire doctrine that was still dominant in her time, despite increasing instances of state intervention and regulation. In this nightmare, the pursuit of individual self-aggrandizement does not prove to serve the best ends of society as a whole. It results only in a chaotic mass of people having no common law. In other words, it results in a completely fragmented society. Taking Marx's suggestion that the "contrast between the power, based on the personal relations of dominion and servitude, that is conferred by landed property, and the impersonal power that is given to money, is well expressed by the two French proverbs, 'Nulle terre sans seigneur,' and 'l'argent n'a pas de maître,'"[9] the extreme end of this lack of sovereignty suggested by commerce is visible in Eliot's image of gambling. In this respect one might compare Eliot's writing to Burke's description of postrevolutionary France as "a common-wealth founded upon gambling"[10]—a description directly referring to the freeing of the French economy at this time but more generally conveying Burke's sense of the import of all the changes brought by the Revolution.

True, Eliot's own writing to a certain extent represents an adoption of laissez-faire doctrine, as one can see in her statement on this issue in one of the essays in *Theophrastus Such*, "A Political Molecule." However, this imagery of gambling in her writing shows how tenuous such a casual belief in this doctrine may prove when one descends from generalities to a representation of social life. This new version of natural law in political science needs a stronger support than "mere" theory, as Eliot might have said. After all, it is significant that one of Eliot's exemplars of honest labor, Caleb Garth, suffers his one great failure when he extends his business operation to a large, speculative scale—that is, when he gambles in commerce. Eliot's insistence in this case, as throughout her fiction, that work be conceived of on a small and immediate scale can be interpreted as a fearful reaction against the economic structure of the national system of life that she seems elsewhere to accept with philosophic equanimity.[11]

It was because the middle-class sense of history was a relatively recent creation that Eliot had to insist on the difficulty of learning this new knowledge even though she presented it, as the middle classes of her time typically presented their ideologies, as universal human truth. This difficulty is not a measure of experience but of the impedance to communication Eliot could expect among her readers. To put it another way, it is a measure of the difficulty of reading in the modern world, as this would appear to an intellectual of Eliot's type who had struggled through the works of figures such as Spinoza, Feuerbach, and Strauss. The temporal dimension given to revelation in her works, which logically seems to contradict the semantic dimension given to universal human nature, cannot be understood within a reasoned argument unless rationality is conceived to be the process of making figurative sense of a discourse: drawing its differences, oppositions, exclusions, and other elements into the construction of fields such as "experience," "psychology," or "natural history," to name just a few of those involved in Eliot's art. The understanding constituted within Eliot's art was never a question of logic or of reason in any transcendental sense; instead, it was a question of manipulating the structures for communication in Eliot's discourse so that they might appear logical and rational. Thus, Dorothea is searching for Eliot's art—or this art is searching for itself by dissimulating itself—in a passage in which she contrasts the assurance of the past to the uncertainty of the present: "But something she yearned for by which her life might be filled with action at once rational and ardent: and since the time was gone by for guiding visions and spiritual directors, since prayer heightened yearning but not instruction, what lamp was there but knowledge?" (*M*, 1: 89).

Dorothea realizes correctly that an outer must be replaced by an inner direction if she is to fit the destiny of Eliot's narrative. However, at this point she has yet to learn that it is only through extreme suffering that she can arrive at a correct definition of this interiority. Dorothea, then, may be seen to figure in her life the narrative given to history through the rationalized articulation of Eliot's discourse. Failing to heed her uncle's oft-repeated conviction that the investigation of any field of knowledge might lead one " 'too far, and nothing might come of it' " (*M*, 1: 287), she has to "struggle out of a nightmare in which every object was withering and shrinking away from her" (*M*, 1: 286) because she has confused the opinionated knowledge that preoccupies Casaubon with Eliot's greater vision of "that complex, fragmentary, doubt-provoking knowledge which we call truth." Casaubon describes himself as being " 'like the ghost of an ancient, wandering about the world and trying mentally to construct it as it used to be, in spite of ruin and confusing changes' " (*M*, 1: 16), with Eliot adding that "he had undertaken to show . . . that all the mythical systems or erratic mythical fragments in the world were corruptions of a tradition originally revealed" (*M*, 1: 23); and so Dorothea wanders in her impression of Casaubon. "Almost everything he had said seemed like a specimen from a mine, or the inscription on the door of a museum which might open on the treasures of the past ages" (*M*, 1: 32). In Casaubon's relation to his work as in Dorothea's relation to him, the tragedy lies in accepting a conception of knowledge as a fixed body of meaning indicated by external signs instead of realizing meaning can exist only in a historical consciousness that accepts the fragmentary nature of any sign and yet understands it in terms of the continuity of the human spirit that binds all fragments, signs, and individuals. Any interpretation more narrow than this is bound to fall into error, or fragmentary partiality.

So tragedy occurs when Dorothea is placed in an eccentric relation to the form of history in Eliot's conception, redemption in her more appropriate placement. Experience in *Middlemarch* is wholly a matter of such categorical distinctions and the plot constructed on their basis. Thus, what Dorothea initially presumes to be the object of knowledge, Eliot presents as a thing of exteriority. It appears Dorothea misconceives Casaubon's nature because she has not begun with a proper historical consciousness and so cannot know the difference between inner and outer life that is so crucial to the appearance of truth in Eliot's writing. She has conceived of knowledge as a substantial object of understanding rather than as the process of understanding, just as she has mistakenly given a substantial characterization to Casaubon that fails to account for the varying aspects of his character over the course of time—just as Casaubon himself, like Lydgate, is looking for an original substance in his research. Thereby, Dorothea is made to bring forth the difference between the past and the present which—along with related differences like those between the inner and the outer, the private and the public, and feeling and science—becomes the basis for the experience of Eliot's characters. "Naturally" there is all the difference in the world between the work Casaubon would have

Dorothea continue after his death—"sorting what might be called shattered monuments, and fragments of a tradition which was itself a mosaic wrought from crushed ruins" (*M*, 2: 54)—and Eliot's reconstruction of the fragmentary present into a spiritual whole. Casaubon conceives knowledge to be exclusionary judgment, whereas Eliot considers it an all-inclusive process of consciousness.

This is how Eliot settles the difference between the past and the present inherent in the form of her discourse: by conceiving history to be an allegory of the human spirit. Although she views historical consciousness as an essentially modern development, this does not so much imply a fundamental break with the past as it does a new kind of understanding of the past. The modern world is novel because of its self-consciousness, but this self-consciousness is also an understanding of the past and a means of approaching the future. It is the very theory of humanity. This is why Eliot may set a novel like *Romola* in a time centuries before her own and yet still discover there the essential story or morality of all her writing: because there, too, it is a question of the allegory of the human spirit. This allegory will be presented in somewhat different terms in *Romola*—it will show the difference between religious law and the promptings of the individual soul rather than the difference between deference before nature and the exigencies of opinions—but in both cases the understanding Eliot develops from the difference is the same. Her argument is that such differences must be understood as part of a continuous process and progress of the human spirit.

It is not just in *Middlemarch* that Eliot showed the mistakes that might be made in this project; Casaubon's is the same misconception of knowledge that affects Bardo de' Bardi in *Romola*, as he lives "among his books and his marble fragments of the past" (*R*, 1: 50), and Mordecai in *Daniel Deronda*, with his mind occupied by "sculptured fragments certifying some beauty yearned after but not traceable by divination" (*DD*, 2: 119), and Merman in the essay "How We Encourage Research," seized by the idea of "the possible connection of certain symbolic monuments common to widely scattered races" (*RS*, 281), and even Silas Marner, as "culture had not defined any channels for his sense of mystery" so that "it spread itself over the proper pathways of inquiry and knowledge" (*SM*, 221). All these figures fail to recognize knowledge as the human spirit in history, misconceiving it as some limited manifestation of that spirit. They mistake fragments for monuments. For Eliot, such knowledge was death, as she indicated by the way Casaubon, Dorothea, Bardo, Mordecai, and Silas all exist at least for a time as ghostly figures akin to the figure of Lisbeth Bede immediately after her husband's death.

This is not to say Eliot would demand that everyone have her historical consciousness in its intellectual form. On the contrary, because she showed that this intellectual consciousness is largely peculiar to the nineteenth century, such a demand would have meant that almost everyone who lived before her time could not have come close to a substantial relation with the human spirit. What she demanded instead was a term that would be the key-word for the multifarious forms that might belong to her allegory of the human spirit throughout history. She needed that word of all words—"the one poor word which includes all our best insight and our best love" (*DD*, 1: 154)—that she found in "sympathy." One can only guess whether the dispersion of desire in the gaps, spaces, and fractures in Eliot's letter to Cross managed to elicit the experience of unity the writer sought to embody in this word.

Chapter 9
Domesticity and Teratology

Our mental business is carried on much in the same way as the business of the State: a great deal of hard work is done by agents who are not acknowledged.

Eliot, "Amos Barton," *Scenes of Clerical Life*

After all, I fear authors must submit to be something of monsters not quite simple, healthy human beings; but I will keep my monstrosity within bounds if possible.

Eliot, *Letters*

Among the adjectives most frequently associated with "sympathy" in Eliot's writing are "growing" and "enlarged." These words are meant to indicate the progressive nature of the human spirit and the corresponding moral structure of Eliot's works. Thus, in *The Mill on the Floss* Eliot opposes "formulas," or opinions, to "the divine promptings and inspirations that spring from growing insight and sympathy" (*MF*, 531). Similarly, there is the example of Philip Wakem, who writes a sympathetic letter to Maggie Tulliver when she appears to have been disgraced by her disappearance with Stephen Guest. He writes of " 'that enlarged life which grows and grows by appropriating the life of others' " and then goes on to speak of " 'this gift of transferred life which has come to me in loving you' " (*MF*, 537). This is sympathy in Eliot's writing: a transferred life that is finally a transfiguration of all society to the "humanity" that is Eliot's metaphor for the human race throughout history. Just as Eliot makes the universal spirit of humanity the measure of individuals throughout her fiction, so does she make sympathy a universal sign of the continuity of this spirit in the everyday experiences of social life. Sympathy is not simply one form of truth among others but the manifestation of truth as immediate social experience, as domesticated universality, and thus as the very surface from which Eliot's realism lifts its representations.

Eliot conceived this term to be the end of art. What she wrote in an early essay, she continued to maintain throughout her life: that "the greatest benefit we owe to the artist, whether painter, poet, or novelist, is the extension of our sympathies" (*E*, 270). As the redeeming word adopted by a leading writer during a time when the middle classes felt themselves extraordinarily threatened by a consciousness of violently diverging interests among different classes in society, Eliot's sympathy is meant to restore a spiritual identity within humankind and thus to elide the questions of social and political identity that had become so pressing during the nineteenth century.

Sympathy represents the life of humanity and so is meant to save Eliot's art from objections to this figure, such as that raised by W. H. Mallock in a satire of the Positivism with which Eliot was associated. He described this movement by asserting that, "viewed by modern science, all existence is a chain, with a gas at one end and no one knows what at the other; and . . . Humanity . . . a link somewhere."[1] Although one certainly may accuse Eliot of this sort of vagueness in her references to humanity, she was by no means unaware of the dangers of this term. It was for this reason that Eliot was concerned to emphasize the individual even while she was returning this figure to society as a whole.

Thus, in her description of how "the fortunes of Tito and Romola were dependent on certain grand political and social conditions which made an epoch in the history of Italy" just as "in the tree that bears a myriad of blossoms, each single bud with its fruit is dependent on the primary circulation of the sap" (*R*, 1: 217), Eliot's attention is judiciously divided among various levels in her narrative. She was always concerned to make humanity arise from the circumstantial situations of her characters and so remain a term filled with living meaning. Insofar as her art succeeded, the Comtian ideal of humanity as a continuous whole that she used to fix the unity of her writing would itself appear fixed within an organic relationship of parts to wholes. Her universal truths would be anchored by the detailed specification of persons and circumstances from which she constructed sympathetic knowledge.[2] This is the most fundamental fable of realism: that parts nourished by detail grow into unified wholes and thus a certain style of representation into substantial truth.

There remains a further problem of definition. An all-inclusive sympathy, which Eliot suggested to be the goal of art, one that transcends all opinions or judgments the way she seems to transcend her writing as narrator, presents the individual as an utterly passive figure in relation to society. The sickroom scene that dramatizes the morality of Eliot's fiction gives more substance to the suffering of the patient and nurse than to the accomplishment of a cure. Eliot has no problem defining a moral consciousness in terms of sympathy; but in defining the means of "healthful activity," she runs into difficulties precisely because of her conception of sympathy, as she indicates in describing Deronda's "many-sided sympathy, which threatened to hinder any persistent course of action" (*DD*, 1: 375). Her morality was admittedly a conservative one, but she could not let it be entirely passive and still hold to her progressive conception of truth.

What saves Deronda, as it does all those who can be saved in Eliot's fiction, is a division between private and public worlds in society that delimits the area in which sympathy and art ought to be actively engaged. Consider a passage from one of Eliot's essays in the *Westminster Review*:

> The sum of our comparison is this—In Young we have the type of
> that deficient human sympathy, that impiety towards the present and
> the visible, which flies for its motives, its sanctities, and its religion, to
> the remote, the vague, and the unknown: in Cowper we have the type
> of that genuine love which cherishes things in proportion to their
> nearness, and feels its reverence grow in proportion to the intimacy of
> this knowledge. (*E*, 385)

This division between private and public worlds in terms of things near and remote is meant to solve the problem of giving sympathy the form of action. According to Eliot, one may survive encounters with public monsters as long as one has domesticated those met in private life. So Felix Holt, to give just one example, finds a happy ending even though he temporarily is sent to prison as a result of misrepresentations about his activity in the riot at the polls. Character, which represents one's successful or unsuccessful relation to these private monsters, carries him through.

Hence Eliot's concern to keep her private life separate from her public identity so that control would proceed from the private to the public rather than the other way around. An author—a public figure—could not be entirely one among other "simple, healthy human beings" because there is a greater sphere of action given to this role than that of common domesticity. However, Eliot regarded this situation as all the more reason for domesticated experience to be valued over the larger scale of commitments that was likely to appear monstrous in comparison. As egoism is the control of the private by the public—as in Hetty's bedazzlement before the idols of society or Gwendolen's submission of her desires to the abstractions of freedom and wealth and power—morality for Eliot is the control of the public ends of society that may be expected to flow from private resolutions and a domestic scale of commitments. Such is the argument of Felix Holt's appeal to public opinion over specific political actions. This is also the logic of his own life, in which he cleans up his house, curing himself of dissipation and refusing to let his mother continue his father's business of selling worthless patent medicines, before he even considers a public role for himself—in which, in any case, he will still be agitating publicly for private reform.

In one of her letters Eliot wrote, "Perhaps the most difficult heroism is that which consists in the daily conquests of our private demons, not in the slaying of world-notorious dragons" (*L*, 6: 147). And the major theme this sentiment forms in all her fiction was struck at the very beginning of her career as an artist, in the description in "Mr. Gilfil's Love-Story" that compares the "poor little heart" of Caterina to the public "stream of human thought and deed . . . hurrying and broadening onward" ("MGL," 156-47). Although it may not be invoked in her later works with the heavily panting sentimentality that encompasses it here, this type of comparison was a favorite device of Eliot's. It is always employed to mark her systematic refusal to depreciate individual feeling in favor of a wider perspective on society, the world, and the world's history.

Through devices such as this kind of comparison, Eliot would devote her writing to the private histories of individuals and urge the reader's sympathies for their feelings. She would argue against the "great philosopher" who emerges "into the serene air of pure intellect, in which it is evident that individuals really exist for no other purpose than that abstractions may be drawn from them—abstractions that may rise from heaps of ruined lives like the sweet savor of a sacrifice in the nostrils of philosophers, and of a philosophic Deity" ("JR," 356). She would refuse to sacrifice her sympathy for individuals and for the circumstances of individual feeling to a larger purpose of her own—yet she would also urge her characters to grow out of sympathy with their own feelings.

In her letters Eliot preached "*absolute* resignation" and the "austere" conclusion "that a human lot in which there is much direct personal enjoyment must at present be very rare" (*L*, 4: 499). Through her fiction she makes this same argument in her narrative commentary and forces her characters to suffer its realization in their lives. As often as she demands that her readers turn their attention to the feelings of her individual characters, she demands that her characters learn to sacrifice their feelings to a wider social commitment. As she comments in *Daniel Deronda* when describing Gwendolen Harleth listening to Deronda's plan to establish a Jewish nation,

> There comes a terrible moment to many souls when the great
> movements of the world, the larger destinies of mankind, which have
> lain aloof in newspapers and other neglected reading, enter like an
> earthquake into their own lives . . . Then it is that the submission of
> the soul to the highest is tested, and even in the eyes of frivolity life
> looks out from the scene of human struggle with the awful face of
> duty, and a religion shows itself which is something else than a private
> consolation. (*DD*, 2: 422-23)

Eliot's continual argument against egoism is that feeling must be turned away from oneself and toward one's responsibilities to others. That this transformation is demanded so insistently shows how strong she believes the contrary attachment to private feelings to be, whereas her equally insistent demand that her readers sympathize with the feelings of her individual characters shows the opposing danger she recognizes in the tendency to sacrifice feelings for others in a dedication to what then would become a public duty without value. It is thus that the structuring of her discourse, with its regulating difference between the categories of the private and the public, is made a universal moral dialectic. Eliot wants to turn individuals toward some sort of social responsibility, yet she would not have this responsibility be so "inexorable, unbending, unmodifiable"—as she describes Tom Tulliver (*MF*, 516)—that it would utterly efface what she regards as the vital importance of individuality. She needs some play in her system, a space of discretion, in which this discourse that determines the structuring of her representation of social life may appear to arise in the form of possibilities seized from nature rather than art.

This is the space of experience in Eliot's fiction—the space in which characters collide with the structuring of her art, and with their own constitution as characters, as if they are undergoing crises, learning, and growing independently of the author's will, which is given over to merely recording their progress. In fact, the significance of Eliot's intrusive commentaries throughout her fiction is precisely this: that they construct a field of representation within her writing that appears as a reflection upon a separate field of observation and thus makes the one appear formally independent of the other, as if Eliot's dramatic and expository descriptions of characters and events were not just as completely prescribed by the nature of her discourse.

Of course, to an extent this analysis may be made of any realist art—of any art that appears neither theological nor ideological in its style of representation. But it is particularly significant in relation to Eliot's writing because her realism is so accomplished a system, its constitutive devices—such as the difference between private and public worlds—so "natural" to the modern world, and its claims to an unprecedented humbling of art before ordinary human life so insistent and so demonstrably persuasive to her readers and critics.

What is negotiated in the balancing act maintained in Eliot's writing is a division between private and public worlds that would submit the private to the public and yet would preserve within that submission an impression of the sacrifice it entailed. This figurative event is precisely what Eliot means by sympathy and therefore constitutes as well the structure of memory and social history in her fiction, in which the past is nostalgically enshrined while progressively improved. Sympathy is always brought about by "sad experience," but it is the outcome of a "growth of higher feeling within us" that proves so valuable that "we can no more wish to return to a narrower sympathy, than a painter or a musician can wish to return to his cruder manner, or a philosopher to his less complete formula" (*AB*, 547). It is the progress of thought and of art, as well as the progress of individual morality. One's desires are fragmented when one is moved to identify with others in society, but the painful sacrifice entailed by this movement is memorialized within the saddened, subdued, or tragic feeling that Eliot describes sympathy to be in the space it opens within the individual.

Moreover, in Eliot's reckoning, what one becomes conscious of through a sympathy with others is the way their private desires, too, are fragmented within the public world. Therefore, one's feelings for others increase one's understanding of oneself. Ideally, the situation would be perfectly reflexive and coextensive with all society. As Eliot writes, "In many of our neighbors' lives, there is much not only of error and lapse, but of a certain exquisite goodness which can never be written or even spoken—only divined by each of us, according to the inward instruction of our own privacy" (*DD*, 1: 184). To Eliot, self-consciousness properly comprehended is social consciousness, or sympathy. It is because it so perfectly represents this negotiation between private and public worlds that sympathy is such a key word in her writing.

In making a psychology of this term of sympathy, as opposed to a theology or ideology, Eliot tries to show exactly how law may be transferred from the world it used to occupy in external nature to its new home in the spirit of humanity. She does so by asserting the crucial importance of one person perceiving another as the theater of his or her actions. In other words, she does so by personalizing society and thus domesticating history. As she writes of Deronda's significance to Gwendolen,

> It is hard to say how much we could forgive ourselves if we were secure from judgment by another whose opinion is the breathing-medium of all our joy—who brings to us with close pressure and immediate sequence the judgment of the Invisible and Universal which self-flattery and the world's tolerance would easily melt and disperse. In this way our brother may be in the stead of God to us, and his opinion which has pierced even to the joints and marrow, may be our virtue in the making. (*DD*, 2: 379)

This is how opinion is policed: by its role as conscience and thus as a personalized substitution for external law. Humanity is spiritualized, made "Invisible and Universal," so that all social relations may take on the aspects of a spiritual drama, may be dominated by a moral interpretation of all conflicts and events that appears only natural and rational, and so may be seen at every moment as the mediation of a unified society. This is modern religion: a sentimentalized view of social relations in the form of a normative psychology. It was to the development of this field of discourse that Beatrice Webb referred when describing the major change of the Victorian period as "the transference of the emotion of self-sacrificing" and of "the impulse of self-subordinating service, from God to man."[3]

So Eliot writes of Esther Lyon, "The first religious experience of her life—the first self-questioning, the first voluntary subjection, the first longing to acquire the strength of greater motives and obey the more strenuous role—had come to her through Felix Holt" (*FH*, 276). Esther, who has believed her life and thoughts to be "a heap of fragments" (*FH*, 366), comes to think Felix Holt is making "an imaginary commentary" within her thoughts (*FH*, 372) and further imagines that "some time or other, perhaps, he would be to her as if he belonged to the solemn admonishing skies, checking her self-satisfied pettiness with the suggestion of a wider life" (*FH*, 366). In such a relation, too, does Dorothea stand to Will Ladislaw. As Eliot comments, in terms that recall her descriptions of the therapeutics of suffering, "There are natures in which, if they love us, we are conscious of having a sort of baptism and consecration: they bind us over to rectitude and purity by their pure belief about us; and our sins become that worst sort of sacrilege which tears down the invisible altar of trust" (*M*, 2: 360). Thus it is that religion is domesticated, psychologized, and made the example as well as the proof of a universal human spirit. Conveyed by this imagery at the same time is a conversion of ideological opinion into spiritual truth because these "natures" acting to influence others are moving them to adopt specific ideals and actions. The invisible commentary individuals frame for each other in Eliot's fiction is thus constituted, in part, by the sublimation of politics in the rules of sentimental psychology.

While Eliot portrays them standing in the stead of angels or God to each other, individuals also stand in the place of a class in the process of appropriating this imagery, which in earlier theories of society was given over to kingship and to aristocratic paternalism. As the middle classes take themselves to be the godhead of society, a man like Deronda may appear as "a priest" (*DD*, 2: 34), a woman "whose nature is an object of reverential belief" may become "a new conscience to a man" (*DD*, 2: 17), or a child may be the leading form given to this appropriation of power, as in the case of *Silas Marner*'s Eppie, who takes the place of the "white-winged angels" that Eliot says are no longer seen (*SM*, 352). Although this figure of the interpreter-savior appears much more fully developed in Eliot's later novels, it is important to see that it represents no break from her early work. It simply develops the logic of a comment such as the following one from "Janet's Repentance": "There is a power in the direct glance of a sincere and loving human soul, which will do more to dissipate prejudice and kindle charity than the most elaborate arguments" ("JR," 311). The figure of the interpreter-savior is sentimentality given the psychological form of "character." In this form its only difference from such a sentimental remark is that psychology may appear to the modern reader a more complex and convincing field of explanation than the field represented by "the direct glance of a sincere and loving human soul."[4]

Examples like those involving Gwendolen and Silas Marner do represent the more fortunate instances of influence in Eliot's work. Some of her characters have much more difficulty taking others as a religious theater for their actions. For instance, Eliot portrays a more complex version of this kind of relationship when she describes the sympathy Romola has for Savonarola, who can offer her only a "stumbling guidance along the path of reliance and action which is the path of life" (*R*, 1: 343). And in a passage in *Daniel Deronda*, Eliot seems to come face to face with the potential amorality of her psychology: "The beings closest to us, whether in love or hate, are often virtually our interpreters of the world, and some feather-headed gentleman or lady whom in passing we regret to take as legal tender for a human being may be acting as a melancholy theory of life in the minds of those who live with them" (*DD*, 2: 285). Nevertheless, this moment and the related qualifications that Eliot places on this psychology are integrated within her narratives only as abnormal, flawed, or degenerate instances of what ought to pass for the "legal tender" of humanity. The ideal relationship is represented as one that may be obtained in life as long as one is moved to experience the force of sympathy.

This psychological field of representation perfectly exemplifies the middle-class assumption that there can be no social question of any sort—political, economic, educational, and so on—that is not primarily a moral question. Despite the way social issues were approached through the systematic definition, collection, and interpretation of facts in institutionalized fields such as political science, psychology, and sociology, it was virtually inconceivable to the middle classes of Eliot's time that any kind of judgment could be advanced that did not in some way represent a moralized truth of human relations demonstrable in the relation of one individual to another. So strong was the sway of sentimentality that no matter how great the scale of social events might be—war, mass poverty and unemployment, the structure of national authority, and so on—it could be addressed by way of examples of individual relations on a domestic scale. Thus it was that all except the most eccentric cases of poverty would be treated in the terms of individual failure and renewal, that "self help" would be defined as the mechanism of social mobility, that investigations of the lot of the poor would always link their social to their religious condition, and that education in the reformed public schools for the elite as well as in the popular system would be regarded above all else as moral training. Even in those areas where issues were predominantly formulated in scientific or technical terms—for instance, in medicine and public sanitation—reforms were advanced within this ideology of moral duty and improvement. Although one can easily see in the moral language of the time the expression of political and economic motivations, environing every public issue was this moral language imagining society in the terms of individual agency and responsibility.

What Eliot's writing does in casting this language into fiction is to make fiction moral, to make the reading of fiction an education in moral sympathy, and above all else to provide for the class of her readership dramatic images of the ideals already enshrined in their social theories and practices. The invisible commentary Eliot's individuals frame for each other is the discourse of a class presented as the discovery of psychology. The great emphasis Eliot places on the importance of this relationship in which one person comes to serve as a conscience for another shows how aware she was that this means of replacing the laws of divinity and tradition could be only an ideal in her society. However, she advanced this ideal as the true nature of society. Any differences between the images it furnished and the actual state of society would not be regarded as contradictions to the ideal but as instances of imperfect enlightenment or degenerate humanity. This is how middle-class moralists typically regard any social issue that is not in accord with their ideals: by terming it a manifestation of ignorance, if not of violence. Such an approach ensures that the conscience of the middle classes will be regarded as an "invisible and universal" direction within society, no matter how imperfect the evidence may be in this regard and no matter what challenges may be raised against this psychologizing of all social organization. It is thus that history is transcended by the middle classes, that the middle-class mind is made the structure of communication within society, and that the ideological force of sympathy is dissimulated as the universal spirit of humanity.

This is not to deny that Eliot and her readers experienced the situations that she describes under the name of feeling; it is not at all improbable that they were moved to tears or experienced some heartfelt response. In other words, she and her readers were not necessarily hypocrites, as in the charge leveled against "eminent Victorians" by many of the writers following this age. To so describe them would be to debase the usual meaning of hypocrisy and to mystify the powers that may accrue to the sincere ideologue, which Eliot, by all accounts, appears to have been. Ultimately, the distinction between hypocrisy and sincerity is itself a device of middle-class discourse. It is a sentimental diversion from the political point of the issue, which is that feeling, too, has a meaning and a history that are culturally and class specific. Feeling, too, is a representation and must be analyzed as such if one is not to be bewitched by the theory of feeling that functions as a universal reality for the middle classes, though in fact it is an aspect of their development and of their self-conscious definition as part of society.

This point becomes even clearer if one analyzes a second way Eliot seeks to give a concrete definition to the word sympathy: by defining its value in terms of work done close at hand. As Eliot put it in one of her letters, "You know I care as much for what is called private work as for public, and I believe in its incalculable efficacy" (L, 6: 106). Within this topic, too, Eliot negotiates a division between private and public worlds that would submit the private to the public but would preserve within that submission an impression of the sacrifice that this entails. Whereas this is accomplished psychologically by her emphasis on the importance of one person taking another as the theater of his or her actions, it is accomplished in regard to work through her emphasis on personal labor: labor done in the immediate presence of and for the immediate benefit of others. Doing one's duty on a private rather than a public scale ensures that one's conception of duty does not become so great and abstract that it ceases to represent true duty by overwhelming all recognition of the private desires and individual lives given over as a sacrifice to it.

It is with this neglect of the individual that Dorothea taxes her uncle's self-satisfaction when she is speaking to him of his Reforming politics: " 'I think we have no right to come forward and urge wider changes for good, until we have tried to alter the evils which lie under our own hands' " (M, 1: 405). To be sure,

Eliot shows Dorothea's own plans for work to be impractically idealistic, and her second husband does become a public man working in the cause of Reform. Nevertheless, what goes without question in Eliot's representation of Dorothea and in her representation of Dorothea's uncle is that work done close at hand—private work—ought to take precedence over any other. She emphasizes this point in the novel through the negative examples of Casaubon and Lydgate and Bulstrode and through the positive example of Caleb Garth. When Eliot depicts Caleb as one who is a skillful farm manager but a failure at business on a wider commercial scale, and when she writes, "It must be remembered that by 'business' Caleb never meant money transactions, but the skilful application of labor" (*M*, 2: 127), her point is to maintain this distinction between sentimentalized labor and the comparative monstrosity of work or manufacture on a scale exceeding the figure of the individual.

In Eliot's fiction the importance of work of this private sort is voiced by characters such as Adam Bede, Felix Holt, and Romola as a contrast to the overweening ambitions of characters like the younger Lydgate and Dorothea, and more generally in contrast to what Felix would call a Byronic infatuation with the infinite. So Adam Bede says that " 'the best o' working is, it gives you a grip hold o' things outside your own lot' " (*AB*, 118), and Eliot described Silas Marner's obsessed weaving as a demonic activity and yet allowed him to say, when he had been blessed through his devotion to Eppie, " 'I should ha' been bad off without any work: it was what I held by when everything else was gone from me' " (*SM*, 386). One is reminded of the description of work in Keble's *The Christian Year* (in which sympathy is also a key work): "The trivial round, the common task, / Would furnish all we ought to ask; / Room to deny ourselves; a road / To bring us, daily, nearer God."[5]

Of course, labor in Eliot's time and in the times of which she wrote would exceed the individual because it was given over to profit, even if one ignores for the moment the other determinations of labor in these times that would show her representations to be those of middle-class sentimentality.[6] However, it is precisely Eliot's point to displace the perception of labor from a social to a cultural ground, which is what the world of private work is. Like the related delimitations of private as opposed to public phenomena throughout her writing, this form of work has no basis in the structures or practices of society except as these were subject to interpretation by middle-class disciplines such as psychology, art, charity, and religion.

This is the rule of sentimentality: to find the private arena away from the public arena, in the intimate details and personal commitments of individuals in their immediate surroundings, tasks, and relationships, and thus to discover the true wholeness and unity of the public world. Approaches that might seem more direct—such as political measures or representations of society on the scale of classes, institutions, or governmental organization—are taken to be detours from the domesticated scale of experience that drives individuals within themselves in the search for their social identity. Doing private work is so important in Eliot's fiction that even when it is madly pursued it may still possess the virtue of taking one outside one's self and directing attention away from the state of one's own feelings. All the while Eliot's fiction is designed to draw her readers' attention away from their private concerns to this symbolic sacrifice of individual feeling.

Of course, there is no such denying of the readers' selves taking place. If they identify with the form of Eliot's representations in this instance, it is because the sacrificial mode of private work appeals to their perceptions of themselves. However, Eliot's irony has room for even this recognition, as in her description of Maggie Tulliver when she first reads Thomas à Kempis and too eagerly takes up a life of renunciation, or in her description of Dorothea liking to give up things, as her sister says, when she is a young woman. It is this quality that distinguishes Eliot's sentimentality from the run-of-the-mill variety of this mode of representation in her age: that she could strain it through an intense sense of irony and yet strengthen it by means of this intellectual discipline.

Silas Marner is particularly interesting in terms of this topic because of the way he retreats from the world and gains his miserly riches by occupying himself as a weaver. In doing so he stands in stark contrast to the general fate of the handloom weavers, who were one of the better-known casualties of the change to an industrial economy in England. They had been declining economically since the Napoleonic Wars and, especially in the 1830s and 1840s, were widely publicized because of their desperate plight; yet Eliot chose to make the subject of her novel a handloom weaver who becomes rich through his work.

To be sure, the beginning of the novel is set before the end of the wars, when this group of workers most dramatically began to face difficulties. And despite the fact that J. H. Clapham has noted Silas would have had to have been "one of the last representatives of his class"[7] and that in any case only a truly exceptional weaver could have amassed the riches attributed to him, there is no reason to think Silas was ever meant to be a representative type. On the contrary, Eliot gives one every reason to read this novel as a romance as well as a realist narrative.

Even with this understanding, however, the notorious history of the handloom weavers during the first half of the nineteenth century makes Eliot's decision to show Marner with his "guineas rising in the iron pot" (*SM*, 232) a significant one, to say the least. It becomes all the more intriguing when one sees, from a reading of Eliot's other works, that she was entirely familiar with the weavers' history and used it in other works in entirely conventional terms. In "Amos Barton" she refers to "the time of handloom weavers" when "every other cottage had a loom at its window, where you might see a pale, sickly-looking man or woman pressing a narrow chest against a board, and doing a sort of tread-mill work with legs and arms" ("AB," 23). Similar references appear in *Middlemarch* (1: 339) and *Felix Holt* (6). Given this context, one can see how her representation of Silas amounts to a symbol of her entire approach to labor. Her approach strips his labor of the social reality it had in Eliot's age so that it may become a pure representation of morality perverted and then reclaimed through the private work of raising Eppie and through the psychological return for investment in her. It even allows Eliot to generalize the significance of his obsessive weaving and hoarding in terms of public work set loose from its moorings in private feelings: "The same sort of process has perhaps been undergone by wiser men, when they have been cut off from faith and love—only, instead of a loom and a heap of guineas, they have had some erudite research, some ingenious project, or some well-knit theory" (*SM*, 232).

Thus, the most sentimental aspect of this novel is not its fairy-tale transformation of gold into girl and the description of the affection that develops between her and Silas but rather its designation of the protagonist as a weaver. In this one feature, which actually enables Eliot to characterize as a maniacal perversion the gaining of riches by a weaver at the very time in English history when, as her readers well knew, weavers were being doomed to starvation, one sees how thoroughly the moralizing nature of middle-class discourse can dominate social reality and force even its harshest aspects to appear as a redeeming expression of the human spirit. Although Marx described the miser as "a capitalist gone mad" who "acts in earnest up to the Gospel of abstention,"[8] what one sees in *Silas Marner* is a symbol of the madness implicit in the culture Eliot made a religion. One sees the perverse transformation of the symbolic figure of a laborer starved by capitalism into the symbolic figure of a psychologically wounded capitalist.

True, this conception of private work drawn from Eliot's culture is modified in her novels. Although this negotiation of private and public worlds is a doctrine of nineteenth-century society—that is, an aspect of laissez-faire doctrine in accord with the tradition of individual philanthropy among the gentlefolk of England—Eliot does not adopt this uncritically. She conceived of society in personal terms, so that the model for social commitment would be essentially unchanged from the example of those ladies in Jane Austen's novels who visit the sick and the poor, doling out their blessings from a hamper of soup and sympathy; but she did show some exceptions. Will Ladislaw becomes "an ardent public man" working for Reform (*M*, 2: 424); Daniel Deronda seeks "some sort of social captainship" that would come to him "as a duty" and finds it in the mission of unifying his people (*DD*, 2: 366); even Felix Holt wants to be "a demagogue of a new sort" when he leads the working classes to the realization that they should look for work close at hand. Moreover, in the essay "The Modern Hep! Hep! Hep!" in *Theophrastus Such*, Eliot argued against the idea of a morality based merely on private life and relations and not on public responsibilities.

However, these modifications do not change the basic theme any more than the doctrine of psychological influence in her work is changed by the modifications she placed on it. They merely give the impression that this theme is judiciously balanced. It is significant that the public work of Ladislaw and Deronda is mentioned only as their future, while the figures Eliot shows actually assuming a social commitment on a large scale—Felix Holt and Savonarola—are embroiled in mob violence and personal failure. Although even so extreme a figure as Savonarola is granted much commendation from Eliot in her role as a narrator, *Romola* is designed so that its most persistent impression is that the best and certainly the safest work one can do is that which can be physically grasped within one's own hands. Purposes beyond this immediate touch of the individual are associated with futile philosophy, misguided science, and "machinery" that cannot truly address humanity. Even in the cases of Deronda, Felix Holt, and Savonarola such virtues as their large-scale commitments possess are established by the aid they give as individuals to other individuals: Deronda to Hans Meyrick, Gwendolen Harleth, and Mirah Cohen, Felix to Esther Lyon and the citizens he protects from the lower-class mob, and Savonarola to Romola and other faith seekers. This is the balancing act of Victorian sentimentality, constructed in equal measures of a Tory fable of the past and a Whig fable of individual responsibilities under the conditions of capitalism, as these superficially opposed viewpoints were absorbed within the middle-class culture exemplified by Eliot's works.

Just as Eliot would preserve the fond memory of the egoistic gratifications and aspirations of childhood while drawing the austere moral of their inevitable sacrifice, so would she preserve the memory of a time before duty grew larger than the field of personal relations in small provincial towns while showing that relations on a merely personal scale are no longer adequate to a consciousness of the English nation in the industrial age. It is thus that Eliot's negotiation of the difference between private and public worlds also provides the structure of her nostalgia for childhood as well as the structure of the history she saw as England's from the beginning of the nineteenth century to her own day.

Wherever one chases down the key words in Eliot's writing—sympathy, humanity, duty, spirit, and so on—they are bound to appear divided against themselves because the referential basis of her realism is ultimately its own constitution as a field of signification. On one hand, this merely means Eliot's art cannot signify a ground outside itself but must constitute as this ground its own insistence on such referentiality, so that any rigorous analysis of this ground will have to be an analysis of the forms that stipulate reality within a certain discourse. Such an analysis is one purpose of this book. On the other hand, because it appears more "philosophically" than in the works of other realist writers, more self-consciously elaborated as a theory in her fictional as well as in her nonfictional writing, this slippage within Eliot's terminology represents an aesthetic agon of a particularly intriguing kind: a contest within the conception of the sacred.

In her art Eliot reaches out to the problematic power of the culture in her society. It is as if she is pinned to the double meaning of *sacer*, in which the holy and the accursed, attraction and repulsion, shadow each other etymologically, as they do within the designation of law in Eliot's art. She cannot accept the intimacy of such antitheses—she cannot accept the *language* of her art—yet she is always drawn to the contemplation of the possibility of this intimacy. She writes, "I think aesthetic teaching is the highest of all teaching because it deals with life in its highest complexity. But if it ceases to be purely aesthetic—if it lapses anywhere from the picture to the diagram—it becomes the most offensive of all teaching" (*L*, 4: 300-301).

According to Eliot, under the name of sympathy art religiously deals with life and is a means for drawing the spirit of life out of individuals and into the public world. So Eliot often represents ideals in her writing as being "poor ghosts" that may be "made flesh" so that "they breathe upon us with warm flesh, they touch us with soft responsive hands, they look at us with sad sincere eyes, and speak to us in appealing tones" ("JR," 346). Whereas her negotiations between private and public worlds help to form the substance of her "experiments in life," she conceives the end of her writing to be more than the merely hypothetical representation that the word experiments might suggest. Optimally, it leads to an expression "more sure than shifting theory"; in fact it becomes life itself. As she writes, "I become more and more timid—with less daring to adopt any formula which does not get itself clothed for me in some human figure and individual experience, and perhaps that is a sign that if I help others to see at all it must be through that medium of art" (*L*, 6: 216-17). In this conception of her medium, she finds the ideal mediation of the spirit of humanity as it appears in history. She finds humanity not in ideas alone or in the simple flesh of man but in the practice of her discourse, which unites these. She conceives art at its sacred best to be the solution to the differences between private desire and public duty, the individual and society, ideas and flesh, and the artist and the public.

At least the spirit may so move her on some occasions, when the hierophant she considers to be art takes a relatively simple form. However, as the distinctions between private and public worlds and between the artist's private desires and art's public responsibilities are negotiated in Eliot's writing, more vexing problems arise than those previously noted. At times the sympathetic solution of sentimentality may even seem to fail, for these negotiations forming the drama of her narratives and the representation of her consciousness as an artist cannot be formulated in clear terms unless it is possible to distinguish private from public motives with clarity. One cannot accommodate these to each other, submitting the private to the public while maintaining an impression of private sacrifice through the rule of sympathy, unless one can tell them apart in the first place. To do so, as Eliot sometimes recognizes, is not an easy task. In fact, domesticity may appear as teratology.

Thus, when commenting on Savonarola's public career, Eliot notes the "doubleness" introduced into action "as the complications of life make Self inseparable from a purpose which is not selfish" (*R*, 2: 159). Given this recognition, how are Eliot's negotiations to be brought to a secure conclusion? Rather than achieving the sentimental structure in Eliot's works that submits the private to the public while maintaining a memorialized impression of its sacrifice, they would seem to result in a vacillation between an impersonal duty that obliterates desire and a personal desire that shatters the world of duty, as in a perpetual tug of war between Tom and Maggie Tulliver. The language of her art would appear as language rather than life and as such would be an accursed or "most offensive" teaching. It would resemble a diagram in which the relation between terms looks so technical that they could float past each other, like ghosts, without any semantic disruption. If the doubleness Eliot writes of should not be resolved, there would seem to be no way to conclusively define the spirit of humanity in the achievement of a novel or in the actual course of life. At best it would be only an ideal, an opinion offered to society, and thus a representation of the failure of communication. Eliot would have to recognize that she was fiddling only with the nature of a discourse in her writing, not with history or human life or the human spirit. And one finds, indeed, that even though the themes to which Eliot gives voice in her novels and letters affirm the possibility of a successful negotiation of private and public worlds, the formal structures meant to uphold these themes emerge as fragments when they are closely analyzed. In Eliot's fiction, as in her letter to Cross, there is no coherent division between private and public worlds; rather there is a discourse fragmented by her insistence on this division.

The history given a rationalized formulation in Eliot's division between the private and the public involves the increasing separation of economic from domestic life that created Victorian domesticity, along with the strengthening impression of a life given over to society as a whole because of the change to an urbanized nation characterized by capitalist industry. Eliot's novels represent the effect of this change as a widening of consciousness onto a public scale beyond the literal as well as the figurative horizons that would generally define the world in a traditionally agricultural England, and her negotiations between private and public worlds demonstrate the need for a new way of representing consciousness under the conditions of this change. However, whereas she represents consciousness in the form of these negotiations to interpret the discourse to which she belongs as a result of her place within this changing society, she represents these terms as universal truth because she is so committed to their institutionalization in the moral, political, scientific, and economic discourse of her class that she cannot see her way past them. She sees the modern world of opinion succeeding to the older world of culture, but what she cannot see is that the distinction between private and public worlds at the center of her historical consciousness is the nature of her own society, to which she gives her deference just as blindly as her Boeotian laborers bow to the local squire and the changing weather. The "agents who are not acknowledged" in Eliot's "mental business" are the forms given her writing by the discourse in which she participated.

Romola is especially interesting in this regard. Although set in late fifteenth-century Florence, this novel is one of Eliot's more complex meditations on the division between private and public worlds and most clearly shows the disturbing "doubleness" this division extends throughout life. As she writes of the renegade priest at a time when his sermons are becoming increasingly fanatic, "In the career of a great public orator who yields himself to the inspiration of the moment, that conflict of selfish and unselfish emotion which in most men is hidden in the chamber of the soul, is brought into terrible evidence: the language of the inner voices is written out in letters of fire" (*R*, 2: 67). In Eliot's presentation, this public figure is a combination of the public and the private—is in fact the incarnation of the division that gives life to this opposition. Because he is himself divided and dividing the citizenry of Florence, he represents this fundamental division in Eliot's discourse, thereby reversing the terms of public and private commitment:

> There is no jot of worthy evidence from the time of his imprisonment to the supreme moment, Savonarola thought or spoke of himself as a martyr. The idea of martyrdom had been to him a passion dividing the dream of the future with the triumph of beholding his work achieved. And now, in place of both, had come a resignation which he called by no glorifying name.
> But *therefore he may the more fitly be called a martyr by his fellow-men to all time.* (*R*, 2: 202-3)

He obtains universality, a glorifying name to all time, because in his final resignation—the austere word Eliot couples with sympathy throughout her letters and fiction—he escapes the division between private and public impulse, sacrifice to the future and desire for the present. Yet, Eliot's argument reconstitutes this division. Therefore, in this passage one sees the constitution of her discourse figured in the denial of that discourse, the naming of her morality called forth from nameless silence, in the same way her writing so often refers to unspoken feelings and unknown histories as the basis for the articulation of the feelings and the history she seeks to forward. It is not hard to see Savonarola's preaching as a manifestation of Eliot's own public voice: "His faith wavered, but not his speech: it is the lot of every man who has to speak for the satisfaction of the crowd, that he must often speak in virtue of yesterday's faith, hoping it will come back to-morrow" (*R*, 2: 131).

This wavering internal to Savonarola's speech may be taken to figure the wavering that is the nature of Eliot's discourse as a result of its division between private and public worlds. This division demands that these worlds be regarded as distinct and conflicting entities, between which it is impossible to establish a firm line—between yesterday's faith and today's doubt or between the truth of nature and the uncertainty of desire. Finally, all one can firmly establish as morality is the suffering consciousness of a divided life. This consciousness makes Eliot an exemplary representative of her class—for to make a religion of suffering sympathy is still to justify and idealize the structuring of middle-class life and behavior—but it also makes her a representative of the fear of this class for its foundation in society. It is this quality that makes Eliot's writing a complex exploration of ideology rather than a conventional reproduction of ideology.

Given these considerations, it only makes sense that Eliot's fiction should follow the austerity of the morality represented in her letters. Whatever her idea that one can expect little personal enjoyment in life may owe to her temperament and individual history, it finds significance in her public writings because it corresponds to a social situation that created the idea of private desire as the basis of modern society and as the potential destruction of that society. This is the great secret Eliot's society needed to decipher—the meaning of individual desire now that it had come to bear a character distinct from public ends, even if it was ultimately in harmony with those ends—and so it is not surprising that the spaces of pleasure in Eliot's novels should be secretive and hidden, as in the Red Deeps where Maggie Tulliver and Philip Wakem meet, in the pagan wood of the Chase where Arthur Donnithorne and Hetty have their assignations, in the locked chamber of the late Mrs. Gilfil's bedroom, or in Silas Marner's revelry alone in his house late at night.

All these spaces, except Mrs. Gilfil's bedroom, are in some respect illicit or immoral, according to Eliot's reasoning. However, even such positive or morally neutral enjoyment as she shows is usually presented under the sign of nostalgia or guilt. So Eliot describes the Archery Meeting at which Gwendolen finds such enjoyment and notes, "No open-air amusement could be much freer from those noisy, crowded conditions which spoil most modern pleasures" (*DD*, 1: 101); and she describes how Dorothea loves to ride on horseback and yet considers this exercise a culpable enjoyment "in a pagan sensuous way" (*M*, 1: 8), as in fact it proves to be in the case of Gwendolen's similar taste for riding. She describes Hetty, "that distracting kitten-like maiden" (*AB*, 86), in the dairy, that bower of sensual volumes, colors, and textures, only to take the pleasure in this image as a sign of Hetty's narcissism; and she dilates on the "sweet history of genuine cream," elaborately detailing its deliciousness, while noting that the reader is most likely town-bred and thinks of cream as "a thinnish white fluid, delivered in infinitesimal penny-worths down area steps" ("AB," 7-8). In short, Eliot rarely presents any extended scene of pleasure and, when she does, invariably turns the individual whose desires are being fulfilled toward an image of change that draws the life from that fulfillment.

Pleasure of any intense sort can only be momentary in Eliot's writing and, as such, a temporary and hence dangerous representation of life because her discourse insists on a difference between private and public worlds that makes obscure the relationship between individual feelings and social life. The most melodramatic moments in Eliot's world—Arthur's last-minute arrival and Hetty's pardon when she is on the scaffold, the captain's heart attack felling him just before Caterina would have committed the irrevocable sin of killing him in "Mr. Gilfil's Love-Story," the substitution of Eppie for Silas's gold while he is held at his open door "by the invisible wand of catalepsy" (*SM*, 329), and the reunion of Tom and Maggie Tulliver in the flood of *The Mill on the Floss*—are also a result of this division in Eliot's discourse that I have referred to as the ambivalence of the *sacer*. It is as if the only dramatic image Eliot can form of fulfilled desire must show that fulfillment arriving magically, out of the ordinary course of things she is otherwise so anxious to preserve as the basis of representation, so as to deny the possibility and the desirability of counting on it.

Eliot's austerity makes sense because it belongs to the formation of her historical consciousness, which can understand society only as a negotiation between private and public worlds. Her austere morality is the systematic complement to her sentimentality, the logical development of a habit of mind that so disposes life along private and public axes that the most valued expression of feeling must prove to be in suffering. What one sees in Eliot's suffering consciousness is not her response to the world or to history or to man but to the discourse she has made of the world and of history and of man as a result of her attachment to middle-class values. Her consciousness of suffering is her transformation of these values into a religion. The suffering spirit she recomposes out of fragmented humanity is her way of placing this class on a firm ideological basis, and yet—so much more extreme is her austerity than the suffering in the tradition of sentimental literature—it is also a recognition that this religious basis cannot be as firm as she would have it because her discourse has not offered a clear distinction between private and public worlds. And Eliot is such an exemplary artist of her age because she developed this tortured religion of humankind at the very height of middle-class prosperity in the third quarter of the nineteenth century, as if she were reflecting both this elevation and the changes in English society that would threaten the assumptions of her class in days to come.

Conclusion
Reproduction/Quotation/Criticism

> *What distinguishes the novel from the story (and from the epic*
> *in the narrower sense) is its essential dependence on the book.*
> *The dissemination of the novel became possible only with the*
> *invention of printing. What can be handed on orally, the wealth*
> *of the epic, is of a different kind from what constitutes the stock*
> *in trade of the novel. What differentiates the novel from all*
> *other forms of prose literature—the fairy tale, the legend, even*
> *the novella—is that it neither comes from oral tradition nor goes*
> *into it.*
>
> Walter Benjamin, "The Storyteller; Reflections on the
> Works of Nikolai Leskov," *Illuminations*

In their passage from a handwritten to a typed page, words may seem to acquire a transcendent quality. We may see this quality even in the most banal circumstances, such as those of the classroom. Consider the explanations some teachers offer when requiring students to type their papers. In addition to the advantage in neatness, students are told, typing enables them to look at their work more objectively. They can view their words as text independent of them, open to revision and correction. According to this argument, in giving writing something of the quality of the printed page, typing is expected to impress upon it an appearance of impersonality that makes words appear *as* words, pure and simple. It is supposed to make revisions easier because it separates the words from what the students imagine they have written, leading them to see their words as if they have come from some other origin.

Conversely, in searching for the original manuscripts of books, teachers may seek a sense of the personal and the historical that seems hidden from the published text. Their reasoning is the same as in the first case. They figure that words are changed in an essential way in the process of their reproduction by modern technology.

As one can see even under conditions as common as these, words in the modern world may seem freed of the circumstances that ordinarily limit our perception of things. Responses to this transcendence will be as various as are individual perceptions of any event, so that what is beautiful about it for one may be uncanny or demonic for another. In any case, those who are struck by this transcendence are likely to feel that a drastic change has come over history.

In an essay Benjamin twice quoted in "The Work of Art in the Age of Mechanical Reproduction" (although he did not quote this passage), Paul Valéry suggested the general effect of modern conditions in the following words:

> Works of art will acquire a kind of ubiquity. We shall only have to summon them and there they will be, either in their living actuality or restored from the past. They will not exist in themselves but will exist wherever someone with a certain apparatus happens to be.[1]

After all, on a printed page—or, today, on a video screen—"love" appears as "love," "feeling" as "feeling," "people" as "people," and "language" as "language," no matter what the conditions of a particular text's composition, publication, and distribution may be. While in the act of reading, one meets idiomatic, dialectal, and other usages of language that may interfere with this transcendent quality of the text; but the modern text may seem to sublimate this interference. Considered as an object, the text may appear to rise above history. "Love" is the same word in a poem by Wordsworth and in an essay by Christopher Lasch; and if we are dealing with a recent edition of Wordsworth's writings, even the typeface and paper of the two texts may be the same.

In his 1936 essay on art and technology, Benjamin suggested that technology may alter our spiritual relation to the past. According to his argument, modern technology may strip away the aura, or spiritual uniqueness, that used to characterize the work of art. Though he seeks to regard this event in a "progressive" way, pointedly criticizing Aldous Huxley in a footnote for not doing so, readers of this essay and of his other writings are likely to come away with the impression that Benjamin was made more than a little unhappy when he considered what industrialization had wrought. He begins and ends "The Work of Art" with comments on fascism and war; and when he suggests in another essay that "the capacity to duplicate both the spoken and the written word" has "outstripped human needs," he concludes: "The energies that technology develops beyond their threshold are destructive. They serve primarily to foster the technology of warfare, and of the means used to prepare public opinion for war."[2]

One might compare his reflections on this point to those of Mary Shelley a little more than a century earlier. In *Frankenstein*, too, it appears technology may destroy a spiritual security that art and life once offered. The work of science intended to satisfy human needs seems instead to produce violence and destruction, violating thresholds of all sorts in the process. This historical issue is represented, in *Frankenstein* and in Benjamin's writings, as a problem of duplication.

However, Victor Frankenstein never entirely ceases to believe that technology might spiritualize the modern world in a revolutionary way. By literally bringing to life what heretofore had only been words, artistic images, fantasies, or theories, he might be placed in a position of godlike power over his own creation. Thus, one senses the democratic, equalizing, revolutionary power words were considered to have in Enlightenment ideology. Indeed, this is just the sense of words Frankenstein's creature has when he listens to others talking or reading. To him, the only problem is that people do not live up to the truth of their words. It is significant in this respect that this creature is figuratively identified with the admonitory text that tells his story and through this with the apparatus of book publication that brings him to life—although one must also remember that this apparatus is connected historically with the development of motion pictures, which have finally reproduced him in forms that bear only a nominal relation to the original.

In the perspective I have drawn here, it seems the destruction of our spiritual relation to the past can coexist in the age of mechanical reproduction with an idealist interpretation of words that emphasizes their universality and transcendent identity. As I see it, this perspective accurately describes the ambivalence that traverses Benjamin's writings, which are sometimes so forward-looking that they dismiss the culture of the book in terms similar to those used by Futurists, as when he writes of "the pretentious, universal gesture of the book"[3] just as these agitators for modernity described the book as "a wholly passéist means of preserving and communicating thought" and as a "static companion of the sedentary, the nostalgic, the neutralist."[4] At other times his writings seem nostalgic, looking back toward the very things they are supposed to be looking beyond, as when he says "all things, in a perpetual process of mingling and contamination, are losing their intrinsic character while ambiguity displaces authenticity."[5]

This ambivalence is the consequence of an attitude that asserts its theoretical rejection of "the aesthetics of Idealism"[6] while maintaining and even strengthening an idealist sense of words. "The concepts which are introduced into the theory of art in what follows," Benjamin writes in the preface to "The Work of Art," "differ from the more familiar terms in that they are completely useless for the purposes of Fascism. They are, on the other hand, useful for the formulation of revolutionary demands in the politics of art."[7] Despite his historical approach to art and aesthetics in this essay, he can come to this conclusion because he regards his words as composing an objective text that he expects will be preserved and accurately reproduced through writing, copying, printing, and reading.

In a general sense, of course, philosophical idealism considerably antedates Gutenberg, not to mention the technologies of the nineteenth and twentieth centuries, and in any case is not a simple thing. "Idealism," one might say, is not always "idealism." Benjamin himself suggested that as the apparatus of perception becomes dramatically different in the modern world, so too do the meanings of everything that might seem to have been made familiar through tradition. According to Benjamin, even our perception of the "general sense" of things is altered.

And yet, although he saw technology as having many and varied effects on the nature of art in the modern world, Benjamin does not escape idealism, as one might assume—to take another perspective—from his attitude toward quotations. By all accounts, Benjamin was fascinated with quotations. He collected them, took pride in those he collected, and conceived of a book that might be entirely composed of quotations. He also collected rare books and first editions and in this respect, too, might be seen to be regarding art in an idealist way. As he himself wrote, the collector "always retains some traces of the fetishist and . . . by owning the work of art, shares in its ritual power."[8] Since it is this connection between art and ritual that he saw being altered by modern technology, one might well ask if this footnote to "The Work of Art" does not reflect on its author, indicating a complicity between the idealism he is criticizing and the historical view of things he is trying to promulgate. Still, Benjamin's fascination with quotations seems most interesting in this regard. "To quote a word is to call it by its name," he writes, adding, a few sentences later,

> In the quotation that both saves and chastises, language proves the matrix of justice. It summons the word by its name, wrenches it destructively from its context, but precisely thereby calls it back to its origin. It appears, now with rhyme and reason, sonorously, congruously in the structure of a new text. As rhyme it gathers the similar into its aura; as name it stands alone and expressionless. In quotation the two realms—of origin and destruction—justify themselves before language. And conversely, only where they interpenetrate—in quotation—is language consummated. In it is mirrored the angelic tongue in which all words, startled from the idyllic context of meaning, have become mottoes in the book of Creation.[9]

Quotation appears as the threshold to transcendence in contrast to technological reproduction, which strips art of its transcendence and threatens human destruction if it is taken too far. The narrative of quotation—exile and redemptive return—contrasts with the narrative of history, in which art, wrenched from its original context, can return to that spiritual home only in the form of destruction. What emerges in this difference between quotation and mechanical reproduction is Benjamin's approach to history, which is at once summoned by and cut off from transcendence. Quotation and mechanical reproduction do not appear logically connected in Benjamin's argument, even though they are rhetorically associated through terms like "context," "origin," "aura," and "destruction," because history would collapse if this duplicity were not maintained. In quotation, Benjamin can figure a truth that is other than discourse and yet that appears through the movement of discourse. He needs to represent truth in this form because the only other objectivity his writing might have seems to be that figured by the process of mechanical reproduction, which destroys the notions of originality and of authenticity and perhaps even of authority. At the same time he must assert and deny an objectivity transcending discourse because it appears to him that otherwise there would be no threshold to quotation or to mechanical reproduction and thus no story at all.

In other words, the refractory idealism in Benjamin's writing stems from the fact that it is only in idealist terms that he can articulate his historical analysis. The ambivalence in his writing is the wavering of its terms between history and "history," or between their appeal to a historical objectivity and their implication as rhetorical terms within the very history they are meant to transcend.

To see that I am not merely wrenching quotations out of context in emphasizing this point, consider Benjamin's argument in "The Work of Art" that fascism is the inevitable result of regarding technology as art. "The violation of the masses," Benjamin writes, "whom Fascism, with its *Führer* cult, forces to their knees, has its counterpart in the violation of an apparatus which is pressed into the production of ritual values." Regarding technology as art, it appears, takes it beyond its threshold and thus to destruction. Concluding that all efforts to render politics aesthetic "culminate in one thing: war," Benjamin illustrates his point by quoting a manifesto on the Ethiopian colonial war written by Filippo Marinetti:

> For twenty-seven years we Futurists have rebelled against the branding of war as antiaesthetic. . . . Accordingly we state: . . . War is beautiful because it establishes man's dominion over the subjugated machinery by means of gas masks, terrifying megaphones, flame throwers, and small tanks. War is beautiful because it initiates the dreamt-of metalization of the human body. War is beautiful because it enriches a flowering meadow with fiery orchids of machine guns. War is beautiful because it combines the gunfire, the cannonades, the ceasefire, the scents, and the stench of putrefaction into a symphony. War is beautiful because it creates new architecture, like that of the big tanks, the geometrical formation flights, the smoke spirals from burning villages, and many others. . . . Poets and artists of Futurism! . . . remember these principles of an aesthetics of war so that your struggle for a new literature and a new graphic art . . . may be illumined by them![10]

In his dogmatic conclusion on this point, as in his dogmatic assertion that his own concepts cannot possibly be of use to fascism, Benjamin contradicts his own insistence on a historical view of things. Idealism alone can wield categories in such a way as to assert that certain concepts can be used only for revolutionary purposes and others only for the purposes of fascism and war. As I hope to have indicated, though, this contradiction is more than a simple weakness or infelicity in his writing. It is a significant contradiction, one that reproduces a general problem in dealing with the issue of history in the modern world; and its analysis can lead us to see "The Work of Art" from a perspective that is valuable for understanding my own argument, as well as Benjamin's.

To concentrate on the instance of language, it can seem as if the world now leads us to perceive words uninflected by any context short of the universal. As so much romantic and postromantic literature testifies, the human voice, the individual touch, and local culture in all respects seem to give way in the latter half of the eighteenth century to an image of a rationalized communication that can be endlessly reproduced and universally translated. Such is the fable of history that began to be popularized in the second half of the eighteenth century, a fable with which I have dealt in my discussion of works by Eliot and other writers of the nineteenth century.

Even if this fable is accepted as history, though, the spirit in which it is taken is an elusive thing, as one can see in the difference between Benjamin's foreboding essay and the cheerful piece by Valéry from which he takes his epigraph. Moreover, although one need not praise this image of communication (as does Jürgen Habermas), one is no less captivated by its idealism when one asserts (as does Hans-Georg Gadamer) the authenticity of an origin we have lost, neglected, or betrayed. And one is still captivated when, sensing the breakdown or falsity of the universal, one is tempted to see words as so much aleatory froth: signs bound to no absolute beginning or end and therefore groundless, free-floating, and unmarked by history. Jacques Derrida never ceases to remind us that we do not escape idealism so easily, but some of those who have aligned themselves with his writing have not been so modest in their assertions.

In my approach to literature in this book, I have tried to avoid giving uncritical acceptance to this modern sense of things. I have tried to avoid accepting fable as history while insisting on the possibility of critically analyzing social history without making dogmatic judgments. Of course, the foregoing sketch of the modern sense of things is very crude and, yes, dogmatically oversimplified. But it serves as a way into the conclusion drawn from my study of nineteenth-century literature, which I have been able to deal with at a more satisfactory length. Through this historical description and analysis, I have tried to develop a theoretical argument: that every form of discourse is fundamentally political in a way we cannot interrogate, cannot even recognize, unless we are committed to changing the discourse that seems natural to our own lives. According to this argument, we must recognize literature as being political as well as social if our sense of history is not to be a form of idealism automatically reproduced, or quoted, from the past.

Benjamin saw art as becoming political when it ceased to be bound by tradition: "But the instant the criterion of authenticity ceases to be applicable to artistic production, the total function of art is reversed. Instead of being based on ritual, it begins to be based on another practice—politics."[11] In this view of things, it seems as if the category of "the cult," with which Benjamin associates art before the modern age, is in some way detached from the struggles over inequities of power that are described by "politics." The rest of Benjamin's essay—and his other writings—would give one the impression that he never meant to suggest such a conclusion. Nevertheless, he is driven to it, as it were, by the very way he names "art" in relation to "politics." Even while tracing historical changes in its nature, he still treats art as an object that is coherent, homogenous, universal, or, in a word, ideal in its nature.

One could say that language itself, rather than the modern world, drives Benjamin toward this conclusion. It is as if he is led by the word "art" to see identity even though other passages in his writing argue against the identity in question. To put it simply, "art" is reproduced as the same word in different passages of his writing although the objects to which it refers are described as differing radically from one another. The result is a problem of rhetorical form: a problem that could be described as the problem characteristic of quotation, which displaces words from one context to another and in so doing may completely change them. In effect, Benjamin's writing in this essay is bedeviled by its topic: the issue of reproduction or duplication. The monstrous issue that so disturbed Shelley's novel reappears in "The Work of Art" a century later and disrupts its categories, carrying them beyond their thresholds until it may appear that all the sense of the text has been appropriated by a play of metaphorical identities and differences.

Thus, as Benjamin deals with the relation between art and politics in this essay, it seems he knows and yet does not know that these terms cannot remain themselves in all places and times. In effect, traditional art is detached from politics in this essay because Benjamin could not find any other way to name this object while he worked to describe the changes he saw it undergoing in the modern world. For lack of a more flexible way of putting quotation marks around the objects of historical discourse, he was driven to adopt an idealist view of art even while he was devoting himself to criticizing this view. In this respect, his fate is common among critics, especially Marxist critics, who have sought in this century to reject the view of things represented by the figure of the liberal intellectual in the nineteenth century. Jurij Lotman and Jan Mukarovský are among the other critics who have described the historically changing nature of art, but their work, too, is troubled by a commitment to idealist definitions of aesthetic functions.

One consequence of this troubling idealism is the romantic aura Benjamin's essay may have for readers today. More specifically, the consequence is the existence of passages like the following, which, as translated by Harry Zohn, reproduces the self-contradictory appearance of *Kunstwerk* in the original:

With the different methods of technical reproduction of a work of art, its fitness for exhibition increased to such an extent that the quantitative shift between its two poles [of cult value and exhibition value] turned into a qualitative transformation of its nature. This is comparable to the situation of the work of art in prehistoric times when, by the absolute emphasis on its cult value, it was, first and foremost, an instrument of magic. Only later did it come to be recognized as a work of art. In the same way today, by the absolute emphasis on its exhibition value the work of art becomes a creation with entirely new functions, among which the one we are conscious of, the artistic function, later may be recognized as incidental.[12]

According to this passage, "the work of art in prehistoric times" is a contradiction in terms. Strictly speaking, there is no such object. Nevertheless, this logical impossibility is a rhetorical reality in Benjamin's argument because his lingering adherence to a nineteenth-century conception of art interferes with his attempt to analyze art as a historical phenomenon. His writing does not appear as a homogenous discourse, then, but as a criss-crossing of discourses, including the discourse of ninetenth-century idealism.

This consideration might seem to lessen the value of Benjamin's writing. However, I think the situation is otherwise. It simply indicates the historical condition of all critical understanding: the condition of conflict and heterogeneous definition that cannot be ideally reconciled within any theory, text, or name.

Hence the importance of an analysis of the specific form of idealism practiced by the liberal intellectual. To dismiss all forms of idealism under the same name would be to leave ourselves as helpless and alienated as we are if we take for granted the sense of things that seems to grow naturally from the practices of contemporary society. It is only by insisting on the issue of history that one can resist the sense of complacency—and its twin, the sense of fatality—with which we are otherwise led to carry on our lives. We have to see history in the practice of critical activity, as well as in the object of critical activity, if we are to try to understand contradictions like those that appear in Benjamin's essay and, in other instances, if we are to understand the apparent absence of contradictions in certain writings.

To develop this argument, I have tried to describe the peculiarities of phenomena such as words, histories, characters, novels, truths, quotations, and authors, as they appeared to liberal intellectuals in the nineteenth century. Furthermore, I have tried to suggest the critical implications of this description for any approach to language, literature, and history. In analyzing some of the most important figures that came to life within the world of discourse that was reality for liberal intellectuals, I have tried to emphasize how rhetorical powers always play a great role in social history. In this regard, it is of more than incidental significance that the discourse of the liberal intellectual still has considerable power in contemporary society, despite the fact that intellectuals today are very different creatures from the nineteenth-century figures whose rhetoric and poses they may reproduce.

Historical approaches to literature have sometimes been criticized for reducing a work to an extraneous context, such as the psyche of an author, the events of an era, or a philosophical worldview. In some cases, this criticism has been justified. However, my approach does nothing of the sort. In fact, my argument is that the categorical division between "text" and "context" is misleading. Rather than reducing a text to a context, a historical approach should show that the text is an imaginary unity. It is a phantasm created by the way material forms (such as the printed word) are institutionalized within forms of discourse: religious, educational, aesthetic, hermeneutic, and so on. The text is a rhetorical and thus a political effect, not an objective reality.

In other words, what we call "the text" is inconceivable apart from what we call "context." The text does not exist as an isolated object, much less as a transcendent one. It is only by virtue of a naive literalism that anyone can see words on a page surrounded by blank space and believe we can read "the text itself," as in the popularized ideology of New Criticism. A similar naiveté, more or less willed, leads to the conclusion that we can read as individual subjects, as in liberal humanism and some varieties of reader-response criticism, such as the psychoanalytic work of Norman Holland. The conclusion that we can experience the text as a totally liberated *jouissance*, as in some of the work of Roland Barthes and Julia Kristeva, also follows a process of figuring in which history is repressed.

Literature does not come to us in isolation from the historical world. The idea that it is so isolated can only be a political statement with a significance determined by the conditions in which it is made, disseminated, and interpreted. We are not given literature as "literature" pure and simple; we are not given "language" and "words" *tout court*. From any beginning one may care to name, things such as "literature," "language," and "words" are presented as discourse. They have no existence apart from discourse, and their existence as objects of discourse is not universal. It varies over history and, in any historical situation, over socially instituted differences such as those of race, class, and gender.

This is not to make discourse a transcendent term—what Kenneth Burke would call a god-term. Despite Victor Frankenstein's dreams to the contrary, we cannot master our own creation. As I have emphasized throughout this work, although specific discourses may have a dominant or hegemonic power, there is no "discourse" pure and simple, just as there is no "language" or "literature" in this sense. There are always only discourses, plural and heterogeneous, no matter where one draws the line that isolates for analytic purposes a particular discourse from another. In the general sense I am using here, "discourse" simply becomes shorthand for an insistence that literature, like any other reality, is a social and political construction.[13] In this general sense, discourse no longer describes a linguistic object but the condition of existence of any object of language. It stresses that discourse constitutes the appearance of reality as such.

One can differentiate discourses in any number of ways, which cannot be completely systematized. For example, one might write about the discourse of the family, of historiography, of sex, of desire, of technology, or, as in the present case, of the liberal intellectual. Given this recognition along with the further acknowledgment that discourse must be conceived to be heterogeneous if one is to resist the blandishments of idealism, it might seem that all is arbitrary in the discrimination and analysis of discourse that I am describing here; that we have surrendered a naive perception of historical categories for a perception that is utterly incoherent; or, in the nineteenth-century terms which still have some currency (viz., recent debates over deconstruction), that we have discarded culture for anarchy.

This is not a necessary conclusion. Although they do become more complex in appearance and more problematic in significance, objects do not disappear from history when one refuses to grant an uncritical acceptance to their formal, rationalized, or idealized appearance in society. In fact, it is the contrary approach that is arbitrary, or ultimately based only on unacknowledged assertions of power.

Historically viewed, objects are no longer outlined in an obvious or ingenuous way. However, they still take on definition from the lines of social identities and conflicts. They are defined by the struggle over the power of meaning. Their existence is as real and material as are the signifying practices that constitute the discourses in which they appear. As I have argued, these practices include literature, as well as the work of institutions like government, education, charity, and psychology. Although it is true that within this approach one cannot perceive objects like "history," "peasants," "the novel," "art," "the individual," and "desire" with the smug assurance of a securely distanced spectator, they still remain definite objects. Moreover, one's analysis of them is even more open to social evaluation and judgment than analysis of a more traditional sort because the historically minded critic cannot take refuge in universal truths, feelings common to all of humanity, obvious facts, formal necessities, beauty, rationality, maturity, wisdom, and such like chat.

Rather than making the critical enterprise arbitrary, an emphasis on the relative and heterogeneous nature of differences in discourse is a salutary reminder that any form of discourse, including critical discourse, is fundamentally political. In any historical situation, in any society, there is no neutral position, no neutral line. Unless one is still captivated by idealism, it is this conclusion that is implied by the recognition that there is no absolute ground to signification.

Granted this conclusion that literature is social and political from its beginning, the integrity, unity, and harmony traditionally attributed to great works—or to any works—must be discarded. These conceptions are displaced by a view of the word, the sentence, the novel—any isolable unit of discourse—as being riven by the contestation over meaning in society. In this view, as Mikhail

Bakhtin and Michel Foucault, among others, have suggested, words are not neutral, abstract, or transcendent marks on a blank page. They are the sites of historical struggles; and these struggles do not cease when professors, easing back in armchairs or sitting before typewriters, compose their thoughts.

Of course, one can read for a variety of reasons and in any number of ways, none of which are scorned within this understanding. There is nothing *wrong* with reading under the impression that one is attaining to a transcendent realm of being. There is nothing wrong with believing, for instance, when one turns the pages of *Adam Bede*, that one is transcending time and space to communicate with the mind of George Eliot and with the human spirit that this mind, in its sublimity and sympathy, so thoroughly comprehended.

But this is not to say that the historical criticism I advocate in this work is simply one brand of reading among others. It does not leave everything as it is. The crucial question here does not concern ways of reading but rather the purposes of criticism. As a social activity, literary criticism is other than reading in the everyday sense of the word. Therefore, this criticism will be entangled in mystification if we do not relate its purposes to its existence as an activity different from reading. Criticism is not practiced by people in general; it is the exercise of intellectuals who are almost always teachers in universities; and it is only by taking these conditions into account that we can decide what we are doing and what we ought to be doing.

Given these conditions, should the purpose of criticism be to propagate a form of truth such as "taste" or (to use a more contemporary example) "meaning"? Or should it be to analyze the way forms of truth such as "taste" and "meaning" are constituted? In other words, should it rather be devoted to studying the politics of rhetoric? As I have argued throughout this book, the advantage of the latter approach is that it leads us to question authority and thus to develop criticism as something other than the compulsive reproduction, or quotation, of a discourse that happens to be institutionalized in the modern world.

Other approaches to criticism may have some advantages in style and formal composure because critics who identify their activity with authority are not driven to turn on their own terms and to displace their own identities. They are not haunted by the past or disturbed by the return of the repressed because they identify themselves with an idealized conception of the past. Given only moderate intelligence and skill, critics of this sort can avoid the obvious self-contradictions that discompose the writing of intellectuals like Benjamin. There is an *ease* in asserting the aristocratic nature of taste, or the meaning a competent, rational, or mature reader must perceive, that is not available to a criticism that resists idealizing history. However, if one asks about the price paid for this ease, it no longer appears so persuasive. It also should be noted that this ease does not indicate a difference between a criticism of pleasure and a criticism of puritanical discipline and self-denial. I have indicated in this book, through the example of George Eliot, that a historical criticism of feeling does not reflect on the reality, legitimacy, or importance of any feeling or sensation. On the contrary, by demonstrating the politics of feeling, it extends our capacity to desire, to feel pleasure, and, even in the most old-fashioned sense of the word, to appreciate literature.

It should go without saying that the practice of criticism is more complex than I make it appear when I imply that it is limited to two types. Again this is a crude outline I have drawn to focus attention on a more central object of theoretical concern in this study: the relation between rhetoric and politics. Since objects of discourse *are* relations, not substantial entities, types, realities, or truths that will stand still for our inspection like soldiers on parade, we must always design new approaches to their understanding. Thus, I have developed my argument about the politics of rhetoric with the more specific issue of the relation between literary representation and social history, and I have advanced the latter argument through the specific instance of nineteenth-century literature and, in particular, the works of George Eliot.

The argument of this design is that one cannot define the relation between literature and society in a satisfactory way if one conceives of "literature" and "society" as independent objects—say, a populated landscape and a book— linked by a dotted line that denotes influence. The picture is only marginally more satisfactory if the line is made reflexive so that the influence can move in both ways; and it is still only a little more satisfactory if we have a number of dotted lines busily intersecting one another and thus suggesting a process of mediation. I do not think I overexaggerate the usual picture of the relation between literature and society; the problem with any such picture is that it still preserves the literary work and society as formally intelligible objects, no matter how complex and variously mediated it may determine the relations among them to be. It is for this reason that writers such as Georg Lukács and Lucien Goldmann could idealize great works of literature and could regard societies as totalities despite the fact that some aspects of their writing might lead one to question such a view of things.

A more adequate description would show there is no fundamental society to which literature must be related in some coherent way (even if this relation is viewed as one of absolute disjunction, as in the aestheticism of the late nineteenth century). If one is not to idealize society, one must consider it an irregularly changing complex of signifying practices that become concentrated, at some points, in institutions. Sometimes these institutions are coherent forms and in their relations to each other give form to society as a whole. However, the appearance of these forms as such is only an effect of rhetorical power. Not that this power is negligible, but it must be understood as a historical phenomenon if one is not to be blind to the way differences of power are materially instituted, maintained, and changed within the patterns of signifying practices that compose society.

Just as there is no "society" pure and simple, there is no "literary work" pure and simple. I have designed this analysis to speak to wider theoretical issues, but it is important to keep in mind that by my argument "literature" is not a universal term. Benjamin, for example, had good reason to suggest that surrealist writings are "not literature,"[14] even though they are commonly regarded as such today. Moreover, as Benjamin also suggested, the fact that objects may be considered art at a particular time and place does not mean they always have been or always will be art. The same conclusion holds for "technology," "the novel," and similar phenomena—including "theory." One can establish a critical relation between terms like society and literary work only by analyzing them as historical forms and by evaluating these forms as political discourse. I have tried to do this with Eliot's work and, more generally, with liberal intellectual discourse in the nineteenth century; and I have at least tried to indicate the implication of politics in rhetorical form on a scale ranging from the level of literature as an institution to that of fine stylistic details in the works of individual authors.

As previously noted, I do not present my analysis as the last word, or the only word, on Eliot's works, or on nineteenth-century literature, or on the discourse of the liberal intellectual—whatever aspect of this study one cares to emphasize. Nevertheless, this kind of historical approach does have a value that sets it apart from other approaches to literature and makes it especially imperative. This approach differs from others in that it does not hold a particular method of reading to be natural, proper, or competent. Instead, it looks to find the significance of ways of reading in the historical relations that constitute social life. More broadly, it looks to explain any signifying practice in terms of the differences of power by which it is instituted and which the people involved in the practice maintain, develop, contest, or transform in their relation with others in society. Therefore, this approach does more than recognize the danger of reproducing history as one form of idealism or another. It recognizes that there is no reproduction of an idea that is not also a reproduction of specific ways of being in the world that exclude, deny, alter, oppress, and destroy other ways of being. To reproduce an idea is also to reproduce a sense of things, to grant certain privileges, to confirm some identities and withhold others, and, in short, to establish power through rhetorical procedures that cannot be neutral toward people in the past or in the present. Rather than making criticism more arbitrary or willful, then, this recognition that the historical conditions of discourse are also political enables criticism to become more demanding, self-critical, and open to revision. Benjamin's occasional dogmatism is nothing to the easeful arrogance of, say, an F. R. Leavis, a Denis Donoghue, a William Bennett, or a John Silber.

When literature is seen not as a response to society but as a social practice, one can see that by the very way one assumes a position as a writer in a particular society one also assumes a certain conception of society. A historical analysis of literature needs to take into account the forms of discourse to which writers are given over in this way, not just the generic and cultural traditions that appear to constitute literature as an autonomous institution. Otherwise, one impoverishes literature. One reduces it to its relation to a particular audience through chat about formal harmony or genius or strength or something of that order. The best alternative is for critics to engage the very possibility of its existence or, in other words, its power to signify.

This does not mean a historical criticism must turn to the conditions in which a particular text initially appeared to establish its meaning. On the contrary, it should leave the fetishism of origins to psychobiographical critics, collectors of autographs and first editions, and religious enthusiasts. In analyzing the conditions in which Eliot's writing appeared and took on meaning in nineteenth-century England, I have not argued that these were the only conditions in which it could have been read at that time and place, and I have not suggested that the meaning that has been found in her work from that time until the present day either can or ought to be constrained by these conditions. In focusing my study on Eliot's identity as a liberal intellectual and the relation of liberal intellectuals to the middle classes, I have not pretended to find an original or critically privileged meaning in her work. What I have tried to show is what meaning this work must have, consciously or unconsciously, for those who identify with the discourse of the liberal intellectual. I have analyzed a politics of rhetorical form, not a phenomenology of reading, although I have tried to emphasize the significance of this analysis by indicating how impressive Eliot's rhetoric has proved to many readers and by describing how these readers must view reality if they take Eliot at her word. In this way I have analyzed literary representation as a discourse in the act of making sense of itself, putting on a face for society, or—in the specific case of Eliot's fiction—making a narrative of itself and thus a symbolic past, present, and future for its assumptions. I have described how the terms of her writing are not the terms of English society past or present but rather those of the discourse in which society appeared to her, thus arguing that history is a matter of political relations or, in other words, that the object of literary representation is always already a representation. This is not to say literature never touches on or refers to the world but that its reference and meaning can be determined only in terms of the historical and political conditions of its existence. It is because they do not recognize the historical struggle over meaning that those who slight this approach must impoverish their imagination, which is to say, their power to change the meaning of things.

Consider in this respect the quotation from Marinetti in Benjamin's essay on art and mechanical reproduction. To be sure, it is as repugnant as Benjamin found it. It appears even worse if one is aware of the other themes interwoven with the glorification of war in the writings of Marinetti and other Futurists. These involved, for instance, a fierce demeaning of women and a rabid nationalism. One cannot even say (as people sometimes try to say in such cases) that Marinetti was simply a foolish and ineffectual intellectual, for he actively supported Mussolini and was a demonstrably influential figure in the cultural life of Europe between the world wars.

Still, Benjamin found this excerpt from his writings *quotable*. It "has the virtue of clarity,"[15] he said; and I imagine most of those who have read Benjamin's essay have been impressed by Marinetti's excited imagery. To say this writing is fascist is to say the truth and yet to say very little if this effect is not explained any further. In this regard, one might also think of writers like Pound and Céline, whose works have even proven impressive to many of the people who find their lives and some elements of their work utterly antipathetic. One might think of an icon like George Eliot, too, whose work can remain so moving even after one realizes its politics. And thinking of a writer as acceptable as Eliot is, a writer as proper under virtually any definitions of literature except those formulated by avowed extremists like Marinetti, one might realize that Marinetti, for all his hyped-up rhetoric, is not a special case. In his writing as in Eliot's, Pound's, and Céline's, politics and aesthetics are not properly separable.

The same is true of Benjamin's writings. In comparison to Marinetti, he certainly comes off well, even if the reassuring ending of the epilogue to "The Work of Art"—"Communism responds by politicizing art"[16]—does not sound very reassuring today. His appearance becomes rather more dubious, though, when one realizes he is capable of writing about "the constructive, dictatorial side of revolution."[17] Perhaps even more disturbing is his preface to a description of a visit to Moscow: "Admittedly, the only real guarantee of a correct understanding is to have chosen your position before you came. In Russia above all, you can only see if you have already decided."[18] To dismiss remarks like these as marginal, regrettable, or historically infelicitous points in his writing, unrelated to its more important moments, would be as foolish as dismissing Marinetti's fascism by saying art is above politics or, conversely, by saying it does not succeed in rising above politics. Measures such as these serve no other purpose but to automatically reproduce our own dogmas about objects (art, life, authors, politics, etc.) and the relations among these objects. In dealing with writers whose work seems especially disturbing to us, as in dealing with the most comforting writers, the only way not to turn ourselves into an unconscious apparatus of reproduction is by resisting the impulse to make the work coherent and homogenous and thoroughly meaningful. It is only through such resistance that we can get at the rhetorical powers which shape our lives and thus prepare ourselves to work against even those dogmas that seem most perfectly and obviously true.

In the case of Marinetti's quotation, one consequence of this viewpoint would be the realization that it is not really about the Ethiopian colonial war, at least not in the sense in which we usually speak of the subject of a piece of writing. Nor would it be satisfactory to say this passage is about war and technology or even about the relationship between art and war. In this respect,

Benjamin's presentation is inadequate. What is at stake in this passage, as Marinetti announces, is the power of rhetoric. The object of his description is not war but an established rhetoric of war that allows for aesthetic terror but not for "terrifying megaphones"; for beautiful human bodies but not for a beautiful "metalization of the human body"; for flowery landscapes or for soldiers fallen like the flowers of their country but not for "fiery orchids of machine guns"; for the aesthetic organization of a picture of war but not for a picture, or "symphony," that includes "the stench of putrefaction." Viewed in this way, Marinetti's writing not only appears related to that of other writers who came out of World War I, such as Hemingway and Siegfried Sassoon, but also challenges the work of these writers.

Marinetti may be displacing the traditional rhetoric of war with an obscene celebration of it, whereas these other writers are seeking to displace it with a chastened realism. However, a consideration of Marinetti's writing might lead one to ask whether the writing that rebelled through realism did not in fact represent an aesthetics that might be as duplicitous and as repressive toward reality as the aesthetics it was supposed to be countering. Without suggesting that *A Farewell to Arms* and Marinetti's manifesto are in any way equivalent, one can still ask whether the antiheroic and laconic rhetoric with which Hemingway approached the subject of war does not reproduce in a different form (for instance, in a sense of fatalism) the submission to honor, duty, and country that appears in the officially institutionalized literature he criticized. Certainly anyone familiar with a contemporary movie like *Apocalypse Now* should be hesitant about deciding the difference between a celebratory and a critical aesthetics; in this respect, one might say Marinetti's manifesto has the virtue not only of clarity but also of honesty. It is a perverse honesty, one that uncritically submits itself to social authority; but it might be said to represent more accurately than the work of writers like Hemingway the hideous power of modern governments to construe destruction as beauty. Benjamin did point to this quality in Marinetti's writing; but in judging it to be the inevitable result of all efforts "to render politics aesthetic," he so oversimplified the representation of reality in the modern world that he inevitably was led to his own dangerous representations—such as his statement that "Communism responds by politicizing art," which appears so cruelly ironic today in relation to the critical meaning Benjamin intended it to have.

There is still more to be said about the significance of this quotation from Marinetti. For instance, in a historical analysis of this quotation one would expect a discussion of the relation between Marinetti's exaltation of war and his professed hatred of women, the traditional family, and sentimentality. For present purposes, though, the foregoing analysis should be sufficient to develop my point: that meaning is not fixed in a text, in relations among texts, or even in relations among texts and individual readers; it is produced by the way texts are defined and institutionalized within discourse. The advantage of developing a historical discourse in criticism is that it leads us to recognize the heterogeneous and relative nature of discourses and thus to confront the politics of the rhetoric by which meaning is produced. Such an approach leads us to see meaning as a struggle, not as an established wealth, property, form, or institution; and in this way it can make the power of imagination something more than rhetoric.

Notes

Notes

Chapter 1. "George Eliot" and the Fables of the Liberal Intellectual

1. C.f. Janet K. Gezari's analysis of the way Eliot's metaphorical language gestures toward a "ground of abstract concepts" in "The Metaphorical Imagination of George Eliot," *ELH* 45 (1978): 98.

2. On the question of Eliot's identity as an intellectual and other points related to my study, see Terry Eagleton, *Criticism and Ideology: A Study in Marxist Literary Theory* (London: Verso Editions, 1978), esp. pp. 102-5. Although there are significant differences between Eagleton's approach and my own, his is the best short analysis of the liberal intellectual—and of the errors commonly made in analyzing this figure—that I know.

Of course, most of Eliot's critics deal with her intellectual background. Among the important works in this regard are P. Bourl'honne's *George Eliot: Essai de biographie intellectuelle et morale 1819-1854* (Paris: Librarie Ancienne Honoré Champion, 1933; reprint, New York: AMS Press, 1973); U. C. Knoepflmacher's *Religious Humanism and the Victorian Novel: George Eliot, Walter Pater, and Samuel Butler* (Princeton: Princeton University Press, 1965), and *George Eliot's Early Novels: The Limits of Realism* (Berkeley: University of California Press, 1968); Bernard O. Paris, "George Eliot's Religion of Humanity," in *George Eliot: A Collection of Critical Essays*, ed. George R. Creeger, *Twentieth Century Views*, ed. Maynard Mack (Englewood Cliffs, NJ; Prentice-Hall, 1970), pp. 11-36; William Meyers, "George Eliot: Politics and Personality," in *Literature and Politics in the Nineteenth Century*, ed. John Lucas (London: Methuen and Co., 1971), pp. 105-30; and George Levine, "Intelligence and Deception in *The Mill on the Floss*," *PMLA* 80 (1965): 402-9.

3. See Raymond Williams, *Culture and Society 1780-1950*, Anchor Book Edition (Garden City, NJ: Doubleday, 1959), p. 38.

Eliot herself used the word "intellectual"; for instance, in referring to a gathering in 1852 of such types as G. H. Lewes, Spencer, Henry Crabb Robinson, Dickens, and F. W. Newman. See Gordon S. Haight, *George Eliot and John Chapman*, 2d ed. (Hamden, CT: Archon Books, 1969), p. 52.

4. See Lewis A. Coser, *Men of Ideas: A Sociologist's View* (New York: The Free Press, 1965), p. 37.

5. For an influential description of this change, see Karl Mannheim, *Ideology and Utopia: An Introduction to the Sociology of Knowledge*, trans. Louis Wirth and Edward Shils, with a preface by Louis Wirth (New York: Harcourt, Brace and World, 1968), p. 139.

6. W. J. Harvey, *The Art of George Eliot* (London: Chatto and Windus, 1969; reprint, Westport, CT: Greenwood Press, 1978) p. 34.

7. Thomas Carlyle, *Past and Present, The Works of Thomas Carlyle*, Centenary Edition, 30 vols. (London: Chapman and Hall, 1896), 10: 5; see also his comments on the new "Philosophical Class" in *Sartor Resartus: The Life and Opinions of Herr Teufelsdröckh, Works* 1: 21.

8. Hippolyte Taine, *Notes on England*, trans. with an introduction by W. F. Rae (New York: Henry Holt and Co., 1876), pp. 242-243.

9. See Alexis de Tocqueville, "The European Revolution," in *"The European Revolution" and Correspondence with Gobineau*, ed. and trans. with an introduction by John Lukacs (Westport, CT: Greenwood Press, 1959), esp. bk. 1, chap. 1; and John Stuart Mill's comment on his agreement with Comte on this point in *Autobiography of John Stuart Mill*, with a preface by John Jacob Goss (New York: Columbia University Press, 1924), p. 148.

10. Quoted by A. S. Collins, *The Profession of Letters: A Study of the Relation of Author to Patron, Publisher, and Public, 1780-1832* (New York: E. P. Dutton, 1929), p. 263.

11. Quoted by Haight, *George Eliot and John Chapman*, pp. 32-33.

12. Quoted by Jerome Hamilton Buckley, *The Victorian Temper: A Study in Literary Culture* (Cambridge: Harvard University Press, 1951), p. 190.

13. Quoted by Haight, *George Eliot and John Chapman*, p. 35.

14. Quoted by John Gross, *The Rise and Fall of the Man of Letters: Aspects of English Literary Life Since 1800* (London: Weidenfeld and Nicolson, 1969), p. 65.

15. Haight, *George Eliot and John Chapman*, p. 33.

16. C.f. Shirley Frank Levenson's discussion of the way Eliot's conception of art represents a widening of sympathy to the point of universality in "The Use of Music in *Daniel Deronda*," *Nineteenth-Century Fiction*, 24 (1969): 317-34.

17. C.f. Jean-Paul Sartre's comments on the way modern intellectuals "take themselves for an elite called to judge everything" with the result that "they think as if they were already living in the distant future and judge our time from the abstract point of view of the future" in *Plaidoyer pour les intellectuels, Collection Idées* (Paris: Gallimard, 1972), pp. 10-11.

Also, c.f. Williams's comment on this change in *Culture and Society*, p. 36; and Louis Bodin's comments on the intellectual as "a public man" in *Les Intellectuels, "Que sais-je?"* 1001 (Paris: Presses Universitaires de France, 1952), pp. 42-43.

18. Quoted by Louis James, *Fiction for the Working Man 1830-1850* (London: Oxford University Press, 1963), p. 29.

19. Charles Dickens, *Our Mutual Friend, The Works of Charles Dickens*, 36 vols. (New York: Charles Scribner's Sons, 1911), 24: 440.

20. For contemporary comments on Dickens illustrative of this point, see George H. Ford, *Dickens and His Readers: Aspects of Novel Criticism Since 1836* (New York: W. W. Norton, 1965), pp. 164-65.

21. See, for instance, Eliot's complaint about a review in *Letters* 3: 302; and comments by a reviewer for *The Daily Telegraph* (1872) quoted in *George Eliot and Her Readers: A Selection of Contemporary Reviews*, ed. John Holstrum and Laurence Lerner, with a commentary by Laurence Lerner (New York: Barnes and Noble, 1970), p. 84.

22. Quoted by Donald Southgate, *The Passing of the Whigs: 1832-1866* (London: Macmillan Co., 1962), p. 22.

23. Quoted by Reinhard Bendix, *Work and Authority in Industry: Ideologies of Management in the Course of Industrialization* (New York: John Wiley and Sons, 1956), p. 22.

24. Quoted by Esmé Wingfield-Stratford, *Those Earnest Victorians, The Victorian Cycle*,

with an introduction by Henry Seidel Canby (New York: William Morrow and Co., 1935), p. 115.

25. Quoted in *Social Policy 1830-1949: Individualism, Collectivism, and the Origins of the Welfare State*, ed. Eric J. Evans, *Birth of Modern Britain Series*, ed. A. E. Dyson and R. T. Shannon (London: Routledge and Kegan Paul, 1978), p. 81.

26. Quoted by Richard D. Altick, *The English Common Reader: A Social History of the Mass Reading Public 1800-1900* (Chicago: University of Chicago Press, 1957), pp. 156-57. (Altick notes [p. 157 n] that the quotation may be imperfect.)

27. E. L. Woodward, *The Age of Reform: 1815-1870, The Oxford History of England*, ed. G. N. Clark (Oxford: Oxford University Press, 1938), p. 429.

28. It is interesting to note that the word scientist was coined in 1840 by William Whewell, who modeled it after the word artist, as if to emphasize the closely intertwined fates of these figures in this century. See S. G. Checkland, *The Rise of Industrial Society in England: 1815-1885* (London: Longmans, Green and Co., 1964), p. 99.

29. On this relationship between professionalism and intellectuals, see N. G. Annan, "The Intellectual Aristocracy," in *Studies in Social History: A Tribute to G. M. Trevelyan*, ed. J. H. Plumb (London: Longmans, Green and Co., 1955); the documents in *Social Policy*, pp. 110-22; and Jacob Taubes's comment about the intellectual's relation to "the new form of legitimation" in bourgeois society, as quoted by J. P. Nettl, "Ideas, Intellectuals, and Structures of Dissent," in *On Intellectuals: Theoretical Studies/Case Studies*, ed. Philip Rieff (Garden City, NJ: Doubleday and Co., 1969), p. 54.

30. C.f. Eliot's description in *Daniel Deronda* (1:56) of Warham's cramming for his Indian civil service exam.

31. Of course, Eliot did show Lydgate's science to be imperfect: "What was the primitive tissue? In that way Lydgate put the question—not quite in the way required by the awaiting answer" (*M*, 1: 154). However, this error is technical or (following Eliot's generalization) philosophical: it does not in any way bring into question the social nature of the medical profession. Knoepflmacher appears to argue otherwise (*Religious Humanism*, pp. 80-83) in describing the error in Lydgate's "scientific view of women" and in his comment that "his physical science is impotent against moral disease." But he comes to the conclusion that Lydgate's failure is marked by the way he "becomes false to his highest ideal: the detachment of empirical truth" (p. 91).

32. For some modern instances, see Harvey's "Idea and Image in the Novels of George Eliot," in *Critical Essays on George Eliot*, ed. Barbara Hardy (New York: Barnes and Noble, 1970), pp. 151-98; Hardy's comparison of Eliot's moral vision to Lewes's description of science in *The Novels of George Eliot: A Study in Form* (London: The Athlane Press, 1959), pp. 78-79; and Felicia Bonaparte's description of Eliot's "habitual" appeal to science in *Will and Destiny: Morality and Tragedy in George Eliot's Novels* (New York: New York University Press, 1975), p. 50.

For comments to this effect by Eliot's contemporaries, see for instance Sidney Colvin's description of Eliot's work in the 1876 *Fortnightly Review*, quoted in *George Eliot and Her Readers*, p. 175; and William Ernest Henley's criticism, quoted in *A Century of George Eliot Criticism*, ed. Gordon S. Haight (Boston: Houghton Mifflin Co., 1965), p. 161.

33. John Ruskin, *Fors Clavigera: Letters to the Workmen and Labourers of Great Britain, The Complete Writings of John Ruskin*, Artist's Edition, 26 vols. (New York: Merril and Baker, 1890), 2: 199.

34. George Macauley Trevelyan, *British History in the Nineteenth Century (1782-1901)* (London: Longmans, Green and Co., 1923), p. 278 n.

35. Quoted by G. H. Bantock, *Education in an Industrial Society* (London: Faber and Faber, 1963), p. 82.

36. Edward Lytton Bulwer, *England and the English*, 2 vols. (London: Richard Bentley,

1833; reprint, Westmead, England: Gregg International Publishers, 1971), p. 122; and Morley, quoted by Richard Stang, *The Theory of the Novel in England 1850-1870* (New York: Columbia University Press, 1959), p. 97.

37. Carlyle, "Characteristics," *Critical and Miscellaneous Essays, Works* 28: 3.

38. Quoted in *Education and Democracy*, ed. A. E. Dyson and Julian Lovelock, *Birth of Modern Britain Series*, ed. A. E. Dyson and R. T. Shannon (London: Routledge and Kegan Paul, 1975), p. 95.

39. Quoted by Q. D. Leavis, *Fiction and the Reading Public* (London: Chatto and Windus, 1939), p. 189.

40. Alfred, Lord Tennyson, "Hail Briton!," *The Poems of Tennyson*, ed. Christopher Ricks (London: Longmans, Green and Co., 1969), p. 484.

41. See also Eliot's essay, "The Too Ready Writer," *Theophrastus Such*, pp. 368-76.

42. Thomas Hardy, *Jude the Obscure, The Works of Thomas Hardy in Prose and Verse*, with prefaces and notes, Wessex Edition, 23 vols. (London: Macmillan and Co., 1912), 3: 405.

43. See Ruskin, *Sesame and Lilies, Complete Writings* 21: 42.

44. Hardy, *The Woodlanders, Works* 6: 146.

45. Mill, *The Spirit of the Age*, with an introductory essay by Frederick A. von Hayek (Chicago: University of Chicago Press, 1942), pp. 2, 25.

C.f. Walter Bagehot's statement about speaking "to the many so that they will listen," quoted by Walter E. Houghton, "Victorian Periodical Literature and the Articulate Classes," *Victorian Studies* 22 (1979): 392.

46. Mannheim, *Ideology and Utopia*, p. 143.

47. Ralph Waldo Emerson, "The American Scholar," *The Complete Works of Ralph Waldo Emerson*, with a biographical introduction and notes by Edward Waldo Emerson, Centenary Edition, 12 vols. (Boston: Houghton Mifflin Co., 1903), 1: 101-2.

48. See Asa Briggs, "Middle-Class Consciousness in English Politics, 1780-1846," *Past and Present* 9 (1956): 65-74; and Briggs, "The Language of 'Class' in Early Nineteenth Century England," *Essays in Social History*, ed. M. W. Flinn and T. C. Smouth (Oxford: Oxford University Press, 1974), p. 154.

49. Quoted in *Social Policy*, p. 27.

50. Quoted by J. F. C. Harrison, *Learning and Living 1790-1960: A Study in the History of the Adult Education Movement, Studies in Social History*, ed. Harold Perkin (Toronto: University of Toronto Press, 1961), p. 233.

51. Quoted in *Class and Conflict in Nineteenth-Century England: 1815-1850,* ed. Patricia Hollis, *Birth of Modern Britain Series*, ed. A. E. Dyson and R. T. Shannon (London: Routledge and Kegan Paul, 1973), p. 132.

52. C.f. Antonio Gramsci's characterization of intellectuals as "the 'salesmen' of the dominant group" in society in *Gli intellettuali e l'organizzazione della cultura* (Rome: Editori Riuniti, 1971), pp. 20-21.

53. Mannheim, *Ideology and Utopia*, p. 144.

54. C.f. Eliot's similar thoughts in *Letters* 3: 111; 4: 65; and 6: 89; and Brian Swann, "George Eliot's Ecumenical Jew, or, The Novel as Outdoor Temple," *Novel* 8 (1974): 39-50.

55. Matthew Arnold, *Culture and Anarchy*, ed. with an introduction by J. Dover Wilson, *Landmarks in the History of Education*, ed. J. Dover Wilson and F. A. Cavenagh (Cambridge: Cambridge University Press, 1935), p. 87.

56. Tennyson, "Love thou thy land, with love far-brought," *Poems*, p. 614.

57. Mill, *Autobiography*, p. 36.

58. Mill, *On Liberty: Annotated Text, Sources and Background Criticism*, ed. David Spitz, *Norton Critical Editions* (New York: W. W. Norton, 1975), p. 44.

59. Ibid., p. 11.

60. Bertrand Russell, "Toleration," in *Ideas and Beliefs of the Victorians: A Historical*

Revaluation of the Victorian Age, with a foreword by Harmon Grisewood (London: Sylvan Press, 1949), p. 273.

61. Quoted in *George Eliot and Her Readers*, p. 56.

62. Mill, "Civilization," *Mill's Essays on Literature and Society*, ed. with an introduction by J. B. Schneewind, *Collier Classics in the History of Thought*, ed. Crane Brinton and Paul Edwards (New York: Collier Books, 1965), pp. 171-72.

63. Quoted in *Working Classes in the Victorian Age*, with an introduction by C. J. Wrigley, *Victorian Social Conscience Series*, 4 vols. (Westmead, England: Gregg International Publishers, 1973), 1: 392.

64. Quoted in *The English Radical Tradition: 1763-1914*, ed. S. Macoby, *British Political Tradition Series*, ed. Alan Bullock and F. W. Deakin (London: Adam and Charles Black, 1966), p. 210.

See also E. P. Thompson's description of how some workers denied the "natural law" of laissez-faire economics in *The Making of the English Working Class* (New York: Random House, 1964), pp. 297-99, 549.

65. See Herbert Spencer, *An Autobiography*, 2 vols. (New York: D. Appleton and Co., 1904), 1: 273-74.

66. C.f. Eliot's similar interpretations of *Antigone* (*E*, 264) and of "Divine Nemesis" (*R*, 125).

Chapter 2. Education and the Transfigurations of Realism

1. On this point and others related to this chapter, c.f. Pierre Bourdieu, "Cultural Reproduction and Social Reproduction," *Knowledge, Education, and Cultural Change: Papers in the Sociology of Education*, ed. Richard Brown (London: Tavistock Publications, 1973), esp. p. 84.

2. Quoted by Harrison, *Learning and Living*, p. 77 n.

3. Quoted by Trygve R. Tholfson, *Working-Class Radicalism in Mid-Victorian England* (New York: Columbia University Press, 1977), p. 38.

4. Quoted by Peter Bailey, *Leisure and Class in Victorian England: Rational Recreation and the Contest for Control 1830-1885, Studies in Social History*, ed. Harold Perkin (London: Routledge and Kegan Paul, 1978), pp. 39, 97.

5. Tennyson, "Locksley Hall," *Poems*, p. 696.

6. On this and other points related to this chapter, see A. P. Donajgrodzki, " 'Social Police' and the Bureaucratic Elite: A Vision of Order in the Age of Reform," in *Social Control in Nineteenth Century Britain*, ed. A. P. Donajgrodzki (London: Croom Helm, 1977), pp. 51-76; and, in the same volume, Richard Johnson's discussion of the ideology of expertise and his analysis of the intellectuals involved in educational reform in "Educating the Educators: 'Experts' and the State 1833-39," pp. 77-107. Donajgrodzki's essay is particularly valuable for its analysis of the assumptions shared by political Liberals and Conservatives in this age, including several rhetorical devices that I discuss as being important elements in middle-class discourse.

7. Annan, "The Intellectual Aristocracy," *Studies in Social History*, p. 247.

8. Ruskin, *Fors Clavigera, Complete Writings* 1: 117-18.

9. Tennyson, "In Memoriam A. H. H.," *Poems*, p. 964.

10. Ruskin, *Sesame and Lilies, Complete Writings* 21: 41.

11. Quoted in *The English Ruling Class*, ed. with an introduction by W. L. Guttsmann, *Readings in Politics and Society*, ed. Bernard Crick (London: Weidenfeld and Nicolson, 1969), pp. 61-63.

12. Arnold, *Culture and Anarchy*, p. 81.

13. C.f. William F. T. Meyers's comment on the riot in *Felix Holt* in *Der Englische Soziale Roman in 19. Jahrhundert*, ed. Konrad Gross (Darmstadt: Wissenschaftliche Buchgesellschaft, 1977), p. 148.

14. E. W. Bovill, *English Country Life 1780-1830* (London: Oxford University Press, 1962), p. 45.

15. E. J. Hobsbawm and George Rudé, *Captain Swing* (New York: Random House, 1968), p. 17 n.

16. Bulwer Lytton, *England and the English* 1: 316.

17. On this and related points, see Richard Johnson, "Educational Policy and Social Control in Early Victorian England," *Past and Present* 49 (1970): 96-119.

18. Quoted in *Education and Democracy*, p. 81.

19. Quoted by Gross, *The Rise and Fall of the Man of Letters*, p. 103.

20. Quoted by Derek Fraser, *The Evolution of the British Welfare State: A History of Social Policy since the Industrial Revolution* (London: Macmillan Co., 1973), p. 117.

21. Quoted in *Education and Democracy*, p. 98.

22. On this debate over the morality of the novel and on Eliot as a test-case in this regard, see Kenneth Graham, *English Criticism of the Novel: 1865-1900, Oxford English Monographs*, ed. Alice Walker et al. (Oxford: Oxford University Press, 1965), pp. 1-6.

23. See, for instance, the *Westminster Review's* 1836 article on education in *Working Conditions in the Victorian Age*, with an introduction by Johns Saville, *Victorian Social Conscience Series* (Westmead, England: Gregg International Publishers, 1973), pp. 204-5.

24. Charlotte Brontë, *Shirley*, ed. Herbert Rosengarten and Margaret Smith (Oxford: Oxford University Press, 1979), pp. 414-15.

25. Quoted in *Class and Conflict*, p. 140.

26. Brian Simon, *Studies in the History of Education: 1780-1870* (London: Lawrence and Wishart, 1960), pp. 334-35.

27. Quoted in *Education and Democracy*, p. 76.

28. Quoted in *Class and Conflict*, p. 291.

29. Ibid., p. 264.

30. Quoted by Harrison, *Learning and Living*, p. 101.

31. Ruskin, *Sesame and Lilies, Complete Writings* 21: 76.

32. William Wordsworth, *The Prelude, Selected Poems and Prefaces*, ed. with an introduction and notes by Jack Stillinger, *Riverside Editions*, ed. Gordon N. Ray (Boston: Houghton Mifflin Co., 1965), p. 275.

33. Carlyle, "Characteristics," *Works* 28: 12.

34. Ibid., 28: 9.

35. Carlyle, *Sartor Resartus, Works* 1: 185.

36. Arnold, *Culture and Anarchy*, p. 30.

37. John Keble, "Monday in Easter Week," *The Christian Year, Everyman's Library*, ed. Ernest Rhys (London: J. M. Dent and Sons, 1914), p. 90.

38. On this point, see, for example, Barbara Hardy, *The Novels of George Eliot*, p. 96; David R. Carroll, "*Felix Holt*: Society as Protagonist," *George Eliot*, p. 124; and George Levine, "Determinism and Responsibility in the Works of George Eliot," *PMLA* 77 (1962): 268-69.

39. Virginia Woolf, *Mrs. Dalloway* (New York: Harcourt, Brace and Co., 1925), p. 152.

40. C.f. Laurence Lerner's description of Eliot "valuing religion in so far as it was a metaphor for conduct" in *The Truthtellers: Jane Austen, George Eliot, and D. H. Lawrence* (London: Chatto and Windus, 1967), p. 42.

41. Carlyle, "Chartism," *Works* 29: 194.

42. See *Essays*, p. 32 n.

43. Quoted in *George Eliot and Her Readers*, pp. 17-18, 163.

44. Hardy, *The Novels of George Eliot*, p. 107.

Chapter 3. Literary Consciousness and the Vacancy of the Individual

1. Carlyle, "Chartism," *Works* 29: 122, 157.

2. Harrison, *The Early Victorians: 1832-1851* (New York: Praeger Publishers, 1971), p. 57.

3. Quoted in *George Eliot and Her Readers*, p. 49.

4. Quoted by Bailey, *Leisure and Class*, p. 105.

5. Quoted by Amy Cruse, *The Englishman and His Books in the Early Nineteenth Century* (New York: Benjamin Blom, 1968), p. 230.

6. Wordsworth, *The Prelude, Selected Poems and Prefaces*, p. 353.

7. Wordsworth, "A Narrow Girdle of Rough Stones," *Selected Poems and Prefaces*, pp. 143-45.

8. Woodward, *The Age of Reform*, p. 512.

9. Carlyle, "On History," *Works* 27: 86.

Also, c.f. Henry Auster's comments on individualism in *The Mill on the Floss* in *Local Habitations: Regionalism in the Early Novels of George Eliot* (Cambridge: Harvard University Press, 1970), pp. 166-69; and the connection made between the novel and the rise of democracy and individualism by Eliot's contemporary W. C. Roscoe, as noted by Stang, *The Theory of the Novel in England*, pp. 51-52.

10. See, for instance, "Janet's Repentance," pp. 356-57; the speech in which Bardo lauds the power of thought in *Romola* 1: 55; and *Daniel Deronda* 1: 415.

11. Wordsworth, "A Poet's Epitaph," *Selected Poems and Prefaces*, p. 119.

12. C.f. Harvey's description of how the "antithesis of narrow and broad, of closed and open, recur throughout her work" in *The Art of George Eliot*, p. 44.

13. C.f. Philip Fisher's suggestion about the ways readers are implicated in Eliot's novels in *Making Up Society: The Novels of George Eliot* (Pittsburgh: University of Pittsburgh Press, 1981), p. 114.

Also, c.f. Hugh Witemeyer's comment on this passage in *George Eliot and the Visual Arts* (New Haven: Yale University Press, 1979), pp. 86-87.

14. C.f. Hardy's description of how Eliot introduces her major characters "in words that are clearly analytic, taxonomic, and instructive" in *"Middlemarch* and the Passions," *Particularities: Readings in George Eliot* (Athens: University of Ohio Press, 1983), pp. 7-8.

15. Valentine Cunningham, *Everywhere Spoken Against: Dissent in the Victorian Novel* (Oxford: Oxford University Press, 1975), p. 144.

16. On this subject of generalization in the representation of character, c.f. Sidney Colvin's comments, originally published in the *Fortnightly Review* in 1873, quoted in *George Eliot and Her Readers*, pp. 99-102; Isobel Armstrong, " 'Middlemarch': A Note on George Eliot's 'Wisdom'," *Critical Essays*, p. 117; and Witemeyer, *George Eliot and the Visual Arts*, p. 77.

17. In relation to this topic of allegory, c.f. Constance Marie Fulmer, "Contrasting Pairs of Heroines in George Eliot's Fiction," *Studies in the Novel* 6 (1974): 288-94; George Levine, "Intelligence as Deception: *The Mill on the Floss,"George Eliot*, pp. 122-23; in the same volume, George R. Creeger, "An Interpretation of *Adam Bede*," pp. 86-106; Carol Christ, "Aggression and Providential Death in George Eliot's Fiction" *Novel* 9 (1976): esp. p. 131; and Hardy, "The Scene as Image," *The Novels of George Eliot*, pp. 185-200.

18. C.f. Harvey's comments on the deceptive appearance of nature in Eliot's fiction in "Idea and Image in the Novels of George Eliot," *Critical Essays*, pp. 192-94.

19. Hardy, *Jude the Obscure, Works* 3: 15.

Chapter 4. Genteel Image and Democratic Example

1. Mill, *The Spirit of the Age*, p. 12.

Also, c.f. William H. Marshall's description of Eliot's concern in *Middlemarch* with "the nineteenth-century collapse of the public ontology" in *The World of The Victorian Novel* (New York: A. S. Barnes and Co., 1967), p. 310.

2. Quoted by Pauline Gregg, *A Social and Economic History of Britain 1760-1972*, 7th ed.,

rev. (London: George G. Harrap and Co., 1973), p. 247. (It should be noted that this widely quoted statement is also quoted in many forms.)

3. Carlyle, *Past and Present, Works* 10: 140.

4. Carlyle, "The Present Time," *Latter-Day Pamphlets, Works* 20: 9.

5. C. B. Cox, *The Free Spirit: A Study of Liberal Humanism in the Novels of George Eliot, Henry James, E. M. Forster, Virginia Woolf, Angus Wilson* (London: Oxford University Press, 1963), p. 23.

6. See Joseph Wiesenfarth, "George Eliot's Notes for *Adam Bede*," *Nineteenth-Century Fiction* 32 (1977): 127.

7. Of course, this line about Adam's obsolescence is also meant ironically, as an insult to the working classes of Eliot's time.

8. C.f. Auster's comments upon the similarity between Arthur and Hetty in *Local Habitations*, pp. 118-19, 130.

9. George Meredith, *The Egoist, The Works of George Meredith*, Memorial Edition, 29 vols. (New York: Charles Scribner's Sons, 1910), 14: 138.

10. C.f. Barbara Hardy's description of how a "disappearance of glamour is an essential part of the process of every novel" of Eliot's in *The Novels of George Eliot*, p. 195.

11. Jane Austen, *Northanger Abbey, The Novels of Jane Austen*, ed. R. W. Chapman, 5 vols. (London: Oxford University Press, 1932-34), 5: 209.

12. See Jerome Beaty, "The Text of the Novel: A Study of the Proof," in *Middlemarch: Critical Approaches to the Novel*, ed. Barbara Hardy (New York: Oxford University Press, 1967), pp. 59-61.

Also, c.f. the discussion of women's special disabilities in her society and Eliot's reaction to them in Kathleen Blake's study, "*Middlemarch* and the Woman Question," *Nineteenth-Century Fiction* 31 (1976): 285-312.

13. Dickens, *Great Expectations, Works* 22: 124.

14. Hardy, *Jude the Obscure, Works* 3: 98.

15. Quoted in *George Eliot and Her Readers*, p. 127.

16. Wingfield-Stratford, *Those Earnest Victorians, The Victorian Cycle*, p. 46.

17. Quoted by John W. Dodds, *The Age of Paradox: A Biography of England 1841-1851* (London: Victor Gallancz, 1953), p. 193.

18. On this point and others related to the question of Eliot's political attitudes and her moral idealism, see Graham Marti, " 'Daniel Deronda': George Eliot and Political Change" in *Critical Essays on George Eliot*, p. 133-50.

19. Quoted by Briggs, *Victorian People*, pp. 11-12.

20. C.f. Brian Swann's commentary on this passage in "Eyes in the Mirror: Imagery and Symbolism in *Daniel Deronda*," *Nineteenth-Century Fiction* 23 (1969): 434-45.

21. C.f. Douglas C. Fricke, "Art and Artists in *Daniel Deronda*," *Studies in the Novel* 5 (1973): 220-28.

22. In relation to this image of art in her novels, c.f. Witemeyer, *George Eliot and the Visual Arts*, esp. chapter 5, "Portraiture and Knowledge of Character," pp. 44-72.

Chapter 5. Imperfection and Compensation

1. On the subject of the relation between Eliot's works and her time, c.f. Lucien Goldmann, "Le structuralisme génétique en sociologie de la littérature," *Littérature et société: Problèmes de méthodologie en sociologie de la littérature, Etudes de sociologie de la littérature* (Bruxelles: Editions de l'Institut de Sociologie de l'Université Libre de Bruxelles, 1967), esp. p. 200. Although Goldmann's analysis of literature, in this essay as elsewhere in his work, is weakened by his notion of the great work and the great artist as well as by his emphasis on totality in society as in the

great work, it is relevant to my argument in this chapter. Also the works of Michel Foucault are, as should be obvious, an important context to my argument in this chapter and elsewhere in this book.

2. Carlyle, "The Present Time," *Latter-Day Pamphlets, Works* 20: 17.

3. J. Hillis Miller, "Narrative and History," *ELH* 41 (1974): 455-73.

4. Miller, "Optic and Semiotic in *Middlemarch*," *The Worlds of Victorian Fiction*, ed. Jerome H. Buckley, Harvard English Studies 6 (Cambridge: Harvard University Press, 1975), p. 144.

For other analyses of Eliot's work in terms of the questions it raises about the difficulties of interpretation, see Cynthia Chase, "The Decomposition of the Elephants: Double-Reading in *Daniel Deronda*," *PMLA* 93 (1978): 215-27; Dianne F. Sadoff, "Nature's Language: Metaphor in the Text of *Adam Bede*," and Elizabeth Weed, "*The Mill on the Floss* or the Liquidation of Maggie Tulliver," *Genre* 11 (1978): 411-26, 427-44; and Fisher, *Making Up Society*, pp. 167-96.

5. On this point, see Williams's interesting suggestion that Will Ladislaw has been "unconvincing" to Eliot's critics because he represents a type of freedom unparalleled in her fiction, in *The English Novel*, pp. 92-94.

6. See William Lovett's mention of this argument in *Life and Struggles of William Lovett*, with a preface by R. H. Tawney (London: Macgibbon and Kee, 1967), p. 147.

7. Quoted in *George Eliot and Her Readers*, p. 35.

Chapter 6. Realism and Romance

1. C.f. Levine's discussion of the traditions of the novel and the romance in relation to *Romola* in "'Romola' as Fable," *Critical Essays*, esp. pp. 80-81, 94; and Knoepflmacher's reference to Eliot as an "anti-Romantic romantic" (although he uses these terms in a sense somewhat different from mine) in *George Eliot's Early Novels*, p. 152.

2. On this relation between narrator and reading public, c.f. Karl Kroeber, *Styles in Fictional Structure: The Art of Jane Austen, Charlotte Brontë, George Eliot* (Princeton: Princeton University Press, 1971), p. 47.

3. It is significant that Byronism was a conventional scapegoat for Victorian morality, as in the famous remark Carlyle gave Teufelsdrökh, "'Close thy *Byron*; open thy *Goethe*'," Carlyle, *Sartor Resartus, Works* 1: 153. This was a tradition already well established when Byron and Wordsworth, Eliot's favorite poet, were made symbolic antagonists in a debate between Roebuck and Mill in the period after Mill's first breakdown. See Mill, *Autobiography*, p. 105. So, too, did W. H. Smith call Wordsworth's rescue of him from Byron "a sort of moral conversion." Quoted by David Roberts, *Paternalism in Early Victorian England* (New Brunswick, NJ: Rutgers University Press, 1979), p. 66. However, this conventionality further indicates how little Byronism or Romance signified specific literary texts and how much they signified a certain order of social belief and comportment, when deployed in this sort of opposition.

4. For some of Eliot's comments on what should be excluded from art, see "Authorship," *Essays*, pp. 437-38; "The Morality of Wilhelm Meister," *Essays*, p. 146; and *Letters* 2: 347.

5. C.f. the way Margaret in Elizabeth Gaskell's *North and South* reads a passage by St. Francis de Sales recommending humility and understands it to mean that she must take a stand outside herself, much as Dorothea understands Thomas à Kempis. (Of course, like other writers in this age, such as Dickens and Thackeray, Gaskell may also be compared to Eliot in terms of her recommendation of suffering and sacrifice as a means to recall humanity to itself.) See Gaskell, *North and South*, ed. with an introduction by Angus Easson, *Oxford English Novels*, ed. James Kinsley (London: Oxford University Press, 1973), p. 345.

6. Williams, *The English Novel*, p. 84.

On this issue of the relation between part and whole in Eliot's work, c.f. David R. Carroll, "*Felix Holt*: Society as Protagonist," *George Eliot*, p. 124; Jennie Calder's remark about family and community identity, *Women and Marriage in Victorian Fiction* (New York: Oxford University Press, 1976), p. 135; and David Leon Higden, "George Eliot and the Art of the Epigraph," *Nineteenth-Century Fiction* 25 (1970): 133-34.

7. Briggs, *Victorian Cities*, p. 331.

Also, c.f. G. Armour Craig, "Victims and Spokesmen: The Image of Society in the Novel," *1859*, esp. pp. 233, 246.

8. Karl Marx, *Capital: A Critique of Political Economy*, ed. Frederick Engels, trans. Samuel Moore and Edward Aveling, rev. Ernest Untermann, *The Modern Library* (New York: Random House, 1906), p. 305.

9. Quoted by Maurice J. Quinlan, *Victorian Prelude: A History of English Manners 1700-1830, Columbia University Studies in English and Comparative Literature* 155 (New York: Columbia University Press, 1941), p. 235.

10. Hardy, *Tess of the D'Urbervilles, Works* 1: 25.

11. Quoted by Thompson, *The Making of the English Working Class*, pp. 361-62.

12. Nathaniel Hawthorne, *The English Notebooks*, ed. Randall Steward (New York: Russell and Russell, 1962), p. 463.

13. Dickens, *Bleak House, Works* 16: 98.

14. Quoted in *Working Classes in the Victorian Age* 1: 82.

15. Young, *Victorian England*, p. 151.

16. Briggs, *Victorian Cities*, p. 53.

Chapter 7. The Supervision of Art and the Culture of the Sickroom

1. On this point, c.f. Carol Christ, "Aggression and Providential Death in George Eliot's Fiction," *Novel* 7 (1976): 134.

2. In characterizing Eliot's writing, I use the word "utopian" advisedly. She contrasted her writing to "avowed utopias," arguing that it ought not to lapse "from the picture to the diagram" (*L*, 4: 300). Her discussion of this point makes it clear, however, that it is the utopian appearance, not the motivation, that she thought necessary to avoid.

3. William Makepeace Thackeray, *Vanity Fair* (New York: Modern Library, 1958), p. 646.

4. Simon, *Studies in the History of Education*, p. 365.

5. Geoffrey Best, *Mid-Victorian Britain: 1851-1875, The History of British Society*, ed. E. J. Hobsbawm (London: Weidenfeld and Nicolson, 1971), p. 259.

6. Quoted by Tholfson, *Working-Class Radicalism*, p. 39.

7. Quoted in *Social Policy*, pp. 181-82.

8. Quoted in *Class and Conflict*, p. 323.

9. See C. R. Fay's description of the reaction of his workpeople to Owen's Inspecting Committee at New Lanark in *Life and Labour in the Nineteenth Century* (Cambridge: Cambridge University Press, 1947), p. 58.

10. Young, *Victorian England*, p. 27.

11. Thackeray, *The Newcomes, The Complete Works of William Makepeace Thackeray*, with introductions by W. P. Trent and J. B. Henneman, 30 vols. (New York: Thomas Y. Crowell, 1904), 5: 514.

12. C.f. Cunningham's description of how Eliot "demythologizes the traditional formulas of repentance and conversion" in *Everywhere Spoken Against*, p. 169.

13. C.f. Jay Clayton's analysis of how "George Eliot's defense of 'higher feeling' amounts to a defense of her 'higher' art" in "Visionary Power and Narrative Form: Wordsworth and *Adam Bede*," *ELH* 46 (1979): 669.

14. It is interesting in this regard that Herbert Spencer, Eliot's close friend for much of her adult life, took literally this idea of feelings in organic development as part of his developmental doctrine. See Spencer, *An Autobiography* 1: 507.

15. On the appeal to nonlogical understanding on the part of Eliot and other moralists of her time, see John Holloway, *The Victorian Sage: Studies in Argument* (London: Archon Books, 1962), chap. 1, "The Victorian Sage: His Message and Methods."

16. Woodward, *The Age of Reform*, p. 38.

17. John Goode, " 'Adam Bede'," and John Bayley, "The Pastoral of Intellect," *Critical Essays*, pp. 19, 200.

See also Michael Squires, *The Pastoral Novel: Studies in George Eliot, Thomas Hardy, and D. H. Lawrence* (Charlottesville: University Press of Virginia, 1974), chap. 3 and 4.

18. For instance, c.f. Eliot's comment on England in relation to the French Revolution, *Letters* 1: 254.

19. This incident is widely noted by historians of the period. See, for example, Cole, *A Short History of the British Working-Class Movement*, 2 vols. in 1 ed. (New York: Macmillan, 1927), 1: 110.

20. See Elizabeth Burton, *The Pageant of Early Victorian England: 1837-1861* (New York: Charles Scribner's Sons, 1972), pp. 201-5.

21. Dorothy Marshall, *Industrial England: 1776-1851*, *Development of English Society Series*, ed. Dorothy Marshall (New York: Charles Scribner's Sons, 1973), p. 62.

22. See, for example, Leslie Stephen, *George Eliot, English Men of Letters Series* (London: Macmillan Co., 1920), p. 116; Knoepflmacher, *Laughter and Despair: Readings in Ten Novels of the Victorian Era* (Berkeley: University of California Press, 1971), p. 180, *George Eliot's Early Novels*, p. 31, and "*Middlemarch*: An Avuncular View," *Nineteenth-Century Fiction* 30 (1975): 61; Williams, *The English Novel*, p. 77; Miller, *The Form of Victorian Fiction*, University of Notre Dame Ward-Phillips Lecture in English Language and Literature, vol. 2 (Notre Dame: The University of Notre Dame Press, 1968), p. 113; Felicia Bonaparte, *Will and Destiny: Morality and Tragedy in George Eliot's Novels* (New York: New York University Press, 1975), p. 12; Hardy, *The Novels of George Eliot*, p. 20; David Moldstad, "George Eliot: A Higher Critical Sensibility," in *Victorian Essays: A Symposium*, ed. Warren D. Anderson and Thomas D. Clareson (Oberlin, Ohio: Kent State University Press, 1967), pp. 17-27; Hilda M. Hulme, "*Middlemarch* as Science Fiction: Notes on Language and Imagery," *Novel* 2 (1968): 41; and Jonathan Arac, "Rhetoric and Realism in Nineteenth-Century Fiction: Hyperbole in *The Mill on the Floss*," *ELH* 46 (1979): 679. On this point, see also Michal Peled Ginsburg, "Pseudonym, Epigraphs, and Narrative Voice: *Middlemarch* and the Problem of Authorship," *ELH* 47 (1980): 542.

23. Checkland, *The Rise of Industrial Society*, pp. 276-77.

Chapter 8. Private Fragments and Public Monuments

1. J. Bronowski, "Unbelief and Science," *Ideas and Beliefs*, p. 168.

2. Of course, this is not to say that Eliot's ideas about women and their place in society were entirely conventional or conservative. It is only to say that in the particular instance of this very important code, her writings were in agreement with the stereotypes of her culture.

3. Culturally redeeming, for instance, in giving David's lament for Saul and Jonathan ("In death they were not divided") a modern humanistic interpretation, in accordance with Eliot's reading of Christian and other mythologies.

4. On this subject, see Levine, "Intelligence and Deception in *The Mill on the Floss*," *PMLA* 80 (1965): 406; Jean Sudrann, "*Daniel Deronda* and the Landscape of Exile," *ELH* 37 (1970): 435; Lynne Tidaback Roberts, "Perfect Pyramids: *The Mill on the Floss*," *Texas Studies*

in Language and Literature 13 (1971): 116; Karl R. Kropf, "Time and Typology in George Eliot's Early Fiction," *Studies in the Novel* 8 (1976): 430-40; and Peter K. Garett, *The Victorian Multiplot Novel: Studies in Dialogical Form* (New Haven: Yale University Press, 1980), p. 177.

5. Carlyle, "Characteristics," *Essays, Works* 28:2.

6. Hawthorne, *The English Notebooks*, p. 242.

7. Quoted by Haight, *George Eliot: A Biography* (Oxford: Oxford University Press, 1969), p. 119.

8. C.f. Marx, *Capital*, p. 168 n.

9. Ibid., p. 163 n.

10. Edmund Burke, *Reflections on the Revolution in France*, ed. with an introduction and notes by E. J. Payne (Oxford: Oxford University Press, 1921), p. 228.

11. For other comments on Eliot's imagery of gambling, see Hardy, *The Novels of George Eliot*, pp. 133-34; Bonaparte, *Will and Destiny*, pp. 16-22, 160; Knoepflmacher, *George Eliot's Early Novels*, pp. 240-42; Darrell Mansell, Jr., "George Eliot's Conception of Tragedy," *Nineteenth-Century Fiction* 22 (1967): 160; and Joseph Wiesenfarth, "Demythologizing Silas Marner," *ELH* 37 (1970): 234-47.

Also, c.f. Bailey's comments on the change after midcentury from the view of gambling as "a familiar vice" to its appearance as "a threat to property," *Leisure and Class*, p. 23.

Chapter 9. Domesticity and Teratology

1. Quoted by Buckley, *The Victorian Temper*, p. 200.

2. On this subject, c.f. Avrom Fleishman, *The English Historical Novel: Walter Scott to Virginia Woolf* (Baltimore: The Johns Hopkins Press, 1971), pp. 162-63.

3. Quoted by Fraser, *The Evolution of the British Welfare State*, p. 118.

4. On this subject, c.f. Hardy's analysis of "the hero as mentor" in *The Novels of George Eliot*, pp. 55-67.

5. Keble, "Morning," *The Christian Year*, p. 5.

6. Hence the significance of Adam Bede's self-righteous ire when a lady tries to deny him the price he has decided on for a screen he has made for her. The scene serves to maintain the natural dignity and propriety of morally calculated profit and thus, like all Eliot's representations of labor, represents as ordinary human life a utopian cultural system of values such as that found in the theories of intrinsic value in the works of Carlyle or Ruskin.

7. J. H. Clapham, "Work and Wages," *Early Victorian England: 1830-1865*, ed. G. M. Young, 2 vols. (London: Oxford University Press, 1934), 1: 17.

8. Marx, *Capital*, pp. 150, 171.

Conclusion: Reproduction/Quotation/Criticism

1. Paul Valéry, "The Conquest of Ubiquity," *Aesthetics*, trans. Ralph Manheim, with an introduction by Herbert Read, *The Collected Works of Paul Valéry*, ed. Jackson Mathews, *Bollingen Series*, 45 vols. (New York: Bollingen, 1964), 13: 225-26.

2. Benjamin, "Eduard Fuchs, Collector and Historian," *One-Way Street and Other Writings*, trans. Edmund Jephcott and Kingsley Shorter (London: NLB, 1979), p. 358.

3. Benjamin, *One-Way Street, One-Way Street and Other Writings*, p. 45.

4. Filippo Tommaso Marinetti et al., "The Futurist Cinema," *Marinetti: Selected Writings*, ed. with an introduction by R. W. Flint, trans. Flint and Arthur A. Coppotelli (New York: Farrar, Straus and Giroux, 1971), p. 131.

5. Benjamin, *One-Way Street, One-Way Street and Other Writings*, p. 59.

6. Benjamin, "The Work of Art in the Age of Mechanical Reproduction," *Illuminations*, ed. with an introduction by Hannah Arendt, trans. Harry Zohn (New York: Shocken Books, 1969), p. 244 n.

7. Benjamin, Ibid., p. 218.

8. Benjamin, Ibid., p. 244 n.

9. Benjamin, "Karl Kraus," *One-Way Street and Other Writings*, pp. 285-86.

10. Benjamin, "The Work of Art in the Age of Mechanical Reproduction," *Illuminations*, p. 218.

11. *Ibid.*, pp. 241-42.

12. *Ibid.*, p. 224.

13. Of course, this is not to say that the terms of society and politics exhaust the description of literature or of any other reality.

14. Benjamin, "Surrealism: The Last Snapshot of the European Intelligentsia," *One-Way Street and Other Writings*, p. 227.

15. Benjamin, "The Work of Art in the Age of Mechanical Reproduction," *Illuminations*, p. 242.

16. Ibid.

17. Benjamin, "Surrealism" *One-Way Street and Other Writings*, p. 236.

18. Benjamin, "Moscow," *One-Way Street and Other Writings*, p. 177.

Index

Index

Theory and History of Literature

Daniel Cottom is an associate professor of English at the University of Florida. He received his doctorate in English from State University of New York at Buffalo in 1978 and, until mid-1986, taught at Wayne State University. Cottom is the author of *The Civilized Imagination: A Study of Ann Radcliffe, Jane Austen, and Sir Walter Scott.*

Terry Eagleton is a fellow and tutor in English at Wadham College, Oxford. His books include *The Rape of Clarissa, Literary Theory: An Introduction* (both published by Minnesota), *Walter Benjamin, Criticism and Ideology, The Function of Criticism, William Shakespeare,* and *Against the Grain.*